The Art of Pure Cinema

The Art of Pure Cinema

Hitchcock and His Imitators

BRUCE ISAACS

OXFORD
UNIVERSITY PRESS

Oxford University Press is a department of the University of Oxford. It furthers the University's objective of excellence in research, scholarship, and education by publishing worldwide. Oxford is a registered trade mark of Oxford University Press in the UK and certain other countries.

Published in the United States of America by Oxford University Press
198 Madison Avenue, New York, NY 10016, United States of America.

© Oxford University Press 2020

All rights reserved. No part of this publication may be reproduced, stored in a retrieval system, or transmitted, in any form or by any means, without the prior permission in writing of Oxford University Press, or as expressly permitted by law, by license, or under terms agreed with the appropriate reproduction rights organization. Inquiries concerning reproduction outside the scope of the above should be sent to the Rights Department, Oxford University Press, at the address above.

You must not circulate this work in any other form
and you must impose this same condition on any acquirer.

Library of Congress Cataloging-in-Publication Data
Names: Isaacs, Bruce, author.
Title: The art of pure cinema : Hitchcock and his imitators / Bruce Isaacs.
Description: New York : Oxford University Press, 2020. |
Includes bibliographical references and index. |
Identifiers: LCCN 2019039326 (print) | LCCN 2019039327 (ebook) |
ISBN 9780190889951 (hardback) | ISBN 9780190889968 (paperback) |
ISBN 9780190889975 (updf) | ISBN 9780190889982 (epub) | ISBN 9780190889999 (online)
Subjects: LCSH: Hitchcock, Alfred, 1899–1980—Criticism and interpretation. |
Hitchcock, Alfred, 1899–1980—Influence.
Classification: LCC PN1998.3.H58 I88 2020 (print) |
LCC PN1998.3.H58 (ebook) | DDC 791.4302/33092—dc23
LC record available at https://lccn.loc.gov/2019039326
LC ebook record available at https://lccn.loc.gov/2019039327

9 8 7 6 5 4 3 2 1

Paperback printed by Integrated Books International, United States of America
Hardback printed by Bridgeport National Bindery, Inc., United States of America

For my son, Byron Robert Isaacs

Contents

Acknowledgments	ix
Introduction: The Myth of Pure Cinema	1

I. THE EVOLUTION OF PURE CINEMA

1. Pure Cinema in Context	15
2. Hitchcock's Interlocutors	41

II. THE MECHANICS OF PURE CINEMA

3. The Part Is Greater Than the Whole: Toward an Aesthetic Philosophy of the Fragment	61
4. The Fragmented Frame 1: Expression, Abstraction, Schematization	84
5. Intensified Schematics: Bava, Argento, and De Palma's *Body Double*	108
6. The Fragmented Frame 2: Segmentation	127
7. Music You Can Hear: Toward an Abstract Soundscape	164
Conclusion: The Fractal Image in De Palma's *Femme Fatale*	185
Notes	213
Bibliography	233
Filmography	241
Index	245

Acknowledgments

The major part of this book was written over a period of study leave in 2017; I want to thank the University of Sydney for funding this research semester, which was intensely enjoyable. Stuart Cottle and Nicky Hannan, both brilliant film scholars, were integral to the development and progress of the project; they were not only model readers and researchers but enormous fun to work with. I also want to thank the Sydney Literature and Cinema Group, and especially Kim Wilkins, Peter Marks, Paul Sheehan, Ryan Twomey, Blythe Worthy, Sabina Rahman, and anyone else who read parts of this book and made it better. I work with many excellent people in my department and across the university, who are a constant reminder of the privilege of my position. Mark Ledbury's passion for art, film, and music is completely infectious, and I thank him for the many conversations over the years.

Norman Hirschy at Oxford University Press was simply the most generous (and patient) editor I could have wished for. He was interested in this project from the start, which gave me the confidence to pursue it doggedly. I thank Norm, but also Sarah Gleeson-White, my colleague in the Department of English, for steering me in Norm's direction.

Last, I want to thank my wife, Rebecca Goldsworthy, whose presence is in every thought and word, and my twin brother, Herschel Isaacs, for a life spent talking movies. This book is dedicated to my son, Byron.

Introduction

The Myth of Pure Cinema

I.1. The Hitchcockian Method

This is not a book about Hitchcock. There are many of those in critical circles, and I wouldn't presume to add a great deal more to the landmark studies of scholars such as Raymond Bellour, Robin Wood, and William Rothman, among many others. But it is a book that attempts to situate Hitchcockian cinema, and more specifically an aspect of the Hitchcockian style, in the aftermath of Hitchcock's rich, complex, and sometimes unwieldy filmmaking career. In a series of discussions with François Truffaut in 1962, Hitchcock, then at the height of his influence as a filmmaker and prior to the perceived decline of his cinema in the later 1960s, gestures toward an artistic disposition in the following exchange on *Rear Window* (1954):

TRUFFAUT: I imagine that the story appealed to you primarily because it represented a technical challenge: a whole film from the viewpoint of one man, and embodied in a single, large set.
HITCHCOCK: Absolutely. It was a possibility of doing a purely cinematic film. You have an immobilized man looking out. That's one part of the film. The second part shows what he sees and the third part shows how he reacts. This is actually the purest expression of a cinematic idea.[1]

This notion of a cinematic purity, though vague in Hitchcock's account, and no less vague in Truffaut's attempts to distill what this artistic disposition might be, occurs throughout Hitchcock's reflection on his directorial style. In the exchange above, the inference on Truffaut's part seems to be that Hitchcock's pure cinema materializes most explicitly in *Rear Window*, not only one of Hitchcock's most successful films, but also one of Truffaut's personal favorites. L. B. "Jeff" Jefferies (James Stewart), the protagonist of the film, functions similarly to the apparatus of cinema: from his point of view, the world is depicted through the mechanism of a shot reverse shot, which is precisely Hitchcock's description of the three-part structure of the shot. The entire scenario of *Rear Window*, Hitchcock suggests, is a seamless shot reverse shot: a man's world is reduced to (or framed within) what the camera sees. The once sacrosanct boundary between the world and its reproduction in a film image collapses in this very simple contrivance of a film reduced to what the camera sees.

But Hitchcock takes the purity of the apparatus further in *Rear Window*. In its opening sequence, the film eschews expositional dialogue for the unchecked movement of the camera: the camera pans across the interior of a room to fashion the scenario, story, setting, and character motivation prior to Jeff's introduction. Fittingly, the camera concludes its elaborate pan on a medium close-up of a window and the raising of curtains: the viewer's point of view is now explicitly realized through the visual frame. In the most banal sense, the shot suggests that we (the spectators) are at this moment sutured within the visual construction of cinema.[2] Not only is the world reduced in its entirety to a cinematic image, but the spectator is now also compelled to *see* cinematically. In addition to Hitchcock's shot reverse shot, we can say that the raising of the curtains creates a framed cinematic simulacrum, that is, a world encompassed by the image on the screen. This simulacrum finds its most explicit form in the famous *Rear Window* set itself, which is hardly a faithful reproduction of the Greenwich Village scene in mid-1950s New York. Rather, this is "the Village" reconstructed for the cinematic apparatus, wholly contained within the Technicolor palette of Hollywood cinema of the 1950s; *Rear Window*'s setting is surely one of cinema's greatest sets in the true sense of that word. Following Truffaut, I would suggest that if *Rear Window* is indeed Hitchcock's most explicit manifestation of pure cinema, it is a pure cinema because it is the most radically and self-consciously cinematic—and thus "unworldly"—of the director's works.[3]

The exchange with Truffaut comes in 1962, after a period of what can only be described as Hitchcock's golden age. The mid- to late 1950s brought *Rear Window*, *The Man Who Knew Too Much* (1956), *Vertigo* (1958), *North by Northwest* (1959), and *Psycho* (1960), among other films. Hitchcock follows these films (each in my opinion offering a striking meditation on the formal potential of the cinematic medium) with *The Birds* and *Marnie*, released in 1963 and 1964, respectively, and *Frenzy* (1972), a late Hitchcock masterpiece. I argue that this body of work constitutes the culmination, if not the fulfillment, of a sustained artistic and philosophical approach to cinematic form.[4]

In 1937, almost three decades prior to Hitchcock's attempt to articulate a method in dialogue with Truffaut, he offers the following position on film direction: "This is what gives an effect of life to a picture—the feeling that when you see it on the screen you are watching something that has been conceived and brought to birth directly in visual terms. The screen ought to speak its own language, freshly coined, and it can't do that unless it treats its acted scene as a piece of raw material which must be broken up, taken to bits, before it can be woven into an expressive visual pattern."[5] I'll leave the matter of sound and music design alone for now; like almost every filmmaker working in Hollywood's classical era, sound for Hitchcock occupies a passive space in relation to the overwhelming spatiotemporal frame of the visual image. Yet in this statement, Hitchcock seems to extract from the more nebulous pure cinema concept of his discussion with Truffaut two defining formal components: First, "purity" refers to a mode of signification or communication intrinsic to the medium of cinema; elsewhere, Hitchcock will specify that the medium is comprised of moving images, images *of* movement, and, most explicitly, images of action.[6] Second, "purity" refers to that highly specific though somewhat undefined phenomenon filmmakers refer to as "visuality," or simply "the visual." This was a common position held by filmmakers like Hitchcock and a host of other classical Hollywood directors: their position was that cinema ought to relinquish its aesthetic lineages to the novel and theatre and, in Hitchcock's words, speak "in its own language," the language of moving images. For Hitchcock, the phenomenon of cinematic visuality is both a complex of highly orchestrated formal elements within the film image and a singularity, an essential element of the medium, that which makes the medium what it is.

I've always been fascinated by Hitchcock's statements on directorial method, which display such a cavalier attitude to the history of film aesthetics. Of his contemporary cinema era, in 1962, he suggests: "In many of the films now being made, there is very little cinema: they are mostly what I call 'photographs of people talking.'"[7] While he qualifies this statement by acknowledging that he doesn't see many films, the disdain for a particular cinematic approach implies a steadfast commitment to what he at least perceives to be a coherent and relatively stable method. Such statements on method or directorial approach are commonly offered by Hitchcock with a degree of self-confidence and seeming conclusiveness, but with very little critical analysis to support foundational claims. In my searching through various uses of the term "pure cinema" by Hitchcock and other filmmakers (all Hitchcock admirers), I can find little more on the method of pure cinema than what Hitchcock initially summarizes in conversation with Truffaut in 1962. I can find no more exacting (or expansive) an enunciation of what pure cinema is, how it works, how it manifests in the work of other filmmakers, or how it has developed in other film periods, industries, or aesthetic traditions. The resolution seems to be that pure cinema is the distillation of the essence of the medium, which is in turn further essentialized through a somewhat undefined notion of "the visual." If we seek further elaboration, "pure cinema" is, to paraphrase the director, putting film together to create an emotional experience, or using the camera to create suspense and anticipation, or showing action.

The majority of critics and filmmakers interested in the method of a Hitchcockian pure cinema seem to agree that it is anchored in a visual sensibility.[8] This is cinema that must communicate through the mechanics of the visual-filmic medium. The visual field in its entirety refers not only to a camera, props, sets, and so on but also to the entire significatory system of cinema, including the gaze of the spectator. Yet even a commitment to the visual mechanics of the image tells us very little about a method of visualization or visual style or approach. What is this visual system underpinning a pure cinema form? What is it predicated on? Is it discernible within the film frame? Is it a function of the movement of the camera within space? Is it evident in the relation of pieces of film put together through editing? Again, all of this is implied in Hitchcock's description of his method, yet the conceptual foundation is mired in a lack of detail and precision. Can we say that such a method, self-described, is even coherent?[9] For William Friedkin, the director of the classic car/subway chase in *The French Connection* (1971), the chase sequence is the foundation of the Hitchcockian method: the relational movement within the frame and the montage intrinsic to the chase is the foundation of pure cinema.[10] But again, Friedkin says very little about the technique or style or approach to the chase, or to a cinema of action in broader visual and aural terms. He merely expounds on what pure cinema is not: the cinema that is *not* pure merely photographs people talking; it is expositional rather than active. For Martin Scorsese, the Hitchcockian method is "all ballet. It's like choreography, like dance."[11] Perhaps this notion of choreography—which suggests the ordering of formal elements into a pattern—moves us nearer to a method. Nevertheless, without exacting analysis, what does any of it amount to beyond the most banal tautology—pure cinema is cinema reduced to its "purity," or its "essence"—?

I.2. Hitchcock's Imitators

In this book, I attempt to explicate what a pure cinema might be, and how it might have concretized around and evolved after the work of Hitchcock. I locate the essence of Hitchcock's method in a set of films that remain staggeringly experimental decades after their release: *Shadow of a Doubt* (1943), *Rear Window, Vertigo, North by Northwest, Psycho, The Birds, Marnie*, and *Frenzy*. My argument is founded on the conceptual and methodological achievement of these works, both as singular films and as a sustained cinematic practice over the expanse of Hitchcock's career. However, I engage Hitchcockian cinema merely as a point of departure. This is not a book about Hitchcock but about the potential of a *method* most explicitly demonstrated by Hitchcock in his cinema of the 1950s and 1960s. My focus is instead on filmmakers who used Hitchcock creatively for their own ends, expanding on a methodology that I argue was in nascent form even in Hitchcock's richest and darkest meditation on pure cinema, which I take to be *Vertigo*. To attempt to theorize pure cinema as method, I engage the work of the so-called Hitchcockian imitators,[12] selecting the films of peripheral (from a US-centric point of view) genre filmmakers such as Mario Bava, Dario Argento, Lucio Fulci, and, at least to my mind, the most misunderstood filmmaker of the modern American cinema, Brian De Palma. We see the mark of Hitchcock etched into all of their work, from plotlines, to lines of dialogue, to frame composition, to a musical cue that is so subtle as to be almost imperceptible, to a color filter that appropriates a semiotic and affective prompt from a Hitchcockian image. But in the work of these directors, Hitchcockian stylistic gestures are further complicated within a deeper philosophy of visual and aural cinematic form. These filmmakers engage in an open dialogue with Hitchcockian cinema to explore the intricacies of a unique aesthetic disposition fashioned in Hollywood's late classical period. Perhaps the most provocative or controversial aspect of my position is that I argue that such filmmakers reflexively resituate, and thereby enrich, the Hitchcockian method in relation to industrial and aesthetic sets of parameters.[13]

In spite of his later success within Hollywood's studio system, De Palma's *Sisters* (1973), released through Roger Corman's American International Pictures (AIP), is an early attempt at mastering the Hitchcockian thriller. In this sense, De Palma is obviously an imitator of sorts. But in the films of De Palma's oeuvre, I argue that the act of imitation is a creative reconstruction of cinematic form. This is how the cinema of De Palma, and no less Hitchcock, should be accessed: as a highly fluid, reflexive cinematic commentary. Quentin Tarantino has recently stated, "I'm not the biggest Hitchcock fan and I actually don't like *Vertigo* and his 1950s movies—they have the stink of the 50s which is similar to the stink of the 80s. People discover *North by Northwest* at 22 and think it's wonderful when actually it's a very mediocre movie. I've always felt that Hitchcock's acolytes took his cinematic and story ideas further. I love Brian De Palma's Hitchcock movies. I love Richard Franklin's and Curtis Hanson's Hitchcock meditations. I prefer those to actual Hitchcock."[14] For such an imaginative filmmaker and astute critic of cinema, I confess I find Tarantino's assessment of Hitchcock's cinema of the 1950s bewildering. Nonetheless, Tarantino's criticism of Hitchcock reveals his appreciation for a mode of cinema as reflexive meditation. This desire to see cinema not as blank imitation but in relation to its past is also emblematic of Tarantino's artistic disposition, and is most emphatic in the final act of *Inglourious Basterds* (2009). In the eruption of flame in Le Gamaar Cinema, history and cinema are symbiotic companions, each a reflexive meditation on the other. The oscillating currents between past and present are a tension I explore in a constant movement between the cinema of Hitchcock and the cinema of his "acolytes," to use Tarantino's term. In engaging cinema as intertextual—and inter-imagistic—dialogue, I argue that we can reveal the full potential of a form of imitative cinema.

If there is a single filmmaker underpinning the foundation of this work, it is not Hitchcock but Brian De Palma. The Hitchcockian stylistic gestures in Mario Bava and Dario Argento, and to no less a sophisticated degree in the more obscure horror cinema of Lucio Fulci, reach their full potential and philosophical acuity in De Palma's extensive body of work. I examine a broad range of De Palma's films in subsequent chapters, concluding with a detailed examination of *Femme Fatale* (2002), a film that in my estimation represents De Palma's fulfillment of a career-long meditation on what Hitchcock meant by the term "pure cinema."

In spite of the 2015 release of a successful and highly praised documentary on De Palma's career[15]—directed by another De Palma acolyte, Noah Baumbach—De Palma remains the prodigal child of the American New Wave cinema of the late 1960s and 1970s. Where Scorsese and Coppola pushed the art-house and European New Wave sensibility in films such as *Mean Streets* (1973), *The Conversation* (1974), *Taxi Driver* (1976), and *Apocalypse Now* (1979) and Spielberg and Lucas drove the high-concept studio model that would dominate the Hollywood financial imperative for decades, De Palma has remained peripheral to large (studio) and smaller (independent) industries. Like Hitchcock's films of the 1950s and 1960s, De Palma's films have also remained steadfastly idiosyncratic, flamboyant, baroque, self-reflexive, playful, and perverse. They are emphatically nonconformist and thus have implicitly and sometimes explicitly challenged the grand narratives of American film history. If the legacies of the celebrated American New Wave filmmakers are assured, De Palma's is less so, and his directorial signature is less clearly established. Now at the end of a fifty-year career (as I write this, he is in troubled post-production on a new thriller, *Domino*), what does De Palma's cinema constitute as a meditation on cinematic form and cinematic history? In a recent and all too familiar sentiment in a review piece on Baumbach's documentary, Owen Gleiberman concludes that De Palma was the only—and thus highly conspicuous—Hollywood New Wave director bereft of an artistic vision.[16]

In a filmed interview with Baumbach to accompany the Criterion DVD edition of *Dressed to Kill* (1980), at one point De Palma returns, albeit grudgingly, to a reflection on Hitchcock's influence on his own work: "Hitchcock pioneered all this stuff, and of course, he started making silent movies, where you think visually all the time. And even though I'm accused over and over again of imitating Hitchcock, I've always felt that I've taken the ideas of Hitchcock and tried to develop them further . . . that great visual idea and how it's all choreographed."[17] Interestingly, De Palma draws on a very similar concept underpinning Scorsese's description of Hitchcock's method: cinema as "choreography," as a series of patterns constituting form, presumably an assemblage of the material properties of mise en scène (the configuration of the frame and its contents), montage, narrative, soundscape, and so on. Following this statement, Baumbach inserts a single shot from the final sequence of *Dressed to Kill*. The image opens on a medium overhead angle of Bobbi (Michael Caine) and the nurse he has strangled, now lying dead, splayed on the bed with her uniform open to reveal the lingerie she wears beneath. The camera slowly cranes upward to artificially construct a frame within a frame: Bobbi and the nurse on the left, the asylum patients as (cinematic) spectators voyeuristically gazing upon the action on the right of the frame; the two sections of the frame are partitioned by a balcony rail in an emphatic spatial division in the angle of the overhead shot.

It is a signature moment in De Palma that visually constructs within the mise en scène what I call the "segmented frame." The murder scene, highly sexualized, is a spilling over of repressed desire (Bobbi is a "transvestite" who cannot fulfill his desire without murderous consequences) that brings the spectator and action on the screen into direct and explicit relation. The split screen erupts with the affect of cinema's essential fragmentation; as spectators, we desire the suturing of image and subjectivity, while it remains permanently and frustratingly deferred. In this shot, subjective fragmentation is realized through the segmentation of the cinematic frame, and spectatorial voyeurism is revealed in the sequence to be both sadistic and masochistic. I concur with Adrian Martin and Cristina Álvarez López in their audiovisual essay on De Palma that the director's work (and this exemplary sequence in *Dressed to Kill* in particular) represents a "cinematic [form] of vision."[18] In its explicit marking of the spectator-voyeur within the frame, the scene is an imitation of a familiar Hitchcockian stylistic and thematic approach. And yet, if we take De Palma at his word, could we address the sequence as a reflexive attempt to develop a Hitchcockian pure cinematic style, to explore its artistic and philosophical possibilities, to take it further?

Alongside De Palma, I locate the Hitchcockian pure cinema most explicitly in the Italian *giallo*[19] films of Mario Bava and Dario Argento, who in turn influence the *giallo* productions of Lucio Fulci; Fulci's *Don't Torture a Duckling* (*Non si Sevizia un Paperino*, 1972) is a critical point of contact between an American classical and Italian neo-baroque aesthetics of the image. My argument is twofold: First, De Palma's inheritance of a Hitchcockian pure cinema style is complex and discursive. Gleiberman and similar-minded critics see a grossly oversimplified and unproblematic theft from, or at least egregious imitation of, select Hitchcockian works. This is not a new or original position. Thus, a film like *Body Double* (1984) is merely an imitation of

Figure I.1 The segmented frame: *Dressed to Kill* (1980)

Rear Window (with its voyeurism thematic) and *Vertigo* (in its figuration of the doubled woman). For Gleiberman, *Dressed to Kill* blankly imitates *Psycho* in its reconstructed shower scene and the unanticipated death of the film's star, Angie Dickinson, in the elevator: "The slasher in limp blonde hair and sunglasses made the film seem like a replay of 'Psycho' starring Sandy Duncan, and what De Palma really seemed to be clueless about is that the cathartic shock effect of a killer brandishing a straight razor against a backdrop of staccato violins was no longer the stuff of artful suspense. It was the stuff of interchangeable mediocre slasher films that were feeding, parasitically, off the same 'Psycho' aesthetic that he was."[20] Gleiberman is disdainful of what he perceives to be a paltry imitation of Hitchcock, whom he regards as a "dizzyingly romantic"—and thus original—artist.[21] Despite my disagreement with Gleiberman over the ontological properties of textual reproduction, I find that the convenient identification of all things Hitchcock constricts the general interpretation of De Palma's oeuvre. De Palma's thrillers of the late 1970s and 1980s clearly adopt a formal mise en scène, montage, and narrative structure at least in part indebted to the Italian *giallo* film. While the Hitchcockian legacy-as-theft has been frequently identified by critics, less commonly acknowledged are the overt references to the *giallo*. In the final sequence of *Raising Cain* (1992), De Palma appropriates the structure of the revelation of the murderer in what is almost a shot-for-shot reconstruction of a sequence that concludes Argento's *Tenebrae* (1980).[22] The elaborate camera move that closes Jimmy Malone's (Sean Connery) gunshot massacre in *The Untouchables* (1987) is a relatively faithful reconstruction of a far more complex tracking and crane shot in *Tenebrae* that concludes in the killing of a young woman. Both movements are covered by an expressive tracking motion of the camera; each movement is motivated by a choreographed set piece concluding in a murder. We could take this quotational dialogue or exchange further: against the orthodox interpretation of De Palma's elevator murder scene in *Dressed to Kill* as a Hitchcockian theft, I would argue that De Palma's scene is influenced at least in part by a visual and aural rhythmic sensibility that is clearly *not* Hitchcockian. The final razor slash that kills Kate Miller (Angie Dickinson) in *Dressed to Kill* displays the far more aggressive syntax of shot and cut evident in the most excessive *giallo* cinema. The point is that while De Palma's elevator sequence depicts a figure in disguise murdering a beautiful blonde woman with a blade (which, I acknowledge, is precisely the narrative taxonomy of Hitchcock's shower scene in *Psycho*), the mechanics of the image partake of an aesthetic register nearer to the Italian *giallo*, which is a tradition founded on the spectacle of the action set piece, formal image and narrative repetition, and excessive and gratuitous displays of violence and nudity. Such images of excess are perhaps in their nascent form in Hitchcock's shower scene, but a nuanced analysis of De Palma's Hitchcockian cinematics is profoundly limited without a subtle engagement with the formal cinematics of the Italian *giallo* cinema that reflects on Hitchcock, imitates Hitchcock, and in so doing intensifies a Hitchcockian cinematic style.

In spite of De Palma's claims that he is not a student of the *giallo*,[23] I read De Palma's cinema as *more than* Hitchcockian, and as explicitly informed by the aural and visual mechanics of the *giallo*. This is a critical and undervalued point of contact between De Palma and Hitchcock but, more significantly, between an American genre cinema complex (Hitchcock–De Palma) and the transnational industrial model that informs the Italian *giallo*. A pure cinema espoused in Hitchcock's various accounts evolves through an oscillation between cinematic texts. The works of Bava, Argento, and De Palma are thus in a constant process of reflecting, and in this reflection, *expanding*. We might then begin to address the *giallo* films, or the films of De Palma, as a reflexive, creative, developmental authorship.

In the chapters that follow, I attempt to construct what Gérard Genette has called an "architexture" of the pure cinematic image.[24] In a textual circuit connecting the works of the *giallo* and De Palma, pure cinema emerges through textual dialogue, as one text speaks to another in its myriad aesthetic forms. It seems almost a cliché to resort to Barthes, but if we acknowledge that a text is part of a complex and discursive tapestry,[25] why would we need to see imitation as anything but a reflexive, creative expression of textual pasts and textual presents? It is far more useful to address cinema as what Genette has productively called the "architext" of poetic form, which includes all manner of textual enunciation quite apart from the rigid forms through which texts are usually constricted and ideologically framed. Imitation, in this radical Barthesian sense, is thus also poetic creation, and in this process of creation, historical liberation. In a gesture of radical self-reflexive textual commentary, Genette offers a striking formulation: "The text interests me (only) in its *textual transcendence*—namely, everything that brings it into relation (manifest or hidden) with other texts. I call that *transtextuality*. . . . Under transtextuality I put still other kinds of relationships—chiefly, I think, relationships of imitation and transformation. . . . Finally . . . I put under transtextuality that relationship of inclusion that links each text to the various types of discourse it belongs to. . . . It stands to reason that we should call this the *architext*, and *architextuality*, or simply *architexture*."[26] In the model I propose, this architextual structure materializes as knowing imitation, as it crosses the various circuits that link Hitchcock to the Italian *giallo* to De Palma's oeuvre, each a strategic imitative text, each a reflexive expression in relation to the architextual whole. I move from Hitchcock's words in interviews and critical pieces to his films across a voluminous directorial career, subjecting an experimental, idiosyncratic style to what David Bordwell has called "exceptionally exact perceptions."[27] I argue that if a pure cinema is to be found in Hitchcock, it is to be found in the fragments of images that constitute an aesthetic philosophy and design. But the critical part of my method is to subject the Hitchcockian method to a set of formal analytical parameters that emerge forcefully in the works of filmmakers who, to varying degrees of success, carried the pure cinema mantle further, and often to absurd excesses. In Part II of the book, I attempt to explicate a mechanics of pure cinematic form, examining mise en scène, montage, structures of narration, sound, and music design.[28] But in these analyses, I postulate that pure cinema cannot be fathomed as a hermetic, or even entirely coherent, artistic method, philosophy, or aesthetic style, nor should it be. Rather, my sense of pure cinema is that it is nearer to an artistic disposition imposed upon the raw materials of film form. This book is an attempt to crudely systematize this disposition in its philosophical and aesthetic praxis.

PART I
THE EVOLUTION OF PURE CINEMA

1
Pure Cinema in Context

1.1. Pure Cinema and the Modernist Avant-Garde

Hitchcock's desire to fashion a pure cinematic style was not unique or even original to him. Indeed, the notion of medium specificity, or a cinematic art form composed of cinema's essential materials, is part of a larger discourse on cinema's aesthetic and technological form in the early part of the twentieth century.[1] Cinema quite naturally evolved out of its filiation to earlier and companion art forms: the mise en scène mechanics of performance, set design, framing, and lighting of the theatrical stage; the generic properties of exhibitionist or performative entertainment forms such as vaudeville theatre or pantomime; and the narrational plot structure and voice of the novel.[2] Cinema's early incarnation was as a reflection of theatre's formal staging properties: filming through the "proscenium arch" defined the framed medium for many productions from 1895 to 1912.[3] If we contrast a static image with the radical mobility of the image (through mise en scène and montage) in Griffith's work, we have a sense of the degree to which the earliest cinema was cautious in its enunciation of a new artistic and experiential medium.

The desire for a cinema unaffiliated with earlier artistic forms evolved out of larger European aesthetic, cultural, and political currents of the first two decades of the twentieth century. Aesthetic modernism, as nebulous as that term is in theoretical discourse, encompasses various experimental movements, including impressionism (emerging in the late nineteenth century), futurism (approximately 1909–1920), expressionism (approximately 1910–1930), Dada (1916–mid-1920s), and surrealism (from the early 1920s).[4] There are two critical aspects of aesthetic modernism that impact decisively on early cinematic form, and specifically on the philosophy of pure cinema. First, aesthetic modernism in its various experimental incarnations was concerned with artistic form *and* experience; the artistic discourse that fermented the philosophical foundations of modernism gestures to the intrinsic relation between form and experience, and more explicitly to the capacity of new aesthetic forms to engender new cognitive, intellectual,

The Art of Pure Cinema. Bruce Isaacs, Oxford University Press (2020). © Oxford University Press.
DOI: 10.1093/oso/9780190889951.001.0001

psychological, and emotional experiences.⁵ If we consider Luis Buñuel and Salvador Dalí's famous surrealist film of 1929, *Un Chien Andalou* (An Andalusian dog), we can say that it is a modernist experiment both in the sense of its formal image and narrative experimentation and in its desire to create a new psychological and emotional experience. The significance of *Un Chien Andalou* not only to cinematic modernism but to cinematic form per se is in its reflexive commentary on this emergent newness: the classic slice of the eyeball expresses the filmmaker's desire to theorize the image and the gaze of the spectator, comprised of a mise en scène that shocks and a subtle montage of a cloud obscuring a moon that gestures both to opacity in aesthetic form and experience and to painful illumination.

In its philosophical desire for new form and experience, aesthetic modernism quite naturally and intuitively embraced the cinema as a site of radical aesthetic and political potential.⁶ While impressionism, futurism, expressionism, Dada, and surrealism began their lives in painted, sculptural, and architectural works (among others aesthetic forms), cinema's emergence as a mature or reflexive artistic mode in the late 1910s accommodates the various aesthetic currents of these movements. Modernist art's desire to create new form and experience was appropriately applied to the newest art form, the cinema. It was thus only natural that an artist such as Man Ray would explore the medium-specific potential of the cinema in works such as *Le Retour à la Raison* (1923) and *Emak-Bakia* (1926). Similarly, Buñuel and Dalí's *Un Chien Andalou* is a specific application of the surrealist philosophy to the language of cinema, and Dalí would continue to engage the medium of cinema alongside his paintings for the duration of his artistic practice.⁷ This is to say that while the Hitchcockian notion of a pure cinema is situated very much within a narrative medium, the philosophy underpinning such a practice emerges not with the American studio cinema of the 1920s or within large film industries but within the pocket of modernist artists and philosophers comprising the European cinematic avant-garde. A Hitchcockian pure cinema (and thus the pure cinema experiments of the Italian *giallo* or the cinema of Brian De Palma) is in this sense part of a film avant-garde historical narrative.

Pure cinema, or the *cinéma pur*, was a European avant-garde movement that emerged during the mid-1920s in Paris, initially through the short films of Henri Chomette, and later through the filmmaking and philosophical writing of Germaine Dulac. While *cinéma pur* fermented within the larger aesthetic and intellectual discourses of European modernism, critical to the movement is an experimental visual form that appropriated the newly emergent languages of moving image form, notably German expressionism and the Soviet montage cinema.[8] From expressionism, filmmakers like Chomette and Dulac appropriated an attitude toward mise en scène, with its emphasis on line, lighting contrast and exaggeration, and geometric form; from Soviet montage, *cinéma pur* adopted a philosophy of the creative or intellectual association of images. Susan Heyward suggests that *cinéma pur* is characterized by a philosophy of film "signifying in and of itself through its plasticity and rhythms" and cites René Clair's *Entr'acte* as an early exemplar of the style.[9] In the early scenes of that film, we see a diverse expression of the capacity of the medium: realistic space and time is eschewed for experimental spatial configurations, temporal rhythms, and narrational or imagistic logic. Normative framing and montage are not exactly rejected in such a work. Rather, the work seems entirely oblivious to the normative foundations of an early classical cinematic form founded on symmetry and stability within the frame. In *Entr'acte*, Clair seems drawn to the image as a rhythmic form, that is to say, a formal pattern variation occurring in space and time; for Clair, such variations constituted a "pure cinema as soon as a sensation is aroused in the viewer by purely visual means."[10] We see similar experiments with formal spatial and temporal logic in surrealist cinema of this period, such as *The Seashell and the Clergyman* (*La Coquille et le Clergyman*, Germaine Dulac, 1928) and *Un Chien Andalou*.[11] Heyward's notion of the "plasticity" of the image is quite useful here: plasticity clearly describes the malleability of the Soviet montage form, but it also suggests the formal potential of technologically created aesthetic forms. The inherent plasticity of the image is a defining formal characteristic of the *cinéma pur*.[12]

For Aitkin, the plasticity of the image of *cinéma pur* tends toward formal abstraction. In addition to the attempt to "isolate the fundamental formal properties of shape, form, rhythm and movement of the medium," Chomette's *Jeux des reflets de la vitesse* (The play of reflections and speed, 1925) "studies the abstract patterns created by objects filmed at speed and from different angles."[13] Critical here is the rejection not only of narrative form, or storytelling, but of representational form itself—the automatic image of the cinema that had so intoxicated the early modernists with its replete reality is deconstructed in Chomette's film as so many geometric spatial and rhythmic temporal forms. In Chomette, and most emphatically in Dulac's work, cinema is the materiality of objects within a frame, light, movement, and montage—and nothing else.[14]

Dulac offered perhaps the most sustained and coherent philosophy of *cinéma pur* through two early films, *Disque 927* (1928) and *Théme et Variations* (1928). In Dulac's more expansive and precise philosophy of cinematic form, "the character is not the center of importance in a scene, but the relationship of images to one another."[15] Dulac offers this formulation in 1925 in an article titled "The Essence of Cinema—The Visual Idea."[16] Intriguingly, Hitchcock, and later De Palma, specifically describes pure film as not merely "the visual" or "visuality" but as a "visual idea," attaching the visual characteristics of the image to a larger aesthetic concept. As Hitchcock would argue throughout his career, for Dulac, cinema was also essentially "a silent art. Silent expression is its categorical rule and this sentence from *L'Ecriture* could be applied to those who are its servants: *Their throats will not utter a sound*. We, the authors of films, must assume the difficult task of describing *without words, without phrases*."[17] Dulac's position on cinema's essential integrity is explicit and sustained. As Williams suggests, "Dulac's retroactive emphasis on the filming of natural elements, such as the reflections of light on a pond, corresponded to her ideal of a pure, or integral, cinema, based on movement and rhythm, which in drawing its elements from life itself, owed nothing to the other arts."[18] An interesting and provocative paradox emerges in the complex and somewhat indefinable association of a cinema that draws "elements from life itself" in the mechanical reproduction of this life on film. Clearly the tension between the purity of life (or world) and its reproduction through the apparatus of cinema is full of creative possibility. For Dulac, *cinéma pur* is a revelation of both the purity of the medium and the creative capacity of individual experience expressed through the mechanical images of that form.[19]

Hitchcock appropriates several aspects of the *cinéma pur* model from European avant-garde philosophy and practice, and notably from the principles espoused by Dulac. This is not to suggest that he took an interest in Dulac's films or writing, but that his aesthetic development occurred in relative proximity to the emergence of the *cinéma pur* movement. Dulac's cinema of the visual idea is evident in Hitchcock's fascination with geometric form within the film frame. We see in films such as *The Lodger* (1927), *Shadow of a Doubt*, *Vertigo*, *Psycho*, *Marnie*, and *Frenzy* an emphasis on line, shape, segment, partition, symmetry, asymmetry, and spatial relation. As I will attempt to show in Part II of this book, in Hitchcock's most experimental compositions, we see representation tend toward figure and semantic signifier tend toward abstraction.

There is also in Hitchcock an early fascination with the potential of movement and rhythm within the film frame, and within experimental montage. For Hitchcock, like Dulac, a cinema of movement was also a cinema of rhythm and sensation. This is a movement that is intriguingly but also problematically implicated in the machinic movement and rhythm of modern industrial life, including that of the early film apparatus; I will return to this phenomenal experience of modernity shortly in a discussion of *The Lodger*. For Williams, "Dulac was to become one of the foremost defenders of a conception in which the modernity of cinema was derived from its essence in movement."[20] This is a modernity that implicates the medium of cinema and its new modes of perception afforded the inhabitant of the modern city.

The German expressionist influence on Hitchcock is well known, and the time spent with F. W. Murnau while shooting *The Last Laugh* (*Der Letzte Mann*, 1924) was clearly of enormous import.[21] As early as 1922–1923, Murnau speculated on the possibility of a cinema constituted by "the fluid architecture of bodies with blood in their veins moving through mobile space; the interplay of lines rising, falling, disappearing; the encounter of surfaces, stimulation and its opposite, calm; construction and collapse; the formation and destruction of a hitherto almost unsuspected life; all this adds up to a symphony made up of the harmony of bodies and the rhythm of space; the play of pure movement, vigorous and abundant."[22] Here Murnau sounds very much like Dulac in his emphasis on the constitutive elements of visual form and movement as the essence of the cinematic medium. Like Chomette and Dulac, his notion of a pure cinema derived from a belief in the essential qualities of cinema's visual form, movement, rhythm, and sensation. Hitchcock's time spent with Murnau on the set of *The Last Laugh* had a profound effect on the development of the young director's cinematic style. As Gottlieb suggests, in reflecting on his own method, "Hitchcock always emphasized the importance of Murnau as a visual storyteller."[23] As I will attempt to show in analysis, Hitchcock was a keen philosophical and stylistic interlocutor in this evolution of visual storytelling.

1.2. Pure Film Form: A Mise en Scène and Montage Schema

Hitchcock explicitly aligns pure cinema with montage, or the creative possibilities of editing: "To me, pure film, pure cinema, is pieces of film assembled."[24] There is a famous film segment of Hitchcock's explanation of pure cinema through montage, which amounts in large part to the Kuleshov effect.[25] In the Hitchcock clip, the spectator is presented with a close-up of an old man (Hitchcock). First, we cut to an image of a child playing, and then we cut back as a smile appears on the man's face. "What is he as a character?" asks Hitchcock. "He is a kindly man. He's sympathetic." But what if, Hitchcock suggests, we remove the middle image, a single shot of a child, and replace it with a girl in a bikini. "What is he now? A dirty old man."[26]

While the Kuleshov technique is a fairly obvious form of montage (and we see this from Hitchcock's example), it gestures to a larger philosophical disposition toward the cinematic image as creative possibility. For Hitchcock, much like Dulac, cinema is the essential relativity of images among themselves. I would suggest that in this instance, Hitchcock and Dulac are talking about the openness of the cinematic image in montage. The image is *merely* that: relational, contingent, never fully determined or closed off. On the most basic level, we can say that Dulac's pure montage is emphatically noncontinuous and that it bears no relation to the classical continuity montage that dominates narrative filmmaking. In the classical montage schema, an image is largely determined by its predecessor. In this sense, we can also say that classical continuity tends toward representative realism, configuring a spatiotemporal cinematic frame that, in its artificially imposed continuity, resembles the phenomena of perceptual and psychological experience. Against classical continuity, Dulac understands montage as a liberation from a causal schema, deriving its intensity from the affect of movement and spatial form itself.

While Hitchcock's montage is circumscribed by a popular entertainment context, we nonetheless see an imaginative deployment of the association of images throughout his cinema. Montage is for Hitchcock contiguous with a way of seeing, and his cinema seeks to interrupt the flow of a normative spectatorial perception. While fashioned within the structures of generic narrative form in the majority of his works, Hitchcockian montage is frequently unorthodox, challenging, or perverse; in fact, I would say that montage in Hitchcock frequently embodies the same perverse mode of looking that his many flawed protagonists adopt. Whereas classical montage contrives viewing omniscience, Hitchcockian montage is more often than not a revelation of a fragmented, decentered, and inadequate gaze. We see this traumatic montage schema overwhelming the detective's search for truth in *Vertigo*. Scottie's singular function is to discover the truth of Madeleine's strange behavior. Yet his is not the observational gaze of the classical detective narrative. He follows Madeleine to the florist and enters the premises from the rear. The room is dark and engulfed in shadow. A dolly movement contrives Scottie's point of view, but the movement does not simulate an innocent gaze; rather, the movement of the camera is measured, circumspect, and predatory, as is Scottie's proximate gait in the reverse shot. Clearly this gaze, animated through a predatorial scheme of shot and reverse shot, is not the innocent gaze the spectator anticipates from the all-seeing detective.

Scottie then opens the door onto one of the most striking mise en scène compositions in the film. As in the opening sequence of *Rear Window*, in which a curtain is raised to reveal the simulacral set beyond the window, Scottie's opening of the door functions as a makeshift wipe across the screen:[27] this symbolic curtain is opened from left of frame to right, revealing the image from our hidden position.

The bright light of the florist arrests the spectator in its contrast with the shadowy interior of the backroom. Madeleine is held in relatively shallow focus in an expansive depth of field; here depth of field works against the shallow focus to intensify the image of Madeleine. The out-of-focus surroundings bring Madeleine's figure into stark relief, accentuated by the vibrant colors of the flowers in contrast with the drabness of her gray suit. It is critical to note that, in spite of the general point-of-view positioning, Scottie cannot see Madeleine this way: rather, the perspectival and spatial contrivance creates a fractured cinematic gaze that now encompasses both Scottie's

Figure 1.1 The fractured Hitchcockian gaze: *Vertigo* (1958)

Figure 1.2 De Palma's split-screen effect: *Carlito's Way* (1993)

and the spectator's perception. This image is a rich visual metonym for the fractured Hitchcockian gaze of the protagonists of *Rear Window, Vertigo, Psycho, The Birds,* and *Marnie*. In fact, looking very closely now at this image on my monitor, with its jarring focal length and depth of field dissonance, I find it quite astonishing to see how much this image resembles the manifest fracture of the De Palma split screen effect in a film like *Carlito's Way* (1993).

If we put the two images together—a focal length and depth of field dissonance (*Vertigo*) and a split screen contrivance of a spatial dissonance within the frame (*Carlito's Way*)—we see a disposition toward cinema's relativity of images that informs the montage strategy of both filmmakers.[28]

The composition of the frame in the florist reveals the inadequacy of accounting for a pure cinema method through montage alone. Surely creativity occurs also *within* the Hitchcockian frame. Against pure cinema as montage, Skerry has recently argued that a Hitchcockian pure cinema emerges primarily through mise en scène, that is, composition within the frame. More specifically, for Skerry, the purity of cinematic vision derives from the organization of material within the frame in relation to the "absolute camera" and its capacity for movement.[29] Mise en scène composition is thus a function of both the organization of materials within the frame and its composition through the apparatus, whether that apparatus happens to be stationary or moving, horizontally planed or canted. For Skerry, "in Hitchcock's 'pure cinema' system, both mise-en-scene and montage play equally important roles, but it is my belief that mise-en-scene *must* precede montage as the primary element in the construction of a film."[30]

I have argued, following Dulac, that pure cinema is attentive to the radical openness of the image of cinema in its various mechanical and formal capacities. Cinematic form, then, is not the sole function of montage simply because montage sets a framed composition into a relation with other compositions; the compositional frame and montage are relational *systems* (an argument I take up in chapter 3), animated by an endlessly proliferating relation of images. The semantic content of the shot only makes proper sense in relation to the syntax of the ordering systems of space and time: shots, scenes, sequences, a projected narrative whole, and so on. Film form cannot therefore be realized in montage, but only in the relation between mise en scène composition, montage, and perhaps the most critically neglected aspect of filmic form, soundscape.[31]

Pure cinema is for both Dulac and Hitchcock a philosophical and aesthetic praxis founded upon the full potential of the cinematic medium, which is essentially a medium animated by moving images. While form is deployed in radically different ways across the work of these two filmmakers, I would argue that both filmmakers conceptualize pure cinema as the specific potential of a framed moving image set into relation with other moving images. Hitchcock's unique achievement was to forge an experimental method within the structural parameters of a generic entertainment form. This was a pure cinema that materialized through the industrial structure of mass entertainment cinema and evolved to become increasingly experimental, self-reflexive, and playful in its disposition. In his greatest cinematic experiments, in which the image realizes the extraordinarily complex potential of mise en scène composition and montage (I analyze such a sequence from *Frenzy* later in this chapter), Hitchcock's achievement through film form approaches the radical philosophical potential of Dulac and her European avant-garde contemporaries. It is a cinema in which narrative and representational form is increasingly distilled into the abstraction of cinema's pure formal and phenomenological elements: relations within space, movement, time (and thus duration), perception, affect, and intensity.

1.3. *Cinéma Pur*: Exemplary Mechanical Visual Form in *The Lodger*

The Lodger was produced for Gainsborough Pictures and released in 1927, in the final years of the silent cinema era. In its reflexive commentary on cinematic form, in Donald Spoto's words, the film is "virtually a textbook for Hitchcock's later work."[32] In conversation with Truffaut, Hitchcock similarly describes the film as "the first true 'Hitchcock' movie. . . . It was the first time I exercised my style."[33] Truffaut concurs, suggesting that "the film showed great visual inventiveness."[34] Hitchcock continues: "I took a pure narrative and, for the first time, presented ideas in purely visual terms."[35] While *The Lodger* is frequently noted for the first appearance of the standard Hitchcockian suspense plot—a man wrongfully accused of a crime must prove his innocence—I want to read the film instead as a formal cinematic experiment within a familiar, highly formulaic generic framework. I further want to suggest not only that *The Lodger* demonstrates a flamboyant visual style but that Hitchcock's film is very much part of a larger current of experimental works of the mid- to late 1920s that attempt to demonstrate the technological and formal potential of the cinematic medium.

The film opens with the discovery of the latest victim of the London serial killer known as "the Avenger." While largely expositional, the opening sequence is a complex montage of points of view of bystanders and police officers; rather than establishing character or a more conventional narrative focalization, the montage is purely observational. It becomes clear shortly after this initial montage that the opening movement of the film is not about the discovery of the body (hence the lack of focalization) but is instead focused on the filmic visualization of modern machinic communication: the telegraph, the telephone, and the newspaper press. "Word of mouth," comically rendered at the site of the discovery of the body, is no match for the modern machine in conveying a message. In this sequence, cinema offers the visual expression of the modern industrial process.

At the close of this establishing opening sequence, the film cuts from a close-up on the telegraph machine to a wide long shot of the front of the newspaper room.

It is well noted that this image includes the first of Hitchcock's cameo appearances. When Truffaut asked Hitchcock why he had inserted himself into this scene, Hitchcock replied: "It was strictly utilitarian; we had to fill the screen."[36] This explanation for the director's presence within the shot is patently absurd. The image in which he sits in the foreground is a very deliberate, self-conscious experimental composition. In fact, I would argue that the opening montage of the discovery of the body builds to this single experimental mise en scène. Hitchcock sits in a clearly segmented foreground within the frame; the set is an unadorned room with desk and chair. However,

Figure 1.3 Experimental mise en scène: *The Lodger* (1927)

the image encompasses an expansive, striking depth of field that functions as an exhibitionistic composition. I am therefore distinguishing between depth of field as a form of mise en scène organization utilized in the first decade of cinema and depth of field as a self-conscious artistic gesture, which I attribute to Hitchcock's playful organization of space (and himself within it!) in this shot. While the foreground is emphasized within the hierarchically receding frame, critical to the composition is the emphasis on objects and bodies in middle ground and background, each separated from the foreground by makeshift walls. The depth of field is intensified by a constant flow of bodies across the central axis of the screen, situated in an eye line with the body of Hitchcock in the foreground of the frame, as well as the movement of the blades of a giant fan. The frame is thus animated by the constant movement of bodies and is very much in keeping with Dulac's cinematic frame, which has its essence in movement.[37] The set as a whole is clearly signified as an elaborate artificial construct. One senses in this fabrication the explicit stylistic influence of the German expressionist aesthetic, and of Murnau's *Nosferatu* (1922) in particular.[38] Contrary to the professed utilitarianism of this first cameo, Hitchcock's appearance completes a composition with four discrete spatial planes anchored by a series of geometric frames within frames. For a film that only a moment earlier depicted the discovery of a body and the pursuit of a serial killer (each narrative thread a formulaic construct), it is a visual composition of astonishingly complex and experimental form.

In the depiction of the production of the presses for the following morning's news, *The Lodger* is far more interested in the mechanics of the production of newspapers than it is in the content of the news. From the elaborate composition of the newsroom, the film moves to a focused shot of the machinery of the press; this is cinema's revelation of a modern industrial process, which functions quite similarly to Vertov's revelation of the technological filmmaking process in *Man with a Movie Camera* (1929). From a wide shot of the printing press, we cut into a close-up of the aggressive movement of the paper through the machine, emphasizing the formal geometric shapes of cylinders, rods, and levers, all richly animated through machinic movement.

As Hitchcock indicated to Truffaut, the protagonist does not enter the film for fifteen minutes;[39] this is again an unconventional approach to film narrative. The introduction of the Lodger (Ivor Novello) to Daisy (June Tripp) at approximately twenty minutes instantiates the next formal experimental sequence: an exchange of gazes that are situated through experimental mise en scène and montage. As Hitchcock will do in the famous exchange of gazes in Ernie's restaurant in *Vertigo*, the meeting between the Lodger and Daisy is depicted in a series of specifically cinematic points of view. By this, I mean to suggest that the image eschews character point of view (and thus identificatory stability) for a more complex exchange anchored in the rhythmic and choreographed movement of bodies. Daisy enters the room in the background of the shot; in the right foreground, the Lodger gazes into a mirror, constituting not two but three bodies within the frame.

The reflected body in Hitchcockian cinema is never purely a reflection but also another body, and another incarnation, of the figure within the frame. The sequence now unfolds as a reflexive meditation on the formal potential of the cinematic gaze. After a conventional movement of shot reverse shot (including an unconventional line cross), the Lodger turns to confront Daisy with his gaze.

But this is again an unconventional, experimental relationship configured between those two lines of sight: the Lodger's gaze is shot in medium close-up, but with the camera's viewpoint almost directly confronting the line of his gaze. The movement of Daisy is captured through a close-up of the Lodger's

Figure 1.4 The excessive cinematic gaze: *The Lodger* (1927)

eyes, as he presumably tracks her movement. Yet Hitchcock never establishes a contained point-of-view itinerary, but rather cuts frequently from wide to medium to medium close-up, utilizing several angles, including a number of unconventional reverse angles. The point is that this itinerary of the gaze in *The Lodger* is not especially communicative about character or story. It is certainly not an unproblematic identification between spectator and character. Rather, what this itinerary signifies is an excess of the gaze as identification and a rendering of the gaze as a formal cinematic itinerary. In this dissociation of the gaze of the apparatus from the diegetic gaze, Hitchcock configures something like a pure cinematic mode of objectification. We are seeing "more" than these characters see, and in turn the frame in mise en scène and montage exposes more than is denoted within the diegesis. Unlike the gaze that identifies the central character within a scenario, this cinematic gaze is not naturalistic but choreographed, not innocent but performative and exhibitionistic.

These two sequence analyses reveal Hitchcock's early self-reflexive approach to cinematic form and a particular fascination with visual experimentation in mise en scène and montage. There are numerous examples of

28   THE EVOLUTION OF PURE CINEMA

Figure 1.5 The excessive point of view: *The Lodger* (1927)

Hitchcock's interest in the visual potential of cinema, but *The Lodger* is clearly an early test case because it is the most overt in its desire to experiment with the medium. In his strongest narrative works, as well as in *The Lodger*, one senses that Hitchcock's images trace a fundamental and creative tension between telling stories—the necessity of the entertainment movie industry—and depicting the experience of movement, time, and subjectivity within the frame. Indeed, while there is no evidence of a commitment to, or even interest in, *cinéma pur*, Hitchcock's unique place on the periphery of this intellectual current, at this critical juncture in his career, enables him to transpose an essentially philosophical disposition toward the film image into a larger entertainment narrative. It is unfortunate that Hitchcock never engaged explicitly with the philosophies of the European avant-garde, even as his films displayed a capacity for abstract forms of cinematic representation. The time spent at UFA, in the company of F. W. Murnau, among others, clearly fostered an ideal founded on the medium's capacity for self-reflexivity. Of course, one cannot view *The Lodger* in quite the same way as Dulac's *Théme et Variations* or Buñuel and Dalí's *Un Chien Andalou*, or even Murnau's *Sunrise* (1925), which was an expressionistic experiment produced by Twentieth

Century Fox. Yet if Hitchcock's cinema can be rationalized within a single overarching trajectory, commencing at least with *The Lodger*, it is within a visual and aural trajectory that leans with greater and greater confidence to the potential of formal cinematic abstraction. The desire for an "open" geometric frame is evinced in the experimentation of *The Lodger*, but as I argue in subsequent chapters, it is a nascent form of abstraction, somewhat instrumental and literal-minded. If we contrast the desire for abstraction in *The Lodger* with a similar but now intensified desire in *Vertigo*, we could suggest that, against the Lodger's instrumental desiring gaze, Madeleine Elster achieves a more complex figural form, the expression of a pure or autonomous image over and above representation.

1.4. Medium Specificity and Reflexivity: *Frenzy*

Robin Wood argues that Hitchcock's microscopically planned approach to shooting "is the ultimate confirmation of our sense of Hitchcock's conception of cinema as an artificial construct—the most artificial, perhaps, short of animation."[40] Artifice for Wood refers to the structured, premeditated, compartmentalized nature of Hitchcock's laying out of the scenario for shooting on the set. Wood appears to suggest (and I would agree) that there is little room in Hitchcock's method for change on set, or substantive improvisation, which is the working method of filmmakers as diverse as John Cassavetes, Spike Lee, and John Carpenter. There is little of the natural contingency of film production bleeding onto the Hitchcock set. But reflecting on our previous discussion of *The Lodger*, we can perhaps inflect Wood's position on artifice and conceptualize pure cinema not as aesthetic artifice but as a mode of image and sound expression that explicitly addresses the technological and formal parameters of the medium. The pure cinema mode, and indeed the *cinéma pur* that emerged in the 1920s, is attentive to artistic form itself, and to the capacities of the medium that give form expression.

In *Frenzy*, released in 1972, one of Hitchcock's most experimental, reflexive films, the image frequently oscillates between aesthetic realism, a classical Bazinian register,[41] and the artificial image Wood identifies as the signature of Hitchcock's *metteur en scène* method. The elaborate opening helicopter shot over the River Thames, accompanied by its (ironically) majestic score reveals at the end of one of the most ostentatious shots in all of Hitchcock's cinema the naked, dead body of a woman. The jarring dissonance of the grandeur of the city and its washed-up "refuse"[42] constructs a particularly black, playful, and comedic tone that destabilizes the aesthetic register of the opening section of the film.

Frenzy negotiates two overarching modes of cinematic representation: on the one hand, the naked body in the river gestures to an emerging social realism in the cinema of the 1970s; the explicit nature of the murderer's sex killings is striking in comparison to the relatively saccharine villainous acts of films such as *Rope* (1948), *Strangers on a Train* (1950), or *Rear Window*. Yes, such figures demonstrate psychopathic tendencies, but the Hays code clearly forbade the explicit depiction of sexual deviancy. Now working free of the code, Hitchcock offers the female body in its crude and disfigured physicality, presented most disturbingly in the visage of a strangled women with a protruding tongue.

Alongside this new graphic realism, Hitchcock also wished to depict the alleyways of Covent Garden (the site of his childhood) with a degree of geographical and cultural authenticity.[43] In these realist images, *Frenzy* constitutes Hitchcock's deepest engagement with the larger currents of cinematic realism dominant in Europe and the American art house cinema of the 1970s. The film's unconventional realist style is also a striking departure from the more familiar American studio aesthetic of *Torn Curtain* (1966) and *Topaz* (1969), Hitchcock's two preceding films.

On the other hand, against the realism of a post–Hays Code film image, *Frenzy* presents a strategic return for Hitchcock to a cinematic style founded

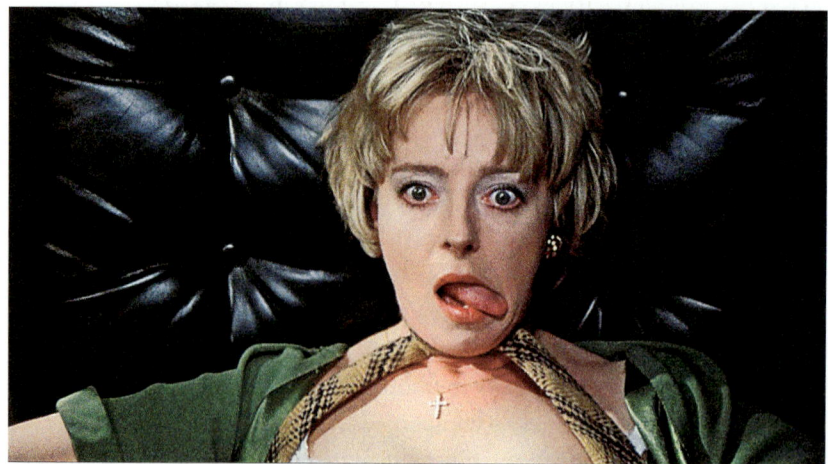

Figure 1.6 Hitchcock's late style: *Frenzy* (1972)

on reflexive, medium-specific experimentation. This formal reflexivity informs the greater part of his oeuvre and, as I argued in the introduction, exemplifies the experimental works of the mid- to late 1950s and early 1960s. In addition to generic plotlines and imaginative narrational strategies, these films demonstrate Hitchcock's self-conscious investigation of the nature of film form, with a particular emphasis on visual composition. In 1972's *Frenzy*, the reflexive Hitchcockian style is more emphatic, and the interrogation of form is intensified and sustained for longer durations.

The negotiation of these two aesthetic and representative modes—realism and reflexivity—is exemplified in the famous sequence in which Babs (Anna Massey) is murdered off-screen by the killer, Bob Rusk (Barry Foster). Babs exits a pub into the naturalistic soundscape of the street—I say naturalistic, though the soundtrack is amplified to capture the location realism of the exterior setting. Babs's entry into the street is matched by the first of a number of expressive "cinematic" movements: the camera zooms tight into Babs's face but holds in a deliberately awkward viewing proximity, achieving a perspective between close-up (the conventional angle) and extreme close-up (an unconventional, almost fetishistic mode of framing).

The zoom animates the frame with an aggressive movement from wide into close-up, registering the presence of the apparatus within the scene, while the completion of the zoom unsettles the frame with its unconventional scale. The realism of the street is collapsed by the extreme shallow focus of

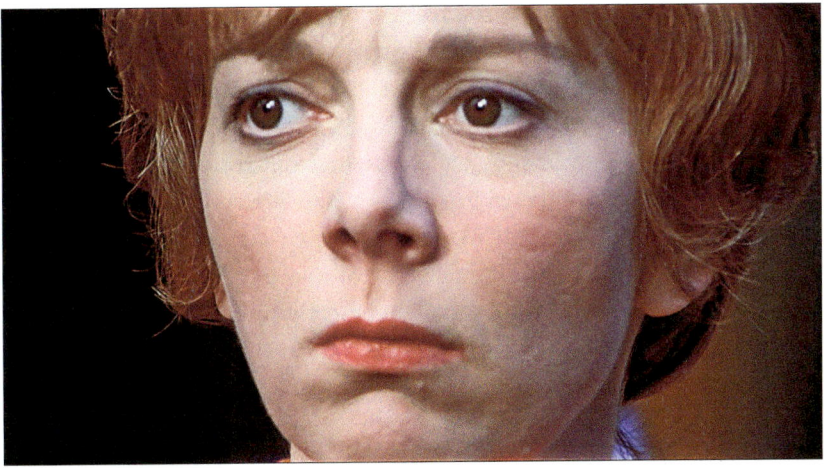

Figure 1.7 The close-up as fetishistic image: *Frenzy* (1972)

the close-up, with the background undefined as a set of abstract shapes in movement. The close-up is further intensified through the loss of the street soundtrack and achieves a moment of greatest intensity in several beats of complete screen silence (1:00:36).[44] The killer's words are then uttered over this silence: "Got a place to stay?" This utterance constitutes a sound image that instantly punctures the hermetic cinematic space, allowing the naturalistic sounds of the street to return and wash over the dialogue that ensues. I would argue that this sudden transition from a realist to reflexive cinematic mode is as sophisticated a rendition of cinema's formal potential as exists in Hitchcock's oeuvre.

In this sequence in *Frenzy*, reflexivity materializes through the complex formal composition of image and sound in relation and in the imaginative attention of the medium to the environment of bodies situated on a busy Covent Garden street. The deliberate and sophisticated play with shot length and scale, perspective, and focus orchestrates movement within the frame, while the duration of the close-up at the completion of the fast zoom unsettles the frame with the presence of a constantly moving apparatus. I would go so far as to say that movement—of bodies within the frame, and of the apparatus that captures the movement of bodies—is the animating force of the sequence. In the multivalent expression of the medium, movement is a function of visuality *and* sound. Thus, a zoom into the stillness of an image (the liminal close-up on Babs) contrives a symbiotic relation between visual and sound images. At what point are the phenomena of visuality and aurality separate in the composition of this image? In what sense can we say that the "sound" of an image bereft of sound—the radical artifice of a perfectly silent cinematic image—is separate from the movement (a zoom) intrinsic to that image? We can take this further still to suggest that sound is intrinsic to the moving image (where it is necessarily extrinsic to the still image of the photograph) and that movement—Dulac's essence of the medium of cinema—is intrinsic to the phenomenal properties of the film soundtrack. Of course, Dulac's early experimental works of the *cinéma pur* movement are silent forms of cinema in the traditional sense of that term. But as we know, silent cinema was never without sound, but merely without the technology required to realize synchronized sound. Dulac's silent cinema, like Hitchcock's, is profoundly aural.

The reflexive movement concludes with a zoom out to a conventional medium two shot (a frame inhabited by two figures), locating the bodies within the environment of the street, instantiating again a point of entry into a realist mode. The soundscape is again amplified, again vitally present. The figures in moving through the street naturally expand the depth of field of the shot; they cross the street laterally, while other bodies move in mid- to deep background. The frame is dense with environmental cues, matched by accompanying aural cues. The long tracking shot captures the continuity and naturalistic movement intrinsic to the realist mode, while the dialogue between Babs and Rusk about the city and their travels anchors the image within the geography of the space. In this clearly marked retransition from a reflexive to a more objective, observational cinematic mode, the sequence captures what Bazin calls the inherent continuity of the real: this is an environment in constant flow, captured through an expansive depth of field, without cutting, containing the world in a single sequence shot and an amplified naturalistic soundscape.[45] The realist modality continues in the cut to the interior of a warehouse and the duration of the dolly shot that frames Babs and Rusk. Depth of field is accentuated within the frame: we see the exterior of the warehouse in deep background, with men loading boxes onto a truck, while Babs and Rusk move through the mid-ground of the shot and come to rest in medium close-up before the camera.

The movement of the camera dollying backward with the walking movement of the characters emphasizes the *flow*, or the "happening" of this movement. We can say, with reference to Deleuze's discussion of movement in the film image, that the movement of the apparatus always configures a *moving*

Figure 1.8 Realist space: *Frenzy* (1972)

image (an image animated by movement) rather than an image *of* movement, or one in which movement has previously occurred.[46] This is why movement for Dulac is such a stunning achievement of the film medium: What other art form can produce a *moving* image? A hundred years of cinema has perhaps taken the gloss off this phenomenon. In contrast to the radical form of movement as process, we can say that a montage that configures movement—for example, the movement of a body from one side of a room to another through a series of cuts—displays only a movement that has occurred, that is *past*. Montage is still of course movement in a sense, having depicted the movement of a body within space, but if we follow Bazin's thinking, it is a lesser movement than that kind of movement that is intrinsic to an image. This is precisely why shot duration was so important to Bazin. In simplest terms, the movement of bodies within the frame and the movement of the apparatus (in the case of *Frenzy*, a dolly tracking the movement of the principal figures within the shot) configure a cinematic movement-in-itself, displaying movement in the process of occurring, but never as a point of origin or destination.

The dolly shot holds for a wholly unconventional (even for Hitchcock) duration of one minute and twelve seconds, concluding one of Hitchcock's most complex camera movements. While not an obvious Bazinian realist image such as we see in Renoir or Welles,[47] nonetheless the dolly shot contrives the continuity of reality in its movement, which is always in a process of occurring. The duration of the movement immerses the spectator in the continuous flow and vibrant energy of the environment.

At the conclusion of the dolly shot, the image cuts to the interior of the apartment building, enacting a sudden and jarring reversion to a reflexive cinematic mode. It is as if the spectator now encounters a wholly different, and deliberately dissonant, image regime. The realism of the Bazinian depth of field and duration ideal is instantly occluded by a cut from exterior to interior. Whereas the movement intrinsic to the dolly shot was animated by the constant flow of the densely packed environment, with its delivery vehicles and market stalls in continuous movement, the camera movement within the interior of the apartment building contrives a purely "cinematic" image itinerary. Realist space and movement is initially punctured by a two shot on the staircase: it is again an excessive close-up, breaching the conventions of classical shot perspective, again almost approximating the extreme close-up ordinarily reserved for fetishistic images.

The two-shot close-up eschews a central focal point: the faces of Babs and Rusk shift in and out of focus, destabilizing the frame and viewing

Figure 1.9 The liminal close-up: *Frenzy* (1972)

perspective. The camera continues to track these bodies on the staircase, holding the shot in what is, quite contrary to the expansive duration of the realistic dolly shot, the excessive, exhibitionist duration of the tracking movement through the interior of the apartment. Against the realism of the preceding dolly shot that is attentive to the environment of the street and warehouse, the tracking shot is attentive to the unnatural cinematic space of the apartment interior; the track says less about the diegetic world than about cinema's capacity to express movement within a tightly choreographed cinematic frame.

The camera pauses at the corner of the staircase, as Babs follows Rusk into the apartment. We hear the voice of Rusk behind a closing door: "You're my type of woman." And then, as if in frustration at not being permitted entry, the camera decides to move, evidently seeking a better vantage point. It begins a slow pan to the right, and down, searching for an aperture; it moves into the wall briefly, but jars back, discovering no point of access. This is a camera with agency and purpose that expresses a desire to see the act occurring behind the door. Turning the staircase, it sees only the innocuous exterior of the apartment and not the sinister interior the facade conceals. With nowhere else to go, the camera retreats further along its original track, its point of entry, and moves out again into the street, its singular gaze collapsing beneath the cacophony of street sounds. We could say that in this moment the instrumental gaze of the apparatus is rendered impotent by the immersive, cacophonous, realist streetscape. The threat of the movement of the interior apparatus is now subdued at the point of exit onto the street.

What is the nature of the *presence* of this cinematic apparatus? What does it mean to say that a camera—or the cinematic apparatus—can desire? The famous tracking shot of *Frenzy* realizes the cinematic apparatus as a libidinal cinematic gaze. Unlike the observational gaze of the dolly on the street, the libidinal gaze of the apparatus within the apartment is highly unstable, deviant in its perspectival configuration, and frustrated at its inability to move where it chooses; it should be permitted entry to all cinematic spaces. Of course, the sequence playfully sutures the spectator's gaze into that of the libidinal gaze of the apparatus; as spectators, we desire to enter the apartment, to enact our desire within the presence of the scene. But this is not the most significant aspect of the sequence, and as I suggested in the introduction, Hitchcock's cinema rarely configures an unproblematic circuit of identification between spectator and character. Rather, what is most striking within the sequence is that the origin of this gaze, no less than the origin of the gaze in which Daisy meets the Lodger for the first time, is the autonomous movement of the camera. The image is the production of a moving, thinking, desiring cinematic apparatus. The reflexive image in this sequence depicts bodies within cinematic frames, and within wholly cinematic regimes of space and movement. Such frames compel the spectator to invest in the image from *within* the cinematic space and from within its formal itineraries. This is to say that the radical potential of the tracking shot in *Frenzy* is to enable the spectator to see through a cinematic gaze, to encounter a world through a uniquely cinematic mode of perception.

1.5. The Purity Thesis Refined, and Cinematic Backdrops

Describing the method of a Hitchcockian pure cinema, Luiza Liz has recently suggested that "it was Hitchcock's deep pleasure in dominating the moving image—his obsessive dedication to make artifice conquer nature . . . that reveals a vast aesthetic sensibility."[48] I have suggested that cinematic purity should not be conflated with aesthetic artifice in spite of the reflexive nature of pure cinema. Rather, purity should connote—as it did for Dulac—the formal and experiential potential of the properties of a medium that sought to differentiate itself from other artistic mediums that had preceded it. In this sense, for Dulac, as for Hitchcock, purity signified an uninhibited expression of aesthetic form. In the set of analyses of a Hitchcockian approach to cinematic form I've offered in this chapter, image and sound exceed the parameters of a classically oriented narrative cinema. A sequence in *Vertigo* or *Frenzy* or *The Lodger* demonstrates in singular moments the capacity of the image to become self-aware and openly referential, to engage the freedom of play in its abstract possibilities.

Hitchcock was also not a filmmaker to shy away from medium-specific effects. We see the striking effect of a glass ceiling that enables the surveillance of the Lodger as early as 1927, or the effect of the "Vertigo shot" in 1958, the production of which Hitchcock elaborates with great pleasure in discussion with Truffaut.[49] We experience the uncanny sensation of accompanying Arbogast (Martin Balsam) as he falls in *Psycho*, a novel cinematic descent accomplished through a simple though ingenious mechanical process.[50] The visibility of the cinema effect in Hitchcock's films becomes more explicit, and more reflexively *cinematic*, in the films of the 1950s and early 1960s. This is a strange evolution toward a cinema of effect, simply because the European and American auteur cinema of this period tends toward aesthetic realism.

The tendency to reflexively situate the image within a larger discourse on cinema's production and spectatorship reveals what Barry Langford has very usefully called "a non-realist order of representation."[51] Hitchcock's films are steadfastly anti-realist in their rejection of social and political realisms prevalent in the cinema of the period. But perhaps more significant is Hitchcock's rejection of the Bazinian image of the real that, at least in Bazin's writing, describes the unique capacity of the film image to communicate the ontological properties of reality. Hitchcock's increasingly flamboyant style through the 1950s and early 1960s very rarely reveals cinema's capacity for aesthetic realism. Rather, as we see in *Frenzy,* Hitchcock tends to eschew reality and its transcendental qualities, deconstructing the "real" into a highly ordered, elaborate set of formal cinematic tropes.

One such trope is the set backdrop, which Hitchcock utilizes in several films to problematize the line between what Bazin called "an aesthetic of reality" and the reproduction of reality on a set.[52] The spectator is initially unsettled by the vibrant artifice of the Greenwich Village set in *Rear Window*. Similarly, the facade of the Bates Motel first seen through torrential rain strikes the spectator as an imagistic trope; it looms over the frame as an elaborate set construction no less than Welles's expressionist design of Xanadu in the opening sequence of *Citizen Kane* (1941). Yet it isn't until *Marnie* that

Hitchcock embraces the full potential of the backdrop to demonstrate the reflexive potential of the cinematic image.

The conventional backdrop functions as an expression of depth within the image, bringing the objects or actions contained in foreground into a seamless relation with the entirety of the frame. Thus, we see in the background of *Rope*'s New York skyline a confluence of buildings descending into shadow with the setting of the sun; the effect is a critical marker in a film otherwise almost bereft of any sensation of passing time. The skyline in *Rope* also sets an actual location and narrativizes the social and cultural norms of that space, which open out in the tensions over class and education within the film's story. But it is important to note that the buildings unproblematically stand in for the city; the image is deep enough, and rarely precise enough, to warrant questioning by the spectator. We could also say that this presentational realism is matched by the long-take cinematography to capture the spontaneity and immediacy of an event unfolding in time.

But we cannot say the same thing of the space of San Francisco in *Vertigo* or the Greenwich Village setting of *Rear Window*, which is wholly contained within the studio lot. If *Rear Window* is, as Hitchcock suggests, a pure cinematic space, I would argue that San Francisco materializes as no less a cinematic image in *Vertigo*. *Vertigo* offers less of an actualization of the city location than a cinematic reconstruction, with the city metonymically encapsulated by a few landmarks: "the Bay," the Mission District, Coit Tower. If Scottie's pursuit is of an apparition (Madeleine), the cinematic city itself, rendered in the opulence of saturated color, is no less apparitional, no less ineffable. In these films, appearing in the mid- to late 1950s, Hitchcock "conquers" the realist space of the city (to use Liz's terminology) and subjects it to an explicitly cinematic topography.[53]

In *Marnie*, the tradition of the matte background as spatial depth within the frame is ruptured by the visibility of the matte construction. In an early scene in the film, Marnie visits her mother at the Baltimore dock. The foreground and mid-ground of the image are comprised of a set construction of a street and a tenement building. Receding from the mid-ground, however, the frame is entirely composited with the foreground action in a matte drawing of the rear half of the tenement building (you can clearly make out the dividing line between constructed set and matte) and what appears to be an absurdly over-scaled ocean liner stationed a few paces from the end of the street.

Figure 1.10 Diegesis as set construction: *Marnie* (1964)

The image is remarkable for its manifest unreality and its incongruity in a tradition of filmmaking in Hollywood that increasingly favored location authenticity. What is Hitchcock doing here? Clearly, the image functions as a special effect of some kind rather than realist representation; it is a marker of artifice rather than authenticity. But why present the image with such compositional incongruity, and especially when the spectator cannot but notice the incongruity between foreground and background?[54]

Michelle Piso has argued that "*Marnie*'s visual composition is extremely controlled, its formal stylization heightened by the glaringly artificial rear projections of the horse rides and the exaggerated, painterly sets of the Edgar neighborhood and Rutland office. These distortions of outside space are not careless flaws.... Rather, they are defiantly airless inventions that underscore and condemn the unnatural quality of the film's depicted world."[55] While these overdetermined cinematic exteriors clearly signify the "unnatural quality" of the film's world (which we could say of several film traditions), far more striking, it seems to me, is the breach of an essential perceptual and ontological realism within the frame. The frame is rent apart by the breach, the dividing line between photographic realism and graphic illustration marked by the line dividing foreground and mid-ground (a photographic composition of a physical set) from the background illustration of the matte. How are we to address such a frame? If our natural intuition is to perceptually engage the cinematic frame as whole (as it is for most of us), this image confounds our perceptual faculties. The frame is internally conflicted, split into so many component parts without resolving into the classical whole of the traditional realist frame. The frame is in this sense an abstract composition of fragments and a basic rejection of what Bazin called the "ontology of the photographic image."[56] In her assessment of the overarching style of *Marnie*, Piso suggests that the film's "denaturalized purism of style . . . recalls the geometrics of Mondrian, the cropped chasteness of Bresson, the angularity of Antonioni's techno-world. The image is cold, silent, intense; its restricted framing creates an abstract and disorienting relation to the body."[57] Thus for Piso, the formal style of *Marnie* shares something of the modernist artist's desire for spatial abstraction and the purity of figures animated through movement.

Reflecting on the several analyses that underpin this chapter, could we begin to suggest that in such effects Hitchcock produced an abstract form of cinema? Or perhaps less grandly, that a Hitchcockian pure cinema projects the possibility of the film image as an abstract spatiotemporal form, even if such a possibility was not fully realized in the cinema of the 1950s and 1960s? Truffaut, perhaps unwittingly, sensed the radical potential of a Hitchcockian pure cinema as aesthetic abstraction. Discussing the crop duster scene in *North by Northwest*, he says, "The most appealing aspect of that sequence with the plane is that it's totally gratuitous—it's a scene that's been drained of all plausibility or even significance. Cinema, approached in this way, becomes truly abstract art, like music."[58] This is a pure cinema that tends toward an abstraction from the whole (whether of a classical aesthetic design or a realist image), splitting into component parts. From *The Lodger* in 1927 to what I've called the radical experiment of *Frenzy* in 1972, the natural trajectory of Hitchcockian cinema is toward abstraction in figure, shape, and movement in an increasingly complex and unrestricted form.

2
Hitchcock's Interlocutors

2.1. Authorship and Imitation

In his excellent study of the Hitchcock–De Palma relationship, Thomas Leitch suggests that "no filmmaker has ever produced a more extended meditation on the work of another filmmaker than Brian De Palma."[1] It is an intriguing term—"meditation"—because it connotes a complex and deep thought process; it connotes reflection. Leitch reads De Palma's quotations of Hitchcock as a reflexive aesthetic strategy, and he suggests most provocatively that "Hitchcock owes as much to De Palma as De Palma does to Hitchcock."[2] In this statement, Leitch seems to acknowledge the intertextual circuit that connects Hitchcock to De Palma, but unlike the majority of assessments of intertextual relationships, Leitch does not construct a hierarchy between an original work and its imitation. He seeks to maintain an analytical focus on assessing the nature of such borrowings, to maintain objectivity, and to assess De Palma's imitation as the reflexive reconstruction of Hitchcockian stylistic gestures; his analysis of De Palma's inversion of the suspense/surprise of the Hitchcock shower scene is a fantastic insight into how a text changes through imitation.[3] In my opinion, Leitch's analysis is unparalleled in scholarship on De Palma, and I use it as a methodological foundation for my examination of the Hitchcock-*giallo*–De Palma textual circuit.

In this chapter, I want to formulate a notion of pure cinema as part of an interlocutionary circuit, and I want to frame this circuit through a very different notion of textual authorship. First, to work with the Hitchcock-*giallo*–De Palma relationship, we must accept that textual enunciation is an iterative phenomenon. Essentially, text is only a closed communicative field in a literal-minded reading that desires a point of origin and its imitation. If instead we attempt to engage text as an open itinerary, we enter a non-chronological, disordered set of textual relations that are, precisely in their ramshackle assemblage, profoundly creative. We might therefore see the interrelations of Hitchcock, the *giallo*, and De Palma, or indeed a plethora of authors, as part of an unwieldy but arresting conversation that privileges textual parts over wholes.[4] Films such as Mario Bava's *Blood and Black Lace* (*Sei donne per l'assassino*, 1964), Dario Argento's *The Bird with the Crystal Plumage* (*L'uccello dale piume di cristallo*, 1970), and De Palma's *Obsession* (1976) utilize the image, sound, and narrative stylistics of Hitchcock as a canvas upon which to expand and creatively develop an aesthetic philosophy and practice. While the pure cinema mode of Bava, Argento, and De Palma is vastly different from the pure cinema mode of Hitchcock, in revealing the essential capacity of the medium to depict visual form, movement, and sound within the frame, I suggest that the *giallo* and De Palma productively consume Hitchcock's style only to regurgitate it in an expanded, intensified form.

2.2. This Is Not an Art Cinema: Pure Cinema and Classical Form

In late 1959 and early 1960, Truffaut and Jean Luc Godard released their first films, *The 400 Blows* (*Les Quatre cent coup*) and *Breathless* (*À Bout de souffle*), respectively, two films that would signal the emergence of the French New Wave. In 1960, Federico Fellini released his most famous, influential and controversial film, *La Dolce Vita*, and established a global reputation on the back of his exploration of the cosmopolitan, alienated European subject; like *The 400 Blows* and *Breathless*, *La Dolce Vita* was a feisty and subversive examination of a national cultural consciousness. Also in 1960, Michelangelo Antonioni released *L'Avventura*, a signature work defining a philosophical style of filmmaking that would henceforth be associated with his oeuvre. Perhaps less flamboyant stylistically than the films of Godard and Truffaut, Antonioni's visual sensibility was no less sophisticated, and no less noticeable to critics; Deleuze would later accord Antonioni's film images in *L'Avventura* a special status in his theories of cinematic time.[5] In Sweden, in 1960, Ingmar Bergman released *The Virgin Spring* (*Jungfrukällan*), a work that would have a lasting impact on the European art film tradition of the 1960s, following only a few years on from *The Seventh Seal* (*Det sjunde inseglet*, 1957) and *Wild Strawberries* (*Smultronstället*, 1957). In late 1959, in New York, John Cassavetes released the definitive version of his experimental feature, *Shadows*, a film that may have had an influence on Godard in his approach to rhythm and pacing in *Breathless*. In 1960, in Hollywood, following 1959's *North by Northwest* and 1958's *Vertigo*, Hitchcock released *Psycho*.

This is a sketchy narrative of an American and European auteur cinema of a very particular moment in film history. Yet placing these films and their influential directors into such close proximity around the release date of *Psycho* is revealing. I would characterize the European art house tradition as a style founded upon two interrelated aesthetic approaches. On the one hand, Truffaut's *The 400 Blows*, Cassavetes's *Shadows*, and Antonioni's *L'Avventura* exemplify a mode of aesthetic realism celebrated by Bazin in his essays on the Italian neorealist tradition; such films bear what Bazin calls an "adherence to actuality."[6] Each filmmaker uses the medium to bring a level of authenticity to the image. Thus, while Truffaut's rush zoom in the final moment of *The 400 Blows* is a highly expressive movement of the camera, its overarching purpose is to bring the spectator into the proximity of a social, cultural, and psychological truth.

The influence of aesthetic realism on the Italian (but also more broadly European) New Wave cinemas has been widely acknowledged.[7] Yet Godard, Fellini, Bergman, and Cassavetes, while clearly impelled by a fascination with the "real" in the 1950s, employ the expressivity and playfulness of a high modernist aesthetic sensibility. Thus, Godard can experiment with point of view, framing, and enunciation in a film such as *Vivre Sa Vie* (1962) to produce images that subvert a classical realist form. Or Michel (Jean-Paul Belmondo) can speak to the camera in the opening scenes of *Breathless* without collapsing the narrative frame of the film; direct address is a modernist trope only in a *non*-avant-garde work, of which *Breathless* is clearly an example. Fellini's fragmented episodic structure in *La Dolce Vita* and authorial self-consciousness in *8 1/2* (1963) represent a clear modernist aesthetic and philosophical sensibility, and the lavish stylistic flourishes in these films are exhibitionist spectacles that demonstrate a degree of textual self-consciousness. Cassavetes's *Shadows* is a jazz film in more than subject matter alone. Its largely improvisatory association of image and sound and its loosely assembled narrative units adopt the principles of jazz musical form. While the film depicts the harsh reality of racial and ethnic conflict in New York of the 1950s, it does so through an expressive cinematic method adapted from a (modernist-infused) musical rather than cinematic aesthetic register.

But where would we situate Hitchcock in these separate, though sometimes related, traditions? Well, for one, I would suggest that *Psycho* is neither a realist nor a modernist cinematic work, and that Hitchcock spent the greater part of his British and American career cultivating an antimodernist aesthetic stance. In Hitchcock, the expressive movement of the apparatus, or narrative ambiguity, or a cut contriving an experimental montage, is a momentary rupture that constitutes a break from the whole, but it is never rationalized within an overarching modernist (or indeed paradigmatic) aesthetic sensibility. Thus, while I agree with Orr that we might read a modernist textual proclivity in a film like *The Birds*, I would in no way describe Hitchcock as a modernist filmmaker or *The Birds* as a modernist film.[8] Hitchcock's narrative and image form, even of the experimental kind we see in films such as *Vertigo* and *Marnie*, require at least a semblance of image and narrative continuity, if not a perfectly hermetic classical continuity. The textual ruptures are what define Hitchcock's cinema as subversive, or as just transgressive enough to trouble the mass cultural establishment. The playful, risqué image of a train entering a tunnel while Roger and Eve consummate their desire in *North by Northwest* is an effective rupture only in relation to the dominant constraints of the Hays Code of production; the image doesn't work outside of the hegemonic structure authorizing acceptable sexual relationships. In a similar fashion, while I could argue that *Breathless* is a crime film of sorts (Belmondo plays the noir protagonist in his mimicry of Bogart) or that *The 400 Blows* is a generic coming-of age-story, such interpretations are obtuse. The cinema of Godard, Truffaut, Fellini, Bergman, Cassavetes, or any filmmaker I would align with the tradition Bordwell identifies as the "art film"[9] utilizes genre tropes only as a reflexive commentary within a modernist aesthetic sensibility. This is why, for example, Michel in *Breathless* must mark out his performance of the noir protagonist by imitating Bogart; without the imitation, we might mistake him for the real thing.

Hitchcock's compulsion to immerse the spectator in story (a larger imperative within the American studio system, and to only a slightly lesser degree in his British-era films) prohibits the kind of experimentation with image and narrative we see in the art house tradition. In conversation with Truffaut, Hitchcock declares, "Making a film means, first of all, to tell a story."[10] A film that seeks expressly to communicate a story embodies what Bordwell, Staiger, and Thompson call the "classical Hollywood narrative," which is a formal aesthetic system that presents a convincing facade of perceptual reality to cover over what is a complex, sophisticated fantasy structure.[11] But "story" signifies far more than narrative action for Hitchcock. It is also a signifier of reflexively modeled *generic* story form. Again, in conversation with Truffaut, in response to Truffaut's categorization of *Strangers on a Train* as a thriller: "It's my good fortune to have something of a monopoly on the genre: nobody else seems to take much interest in the rules for that form."[12] It would be impossible to imagine Godard acquiescing to the rules of a genre form. For Hitchcock, and this is the most important aspect of his formation of a visual style, the tendency toward reflexive generic form and structure inscribes an aesthetic frame that subtends the visual compositional rationale of the film image. I agree with Raymond Durgnat that Hitchcock's "technical flexibility and virtuosity has a smack of the avant-garde about it,"[13] but it seems to me that Hitchcock's stunning achievement in deploying a pure cinema style, particularly in the later films, is situating that style in relation to the limit point of a classical aesthetic paradigm. The synthesis of a reflexive image form and cinema's mass entertainment narrative design constitutes the major expansion of Hitchcock's pure cinema aesthetic from the avant-garde image experimentation of the *cinéma pur* movement of the 1920s.[14] To find a Hitchcockian stylistic legacy that emerges in relative proximity to the release of *Psycho*, I turn to what Mikel Koven calls a "vernacular" European cinema and the curiosity known as the Italian *giallo* film.[15]

2.3. Italian Genre Cinema: The *Giallo* in Mario Bava, Dario Argento, and Lucio Fulci

The *giallo* as a generic form refers quite loosely to a category of the larger Italian genre film corpus known as the *filone*, which includes the *poliziotteschi* (the Italian crime film), the peplum (the " sword and sandal epic" imported from Hollywood), and, perhaps most famously, the spaghetti western, which enjoyed enormous popularity from the early- to mid-1960s to the mid-1970s.[16] I am concerned specifically with the *giallo* as a form of popular exploitation horror cinema,[17] its expressive use of visual and aural form, and its explicit imitation of Hitchcock. In my analysis, I focus on the horror *giallo* with the following narrative structure, which I adopt from Koven's study: "An innocent person, often a tourist, witnesses a brutal murder that appears to be the work of a serial killer. He or she takes on the role of amateur detective in order to track down this killer, and often succeeds where the police fail."[18] While I undertake expansive formal analyses of the *giallo* in subsequent chapters, in this subsection I offer a general overview of the emergence and development of the genre through the films of Mario Bava, Dario Argento, and Lucio Fulci.

2.4. Vernacular Visuality: From Hitchcock to the *Giallo*

> My films are always visually striking because as a critic I liked that sort of film, with strong images. In fact, when I met Sergio Leone, it was maybe the first time in my life that I met a person that also reasoned in terms of images.
>
> Dario Argento

In his description of the Italian *giallo* as a "vernacular cinema," Koven suggests that "vernacular cinema seeks to look at subaltern cinema not for how it might (or might not) conform to the precepts of high-art/modernist cinema, but for what it does in its own right."[23] While his sense of a vernacular mode is defined somewhat loosely in opposition to "popular cinema," the nature of the vernacularism of the Italian *giallo* is described in terms of a baroque experimental form, visual and narrative patterning, exhibitionist spectacle, and excess (in terms of both a formal excess and an excessive effect on the spectator). The common vernacular of the *giallo* is therefore founded upon the explicit and often reflexive exhibition of familiar narrative, imagistic, and sound norms. While the *giallo* story depicts the serial murder of women, it depicts it in a particularly gratuitous and fetishistic way. The design of the spaces in which such set pieces occur complement a formal logic of visual and aural excess. Thus, the excess of (often sexually charged) violence done to the victim is reflected in the intrusive visual design of the set. Colors are lurid and saturated rather than naturalistic or washed. Props are often of large or monumental scale and situated within encompassing architectural spaces, such as museums, galleries, and ornately decorated mansions. Visual excess is complemented by an aural excess in which a soundscape is commonly nonnaturalistic, amplified in relation to the visual source, or, in the most experimental examples in Argento and Fulci, dissonant in musical and sound design.

While he does not explicitly mention her article, it is important to note that Koven is working through Miriam Bratu Hansen's seminal study of vernacular modernism.[24] While Koven uses the notion of vernacularism to valorize the aesthetic form and reception of the *giallo* as a peripheral cinema of the 1960s and 1970s, Hansen's formulation of a vernacular modernism of the classical American cinema is equally provocative for the study of visual and aural form in the *giallo*. Following Kracauer, Hansen suggests that the slapstick comedy (of Keaton and Chaplin, among others) presented modern

American cinema's "reflexive potential . . . to confront the constitutive ambivalence of modernity."[25] Intriguingly, Hansen further suggests that vernacular cinema produces "processes of mimetic identification that are more often than not partial or excessive in relation to narrative comprehension."[26] While I argue that the *giallo* is founded upon neither a modernist aesthetic nor an aesthetic of the American commercial cinema, I would suggest that its vernacularism affords a reflexive engagement (for both film and spectator) with the formal visual and aural properties of cinema. This is to say that the vernacularism of the *giallo* is specifically anchored in its visual and aural medium specificity. It is a vernacularism that, like Hansen's vernacular modernism, is characterized by ruptures and excesses from a classical narrative structure. As such, I contend that the *giallo* is situated within the tradition of a pure cinema form, and it is the European film tradition that most explicitly converses with the Hitchcockian pure cinema of the 1950s and early 1960s. The strongest formal and affective resonance between the films of Hitchcock, the Italian *giallo*, and De Palma is a shared *vernacular visuality*. Simply put, these films and filmmakers share a philosophical and aesthetic disposition toward the film image founded upon an excessive visual and sonic experimentation that did not evolve as a sustained and coherent practice within the European and American art or commercial cinema traditions.

In closing this discussion, I want to make one final distinction between the vernacularism of the *giallo* and other cult cinema forms. As Jeffrey Sconce has argued in an influential piece, the cult film is productively described as a "parametric" text: "As a most elastic textual category, paracinema would include entries from such seemingly disparate subgenres as 'badfilm,' splatterpunk, 'mondo' films, sword and sandal epics, Elvis flicks, government hygiene films, Japanese monster movies, beach-party musicals, and just about every other historical manifestation of exploitation cinema from juvenile delinquency documentaries to soft-core pornography. Paracinema is thus less a distinct group of films than a particular reading protocol, a counter-aesthetic turned sub-cultural sensibility devoted to all manner of cultural detritus."[27] Of course, the *giallo* is clearly part of a larger exploitation cinema, with heavy doses of gratuitous violence and nudity, and without the production value of the Italian prestige films of the modernist auteurs. Yet a critical distinction needs to be made between the mode of exploitation cinema of the paracinema and the *giallo*. Several authors have demonstrated the radically unstable structure of the Italian *giallo* cinema; it was clearly not a film aesthetic founded upon the classical organizational principles that dominated the American cinema.²⁸ Yet neither does the *giallo* exemplify paracinema's "lack of pronounced stylistic virtuosity as the result of a 'conscious' artistic agenda."²⁹ I therefore agree with Sconce that exploitation cinema (and certainly that mode of exploitation cinema he terms "paracinema") represents a stylistic and cultural detritus, rejecting the formalism of an overarching aesthetic system. But this is not the case of the exploitation cinema of the Italian *giallo*. As Argento suggests, and this clearly articulates a position adopted by Hitchcock in discussion with Truffaut in the early 1960s, the *giallo*, in spite of its ramshackle production and reception itineraries, was determinedly reflexive in its engagement with the capacities of cinema; the desire for an expanded and reflexive visuality was intrinsic to its formal and generic structure. The excessive style of the *giallo*, as chaotic as that style can be in the hands of Bava, Argento, and Fulci, must be rationalized within a larger discourse on the history of cinematic style, and especially within a history of those styles in nearest proximity to the *giallo*. The *giallo*'s "excess" cannot therefore be adequately described as a breach of a "closed formal system."³⁰ The rigid dichotomy Sconce casts between the irrational formal excesses of paracinema and the "closed formal system" of a more conventional cinematic frame simply cannot account for the strangeness of the cinema of Hitchcock, the *giallo*, or De Palma, in relation to other American and European cinemas in close proximity. Sconce argues that while the "aesthete['s] interest in style and excess always returns the viewer to the frame, paracinematic attention to excess seeks to push the viewer beyond the formal boundaries of the text."³¹ But in the model of pure cinema I have proposed, founded as it is on textual imitation, one aesthetic imperative does not preclude the other.

2.5. De Palma's American Vernacularism

In a meticulous analysis of the structure of a sequence in *Carlito's Way*, Adrian Martin suggests that De Palma thinks in terms of a formal scene schematic. Martin interprets this notion of a schematic as "a map of the relation of the elements in a scene, especially of the various kinds of *movements* in the scene (of the actors, the camera, the eye-lines . . .) and their interrelation. . . . It is something like an overall *system* for the film, as well as a charting of its moment-to-moment transformations."³² I agree with Martin that the essence of De Palma's schematic of a scene, or even a complex shot, is movement—of objects within a frame, of the frame itself (through the movement of the apparatus), and movement through change from one frame to another (montage). De Palma's visual specificity and eccentricity underpins the schematic layout of the famous pool hall scene in *Carlito's Way*, one of his grandest visual and aural experiments. Martin has done an exemplary job of analyzing the formal complexity of this sequence. I therefore merely wish to draw attention to the unique character of the visual sensibility operating within the sequence and to suggest that the obsessively visual and aural schematizing of the sequence reflects De Palma's visual vernacularism.

In cinematic terms, and more particularly within the register of classical visual form, De Palma's visuality seems to operate in a liminal perspectival and proportional fashion. In his study of De Palma, and in a particularly evocative turn of phrase, Peretz argues that De Palma's films constitute a "passionate witnessing of the broken frame."[33] Indeed, De Palma's frame in his numerous set pieces goes against the grain of formal symmetry, stability, and communication. The frame originates in De Palma as an experimental field of signs, and like Hitchcock, De Palma's formal visuality charges the frame with affective potential. Tracing a fairly conventional schematic, the pool hall scene opens in an establishing shot: we see the interior (or at least the front of room) in a wide-long shot that sets up spatial and character relations.

But this is not a conventional visual schematic that functions to provide spatial orientation and narrative information. Rather, in its formal complexity, it is the schematic itself that arrests the spectator's attention. First, the establishing shot moves with the subtle undulation of an uncomfortable hand-held point of view; the frame is thus destabilized and unconventional as an establishing shot. Second, the room is exhibited as a multiplicity of

Figure 2.1 De Palma's schematic frame: *Carlito's Way* (1993)

frames within the hermetic cinematic frame: a vertical pole sets up the familiar De Palma split screen, weighting the right section of the frame. But on the left of the frame we see the wall recede into the perspectival interior of a mirror. The frames recede into the reflected frame of the mirror, opening out and expanding the interior of the room, appearing almost as a set of receding geometric patterns. The camera moves uneasily. Something is clearly wrong in this scenario (Carlito's nephew will shortly be brutally murdered), and dramatic action is decentered across lines intersecting the frame. While the movement of figures within the frame is confident and expressive, the mood and rhythmic attenuation of the frame unsettles the spectator. We might think of this simple device as a form of dramatic irony expressed by the movement of the camera in relation to the spatial configuration of the frame. In what appears an innocuous movement from exterior to interior, we see the image charged with a complex, reflexive visual and aural register.

De Palma's visual vernacularism in such sequences operates in an intriguingly similar fashion to that of Bava and Argento, or indeed Hitchcock. De Palma opts early in his career to explicitly identify with a Hitchcockian formal and generic legacy. While each of De Palma's early works, and most notably *Murder a la Mod* (1968) and *The Wedding Party* (1969), represents formal cinematic experiments in an era in which formal experimentation had become the norm in the American studio and independent film industry,[34] it was not until the release of *Sisters* in 1973 that De Palma schematized a film through the visual logic of a Hitchcockian template. In an interview in 1973, De Palma notes, "I am also a great admirer of Hitchcock and *Psycho*, and there are a great many structural elements here [in *Sisters*] that are in Hitchcock's movies: introducing a character and then having him killed off early in the film; switching points of view; taking the person who sees the murder and then involving him in solving the crime."[35] Leitch reads the body in the sofa in *Sisters* as a veiled quotation of the body in the chest in *Rope*;[36] De Palma reveals that the sequence was storyboarded as a single elaborate tracking shot, but the limited budget required the movement to be covered in a more conventional master shot pattern.[37]

While I offer an analysis of *Sisters* in subsequent chapters, I suggest here that this early imitation represents a defining point of departure in De Palma's career and that it would indeed continue to define the visual vernacularism of his cinema. Like Hitchcock at a critical juncture in the mid-1930s, after the release of *Sisters*, De Palma explicitly identifies a formal aesthetic disposition within the thriller genre. Speaking again in relation to the visual experimentation of *Sisters*, De Palma suggests, "The reason that I like the genre is that you can work in a sort of pure cinema form. That is why Hitchcock likes it too. It's all images, and your storytelling is entirely through images and not people talking to each other."[38] Here De Palma self-identifies as a meditative (to use Leitch's terminology) Hitchcockian imitator. And if *Sisters* is a fledgling attempt at a Hitchcockian pure cinema, De Palma's imitation of Hitchcock becomes increasingly transparent, cavalier, and exhibitionistic in his thrillers of the later 1970s and 1980s.

De Palma's oeuvre presents a sustained and sophisticated meditation on the capacity of cinema's visual and aural forms. To this end, he departed very quickly from the trajectories of his film school generation colleagues. Scorsese became the American neorealist par excellence in the 1970s, culminating in the striking realist image of *Raging Bull* (1980). Coppola increasingly explored the capacity of the American independent and studio system to realize a genuine art-cinema medium. The Coppola-Bogdanovich-Friedkin venture of American Zoetrope to realize a new American art cinema form in 1969 in San Francisco failed, and Coppola produced *The Godfather* in 1972, perhaps the exemplary aesthetic model of the American sophisticated commercial cinema of the early 1970s.[39] De Palma's closest companion and in many ways the contemporary filmmaker whom De Palma most admired, Steven Spielberg created the new model of a mass cultural American cinema of the late 1970s and 1980s.[40] In the constant friction between the American commercial and art cinema industries, De Palma remained (and remains) an eccentric, and his work remains an aesthetic oddity.

I suggest that De Palma's marginalization within the studio system is convincingly explained by his obsessive, highly specific, vernacular visual style and its concomitant lack of interest in classical narrative exposition, logical development, and plot resolution. Consider a fairly obvious expositional scene in *The Untouchables* that might play very differently in the hands of another filmmaker. Elliot Ness (Kevin Costner) and Jimmy Malone (Sean Connery) sit somewhere at the front of a church in Chicago, discussing how to "get Capone." David Mamet's dialogue is characteristically spiky and engaging: Malone says, "You said you wanted to know how to get Capone. Do you really want to get him? You see what I'm saying. . . . What are you prepared to do?"

In narrative terms, this is what script doctors call a turning point; it is a sequence that will propel the story on a new trajectory, the getting of Capone. But let us consider the sequence instead as a reflexive meditation on the

54   THE EVOLUTION OF PURE CINEMA

Figure 2.2 The two-shot in architectural space: *The Untouchables* (1987)

formal capacity of the visual frame. The image that facilitates the narrative exposition opens on a low-angled two shot of Ness and Malone.

Now the spectator should anticipate a two-shot dialogue to cover the narrative turn. But surely not the composition of *this* two shot. The figures are captured in an extreme depth of field and focus, bringing into relief the architectural space of the church, Our Lady of the Sorrows, on the west side of Chicago. This is not a Bazinian deep-focus image; rather, De Palma juxtaposes the two shot as a medium close-up against the monumental depth scale of the basilica. The image is thus very clearly an explicit depiction of pictorial perspective within the relative stability of the unmoving frame.

The two shot is, however, merely the commencement of De Palma's examination of the potential of the visual cinematic frame in what is otherwise a relatively conventional expositional sequence. As the necessary dialogue exchange unfolds, one senses De Palma's desire to layer beneath the scene a visual schematic: What is the visual (and not purely expositional) purpose and logic of this sequence? The exposition continues: Malone: "What are you prepared to do?" The image cuts to Ness: "Everything within the law." The image then cuts back to Malone, but now on a new angle within the frame. The requisite expositional continuation—"and *then* what are you prepared to do"—is covered again in two shot, but in profile, with Ness in right foreground in close-up and Malone in left background in medium close-up.

When I screened this image recently to a class, a number of students were unsettled by the crudeness of this two shot; the image seemed oddly unfocused. I suggested that De Palma had used a split diopter lens to collapse the space between Ness in foreground and Malone in background. The split

Figure 2.3 Split-diopter segmented framing: *The Untouchables* (1987)

diopter, I explained, was effectively a split in the frame, or what I called a perspectival "seam." What makes this split diopter shot curious is the remarkable clarity and visibility of the seam: rather than masking the seam within the frame (and thus maintaining at least the semblance of perspectival realism), De Palma draws our attention to the seam, and to the radical perspectival/spatial breach. One of the students asked: "What's the point? It looks so fake."

Yes, of course, in a particular visual register defined according to a perceptual realism, it is a terribly fake contrivance of frame space. But the revelation of the unique space of this frame reveals De Palma's continuing exploration of the potential of the cinematic frame as a set of fragments within a whole. Indeed, I would argue that the sequence, while necessarily expositional (this is a gangster film, after all), presents an entry into a deeper, reflexive meditation on visual cinematic form. De Palma's method is to contrast what appears to be a more conventional pictorial perspective in the two shot (providing something like the logic of depth within the interior space of the basilica) with the frame as a series of geometric segments. The split diopter frame thus asks the spectator to question the nature of cinematic space itself, and of cinema's capacity to depict space within a frame. As such, this sequence in *The Untouchables* represents one intriguing example of De Palma's expanded ontology of the cinematic image.

Like Hitchcock, Bava, and Argento, De Palma's visual vernacularism across a forty-year career represents a philosophical and aesthetic disposition. Of course, Scorsese, Coppola, and Spielberg are among the most imaginative and sophisticated stylists of the American film school generation. But I would argue that their visual schematics serve a more emblematic and visible logic of story, character, and thematic development. While Spielberg's early work demonstrates a highly reflexive visual sensibility within a more explicitly molded genre narrative structure, the gradual emergence and development of the "high concept" aesthetic precludes visual and aural experimentation of the kind we see in De Palma of this period;[41] essentially, De Palma's work, like that of Argento before him, underpinned by the logic of a second-tier production system, moves toward greater visual and aural excesses that simply could not be countenanced by the American commercial film industry of the 1980s and 1990s.

Can a camera move be attentive to a formal pattern and structure? Can it articulate as a process of textual exchange or interlocution? In *Carlito's Way*, a generic, tonal, and rhythmic transition occurs with a single camera move. Carlito (Al Pacino) stands against a garish red wall waiting for his nephew to return from making the deal. The amplified soundtrack makes the threat palpable within the space. The incessant beat of the diegetic dance track intensifies the set of relations between Carlito and the other figures in the front of room. The beat functions as an invocation to sudden, violent transformation. The point of transition is initiated by an innocuous medium shot on Carlito. Prior to this shot, the space is covered in a series of angles, each increasing the level of tension within the frame. It is at this point, however, that the threat is confirmed through a slow dolly into a medium close-up on Carlito's face, followed by a set of explicit "Carlito" points of view. The movement from medium to medium close-up—that is, the affect of movement itself, and not the image of a new proximity to Carlito's eyes—formalizes the act of seeing intrinsic to the schematic of the sequence.

What began as exposition and setup is now realized as a formal visual itinerary. And as Martin demonstrates in his analysis, this visual itinerary is only further complicated and enriched as the sequence progresses. The subtle movement of the camera in this moment recalls the excessive movement itinerary of the camera in the staircase landing in *Frenzy* previously discussed. Each movement signifies a transformation within the cinematic frame from a coverage of diegetic space to a revelation of the frame and its intrinsic visual logic.

In the pool hall sequence in *Carlito's Way*, De Palma reminds us of the elasticity of cinematic visuality. This elasticity of form and its capacity for expression—and specifically its capacity to reflexively change, at times gradually and incrementally, at other times with staggering abruptness—is the foundation of De Palma's formal aesthetic. De Palma seems to ask time and

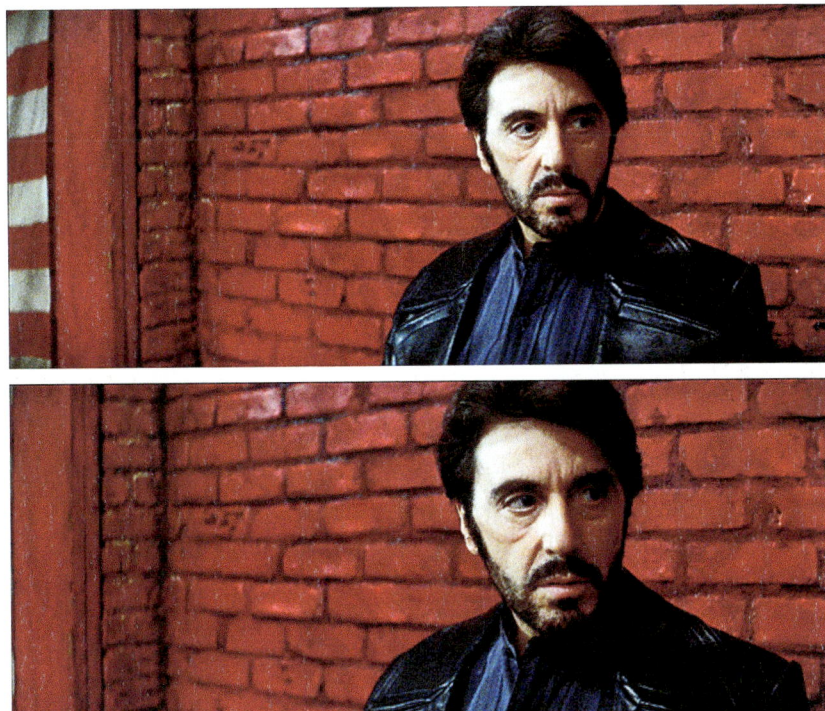

Figures 2.4–2.5 Seeing schematically: *Carlito's Way* (1993)

again in his work: To what extent can visual form richly and discursively *signify*? Can a bodily gesture signify a formal visual itinerary? In what way does a frame and its content, a track, a dolly, a zoom, a cut, a dissolve, a wipe, an iris shot, signify a medium and textual reflexivity, and therein a constantly multiplying set of stylistic exchanges?

PART II
THE MECHANICS OF PURE CINEMA

3
The Part Is Greater Than the Whole
Toward an Aesthetic Philosophy of the Fragment

3.1. Eisenstein and the Myth of Total Cinema

As has already been noted, Hitchcock's notion of a pure cinema is anchored in montage: "To me, pure film, pure cinema, is pieces of film assembled."[1] It's a simple, workable definition of one aspect of film form that had long fascinated filmmakers and theorists. It is also a way for Hitchcock to articulate an aesthetic sensibility and method that would differentiate his practice from the American studio norm. On the subject of montage, Hitchcock's nearest influence seems to be Sergei Eisenstein, for whom montage was not merely a part of cinema but, in a very real sense, was cinema itself. If cinema had the capacity for thought, montage was the mechanics of that thought process. For Eisenstein, montage was also at the root of the specificity of cinema as a technological, aesthetic, and intellectual enterprise. In his most famous formulation, Eisenstein writes, "By what, then, is montage characterized and, consequently, its cell—the shot? . . . By collision. By the conflict of two pieces in opposition to each other. By conflict. By collision."[2] Eisenstein sees this form of montage—the part that, in collision with another part, gives rise to a new idea—as the only legitimate form of montage, and the only element of cinema that constitutes something like an essence of its form. In the more familiar conception of montage as flow or sequentiality (which Eisenstein attaches to Kuleshov), montage is a contained, deterministic system, and the flow represents the unceasing current that carries one cell (a shot) to another. Following Eisenstein, one could argue that in Kuleshov's more conservative vision of montage, sequentiality is the fabric of the whole.

Implicitly challenging Kuleshov, Eisenstein writes: "Conflict within the shot is potential montage, in the development of its intensity shattering the quadrilateral cage of the shot and exploding its conflict into montage impulses *between* the montage pieces. . . . The dynamics of montage serve as impulse driving forward the total film."[3] In this expanded formulation, the total film is a fulfillment of the component parts of the whole less as aggregation than as the potential of a set of dialectical relations. Eisenstein concludes that "we are now seeking a unified system for methods of cinematographic expressiveness that shall hold good for all its elements."[4]

This is a conception of montage that represents one of the monumental achievements of classical film theory. It is also a conception of montage that emerges out of a unique technological, aesthetic, and philosophical synthesis and therefore belongs to the cinema. Yet in spite of Eisenstein's elevation of the montage cell as potential, which is to say, montage that is more than the units in meaningful relation, it seems to me that in these descriptions he attaches too great a significance to the rationale of the part (for example, a shot) within the whole. On one level, Eisenstein's emphasis on the total film makes sense, and it is an aesthetic and philosophical disposition we see in various currents of the *cinéma pur* tradition of the 1920s.[5] An intellectual montage encompasses thought, and in thought the capacity for change. Thus, an overarching change that arises from what Elder describes as "something that exerts a measurable pressure on the consciousness of the spectator"[6] is in some sense necessary to Eisenstein's political project. But surely at the same time, while the collision of two cells creates rather than reveals montage (this is the essential break from Kuleshov), the process of collision brings the part, even momentarily, into stark relief from the whole. If montage is the dialectical relation of one shot to another, it is also the materialization of a very different ontology of the shot, that is, of the shot as *discrete* part, as fragment. This is the intensity of the shot (or, indeed, any formal element within the whole) that precedes organization within a dialectical system.[7]

Rereading montage in the context of the Marxist dialectic, Elder interestingly argues that Eisenstein's montage system was precisely that technological and aesthetic phenomenon in which "elements break with the Whole (which one should understood [sic] polyvalently, as intending the aesthetic unity, the social order, and the Metaphysical One), and contend against it."[8] For Elder, it seems that Eisenstein's montage was predicated not only upon a break with the metaphysical whole, but that the expression of the work of art as the potential for change required a conception of montage as *both* whole and fragment; without the fragment, the whole could not subsist. Furthermore, for Elder, the fragment as part must be sustained "so that when the Whole once again takes [it] into itself, [it] transforms the whole."[9] If Hitchcock was influenced by Eisenstein's thoughts on montage (which is almost certainly the case),[10] it is a form of montage attuned to this capacity of the element to signify itself, even momentarily. Sounding very much like Eisenstein, Hitchcock suggests that in montage "any individual piece is nothing. But a combination of them creates an idea."[11] This is clearly the case for all montage systems. But in an expressive montage, in a montage designed as conflict, the individual piece must sustain a disjunctive (rather than self-evident or organic) relationship with another piece. Thus, in Hitchcock's schema, an "idea" is merely one further materialization of a part that sustains the projection of the whole. Understood in this way, montage is potentially more than a forced collision of shots; it is the materialization of relational *systems*, each abstractly signifying the deferred presence of a metaphysical whole.

While the motif of the fragment is everywhere apparent in Hitchcock's oeuvre—from partitioned or replicated bodies, spaces, lines, shapes, and, more abstractly, figures within the visual frame to the disjointed, striatic patterns in narrative schemas that build cumulatively into complex systems—in the greater part of Hitchcockian scholarship, such motifs of fragmentation are read as symbols, motifs and allegories of desire. An exemplary study of this kind is Allen's subtle reading of Hitchcockian poetics through the lens of a conflicted romantic ideology.[12] But for Hitchcock, the fragment is utilized as more than a cell within a montage system. Rather, in the montage that for Hitchcock constitutes a pure cinema, the fragment is a formal segmentation within the narrative, visual, and aural frame *before* it is a communicative or symbolic sign. It is an irruption within the whole. Thus, we might say that the parallel train tracks as formal segmentation within the frame in *Strangers on a Train* symbolize a splitting off of desire from the normative situation to the deviant,[13] or that the doubled woman of *Vertigo* signals Scottie's excess of desire.[14] But my position is that, prior to such conclusions, we ought to be attentive to the fragment as part of a formal mise en scène and montage compositional system. The fragment is thus a *figure*, or a shape. We could then also say that the mirror reflections of Madeleine in *Vertigo* or Marion Crane in *Psycho* are not just symbolic signs but a rent within the formal classical schema of frame, shot, cut, sequence, movement, narrative, and so on. If Hitchcock's idea of a pure cinema is montage, it is a very particular kind of montage in which fragments build on other fragments, gesturing toward an abstract and always deferred image of the whole.

In my analysis of the mechanics of pure cinema, I attempt to analyze the segmentation of this organic whole of visual, aural, and narrative form into the discretization of its infinite array of parts. And then, in their imitation of Hitchcock, I trace the cinema of the *giallo* and De Palma as a further abstraction of the part from the whole, but in this imitative, reflexive aesthetic gesture, the bond between part and whole is increasingly tenuous, synthetic, and irrational. In such systems deployed within the *giallo* and De Palma's more experimental works, the vibration of the fragment that precedes the whole is intensified, and all the more vivid.

3.2. Beyond the Shot: The Part and the Whole in Hitchcock

We see time and again in Hitchcock an inclination to experiment with the mechanics of film form in relation to the composition of the frame (mise en scène), montage, and sound design. As Bellour argues in his several studies of Hitchcock but most notably in relation to *North by Northwest* and *The Birds*, a Hitchcockian cinema reveals an essential desire to explore shape, pattern, and scheme and, within such parameters, the curious effect of symmetry, asymmetry, movement, rhythm, and what he calls a system founded on the "fragment" in the "double constraint of repetition and variation."[15] Bellour is a critic particularly well suited to Hitchcock's fetishization of film form: his eye is always attuned to the microscopic pattern and its vibration within the systemic whole, and thus lends itself to the aesthetic object that signifies at the microscopic and macroscopic level. This complex relation between the small and large fragment in aesthetic design neatly describes the back-and-forth oscillation of a Hitchcockian film style, as it contemplates the import of an almost imperceptible signifier within the frame (for example, the rotation of the blades of a fan in a depth of field composition in *The Lodger*) or, in relation to a far grander aesthetic scheme, the structure of spectator-character identification in a film such as *Rear Window*. This is to say that Hitchcock's cinema (and especially those experimental works of the 1950s and early 1960s) expresses its artistic intent in terms of very small and very large formal schemas.

I follow Bellour's lead in attempting to conceptualize Hitchcock's cinema less as an uncontaminated "classical style," which is said to express itself in terms of the aesthetic whole, and more in terms of a system that inscribes the relation of parts to other parts, and of discrete parts to the systemic whole. Such relations occur, for example, from one shot to another, or from a sequence that concludes and then instantiates the beginning of a new sequence. But it is important to bear in mind that the relation of one part to another, as

Deleuze tells us, is always also the relation of the part to the whole.[16] I take as a starting point that Hitchcock's cinema is, as Bellour suggests, an aesthetic *system*. Further, I take from Bellour that this is a system of astonishingly intricate design. One of the great pleasures of attempting to analyze Hitchcock is that Hitchcock's cinema seems to subtend from an explicitly indicated schematic of a whole (a genre or plot design familiar to the viewer, even if such designs are subversively deployed) to a plethora of almost insignificant signs that the viewer, critic, and theorist might impose some meaning upon. Hitchcock's *Rear Window* seems just as stimulating for the casual viewer as it is for the analyst like Bellour, who "jots down dialogue, action, and especially shot sequence . . . filling notebooks to the point of absurdity."[17] In this essential relationship of the part to the whole, Hitchcock's cinema manifests as both classical and baroque in its aesthetic sensibilities, both a cinema of classical totality in formal design and a cinema subtended from the whole as expressive fragment.[18]

In one quite obvious sense, Hitchcock is a classical Hollywood filmmaker. His stories conform in large part to Kristin Thompson's formulation of the classical narrative as a "chain of causes and effects that is easy for the spectator to follow."[19] Thompson's point is not just a question of form but also a question of the way in which the mechanics of form inscribe a broad-based but very particular relationship between the film and the spectator. Thus, for Thompson, classical Hollywood style would mean very little if it did not encode the spectator's address of that form. Classical style is predominantly communicative; its overarching purpose is to provide stimulation through the provision of communicational cues that build to an edifice of a story, plot, character, narrative, and a visual and aural compositional whole. In this influential formulation, Thompson is part of a larger community within film studies that has argued persuasively that continuity (the chain of causes and effects) has by and large remained a staple of Hollywood style from the inception of the classical era to its most recent blockbuster films.

This formal classicism could be applied to any number of Hitchcock's films. *Strangers on a Train* reveals a formal parallelism in plot and character that in large part describes an overarching narrative structure.[20] Allen traces the film's formal design, which moves from parallels in story structure (the exchange of murders that constitute the inciting incident of the plot) to the "visual arabesque of patterned doubling";[21] in this instance, visual patterning gestures toward and resonates within a total narrative system. Like Bellour, Allen sees such figures in composition design in terms of a larger system of parts within wholes, which he then relates to Hitchcock's pure cinema "bravura style."[22] Similarly, *Rear Window* builds to a conventional mystery surrounding what the protagonist has seen, and in so doing broadly conforms to Thompson's principle of classical narrative in terms of an inciting incident (where is Mrs. Thorwald?), a series of plot points that bring the protagonist to the source of the mystery, and resolution. For all of *Rear Window*'s playfulness with sexual mores and generic subversion, it is strikingly classical in bringing to fruition what Thompson describes as the emotional intent of the film.

The whole in films such as *Strangers on a Train* and *Rear Window* drafts and validates a normative contract of desire between spectator and film. The classical style closes off the system, bringing stability to the formal (and desiring) whole. In its closed system, the classical style is automatically self-perpetuating, which also accounts for its resilience. In spite of *Strangers on a Train*'s subtle and playful perversion, I think Allen is right to describe the film "in one sense [as] a conventional romance."[23]

And yet, if we recall Truffaut's description of the crop duster sequence in *North by Northwest*, we can see that this totalizing desire of the classical style is limited in its broad-based application to Hitchcockian cinema. Truffaut argues that "the scene is completely silent for some seven minutes; it's a real tour de force.... The most appealing aspect of that sequence with the plane is that it's totally gratuitous—it's a scene that's been drained of all plausibility or even significance."[24] Truffaut's position is based on a critical distinction between an aesthetic of the whole and an aesthetic of the fragment. As a sequence within a chain of causes and effects, that is, as part of the structural whole, it seems almost redundant and absurd; in fact, it is the kind of sequence, handled with less aplomb, that would characterize the formal excesses of the James Bond franchise in the 1960s and 1970s. This narrational gratuity, suggests Truffaut, is key to the function of the sequence: "That's the whole point.... How can anyone object to this gratuity when it's so clearly deliberate—it's [sic] planned incongruity? It's obvious," he tells Hitchcock, "that the fantasy of the absurd is a key ingredient of your filmmaking formula."[25] The scene, in its entirety, makes explicit what Bellour calls "the theatricality of its machinations."[26]

But as an aesthetic of the part, as Bellour suggests, the crop duster sequence points to "a system only because there are several systems, a plurality, an infinity of systems. For if each system generates systems inferior to it in extension, these systems—micro-systems, sub-systems, and so on to infinity, down to the most elementary relationships—never stop marking the displacement of the system in relation to itself, its subdivision onto itself, bearing witness to the fundamental irreducibility of any textual structure."[27] This system is hermetic and self-sustaining even as it integrates into a vast array of formally scaffolded visual, aural, and narrative semiotic systems. The aesthetic of the part is something like a baroque experiment within a legitimizing classical system of signs. The sign as part is exhibitionistic and transgressive, irrational and excessive, and is subdued (but never obfuscated) by its relation to the whole. Bellour's model of a classical Hollywood style is therefore founded on a tension within and between systems, endlessly proliferating across compositional fields. "That is why the narrative," Bellour tells us, "what is usually called the narrative of a film, is always torn between pure narrative surface and the depth of the overall system. Between the two the various systems, segmental, inter-and intra-segmental . . . endlessly restore the fragmented image of this depth."[28]

In a system of textual relations, sense-making, or continuity from one event to the next such that the viewer comprehends the whole, is only part of the formal function of diegetic storytelling. And the particular way in which an event is framed in relation to the whole and then as an event in itself, or as a part, greatly affects the viewer's experience. What would be lost if Hitchcock had elected not to include the gratuity of the crop duster sequence? For Truffaut, it would be a cinema bereft of the aesthetic design that "becomes a truly abstract art, like music."[29]

Such expressions of the part subtended from the whole abound in Hitchcock, though few are as deliberately gratuitous as *North by Northwest*'s crop duster sequence. The shower scene in *Psycho* is a pure expression of the fragment, and perhaps Hitchcock's most explicit articulation of pure cinema as a system of montage. Indeed, I would argue that *Psycho*'s formal regime leans more toward an aesthetic of the fragment than any other Hitchcock film; this is perhaps in some way due to Bernard Herrmann's film score, which is wholly unconventional for its gratuity, a notion I develop in chapter 7. A viewer encounters *Psycho* through a series of complexly proliferating parts within the whole: the distended first-act theft, Marion's flight, the shower scene, Arbogast's death, and so on, each an exhibition of a formal set of systems articulated as shot, scene, and sequence relations, each leaning toward, but without fully embracing, the order of the classical whole. In the virtuosity of the Hitchcockian part, *Psycho* seems far more banal as a classical narrative, particularly in its rational ending of what is ostensibly a system of irrational narrative patterns. I prefer to encounter the apparently closed narrational system of *Psycho* as a facade or screen that masks a radically unclosed, unstable set of systemic relations, lacking in formal consistency or coherence.

The part resonates with an internal vigor and intensity because its duration is less than the duration of the whole, and of a different character entirely. If the duration of the whole distends the experience of time and stitches the film together into a hermetic experiential circuit, the duration of the part functions as a shorter but more intensive phenomenon, and thus affects the viewer as an interruption of the circuit of the whole. The affect of the part is intense and jarring also because, at its root, it is a transgression. Truffaut is thus correct to read the crop duster sequence as a gratuity, because it should not be there; it has no place within the whole. We could say the same of *Psycho*'s shower sequence. Does Marion's death require a sequence of such intensity, and such compositional exhibitionism, so forcefully delineated as a set piece? In the case of Hitchcock's shower scene, the part is always more than what is required of the articulation of the whole. In terms of an overarching classical style, the shower scene, like the crop duster scene, like the set piece of Marnie's theft of funds from the Rutland company, is a gratuity. But in this intensified experience of the part, the viewer encounters the surfeit materiality of the shot, scene, sequence, cut, montage relation, and sound cue, and it is in this sense that Hitchcockian cinema breaks most conspicuously from the classical style and takes on the characteristics of another montage system altogether.

3.3. Excessive Affect: The *Giallo* Set Piece

One of my favorite passages in the Hitchcock-Truffaut dialogue is a discussion about *Foreign Correspondent* (1940), Hitchcock's second American film after *Rebecca* (1940). Clearly dissatisfied with aspects of the film's style, Hitchcock imagines shooting the film in color: "Had the picture been done in color, I would have worked in a shot I've always dreamed of: a murder in a tulip field. Two characters: the killer, a Jack-the-Ripper type, behind the girl, his victim. As his shadow creeps up on her, she turns and screams. Immediately, we pan down to the struggling feet in the tulip field. We would dolly the camera up to and right into one of the tulips, with the sounds of the struggle in the background. One petal fills the screen, and suddenly a drop of blood splashes all over it. And that would be the end of the killing."[30] It's a wonderfully evocative description of a sequence, and an insight into the detail with which Hitchcock choreographs a montage. One could imagine this in Hitchcock's hands, the vibrant colors, the jagged cuts, the fetishistic angles on body parts we see in *Psycho*'s shower scene, extreme close-ups on faces and hands, and the coverage of the space that renders a tulip field sinister and garish, perhaps by moonlight.

But what if the color was lurid rather than vibrant; the cuts intensely jarring, bordering on irrational relations of scale and shape, and the space segmented into a chaotic set of fragments within the frame? Furthermore, unlike a Hitchcockian sequence that intuitively communicates narrative information with economy and elegance, what if the sequence was irrational in its relationship to a narrative whole? What if the sequence, in terms of a classical narrative form, seemed *gratuitous* in its disorder, in its incoherence?

This exchange with Truffaut constituted one point of origin for this book. The revelation for me was the way in which Hitchcock's imagining of a sequence in color intensified the visceral effect of its component parts: a shot of a petal would hold only to be saturated in blood; a pan from the figure would be motivated only by a desire to fix on struggling feet, as if severed from the body. And in Hitchcock's account of how the scene would play out, there is a clear rhythmic emphasis: a movement from stasis and stability (a girl walks in a tulip field / she screams), the building of a set of increasingly jarring, disorienting cuts that fetishize the figure within the frame, and then a release of tension, a rhythmic slowing down of the movement of the sequence, and a visual coda in the form of a dolly movement and reveal: "One petal fills the screen, and suddenly a drop of blood splashes all over it." Imagine if Hitchcock had shot *Psycho* in color, as had been his desire.

In my own imagined orchestration of the sequence through Hitchcock's words, knowing what he would produce through the experimental montage of the shower scene in 1960, I could not help but visualize any number of set-piece murders in Bava and Argento in the 1970s *giallo* cinema. But whereas Hitchcock could only imagine his sequence in color (this is a use of color that must be censored by a black and white palette, even in 1960), color is a visible mark of baroque, exhibitionistic excess in the *giallo*. Similarly, whereas Hitchcock must orchestrate a sequence within an overarching thriller narrative, the *giallo* eschews the classicism of the whole for the fetishism of the part. One suspects that Hitchcock's montage of fragments, even in their colored intensity, would nonetheless be rationalized within the narrative whole, as it was in *Psycho*. But in Bava, and most emphatically in Argento, the whole is dispensed with, or at least neglected in favor of an increasingly baroque experiment with the formal mechanics of the part. In the most excessive, absurd renditions of the set piece, the *giallo* is a form of cinema that "unravel[s] clear storylines and psychologically plausible characters."[31] One of the unique spectatorial pleasures of the *giallo* is its *non*-sense-making relational systems, its frenzied ruptures of organized form through images of intense violence or excessive, exhibitionist displays of style, whether of narrative, visual or aural design.

One could read this formal "unraveling" through the more unwieldy but potentially useful notion of excess. "Excess," suggests Thompson, "is not only counter-narrative; it is also counter-unity."[32] In this influential essay, Thompson attempts to come to terms with the materiality of the screen, which cannot be explained in relation to the whole. There are elements in most films, and in some films more than others, that simply cannot be rationalized within what Eisenstein calls the "total film." I would like to build on Thompson's formulation to suggest that excess, for all that the term might connote in relation to narrative structure, image, and sound composition, is founded upon what I have called an aesthetic of the fragment. As both an element of form and a very particular kind of spectatorial experience, excess derives from the work's transgression of the whole. Working through Eisenstein, I have described a kind of montage that is attuned to both the fragment and the whole. But the excessive textual and experiential itinerary of the fragment is not limited to the composition of the shot, or indeed to the shot at all, but is instead a disposition toward formal *incompleteness*, or irresolution; it is a compositional form always in the process of being unraveled. In his exhaustive examination of the *giallo*, Koven suggests that "these movies are not necessarily for us. . . . These films are an insider's discourse among themselves."[33] The *giallo* is in many ways a transgression of the complete narrative film. This is not to suggest that there is no story in these films, but that story is a peripheral part of a series of performative set pieces. In the *giallo*, all set pieces are distinguished by a degree of gratuity and nonsensicalness we see in Hitchcock's crop duster sequence. But the gratuity of the *giallo* set piece is of a kind wholly different from the Hitchcockian set piece. In Hitchcock, gratuity is fleeting and subversive; even in transgressing the classical norm, it must erase the mark of its own transgression. But in the *giallo*, gratuity is required to reveal the play of the fragment. The *giallo* does not require the spectator to rationalize the meaning of a sequence within a narrative whole, as the crop duster scene must, or as the shower scene must. In the *giallo*, such rationalizing processes obfuscate the pure object of pleasure, which is, following the work of Shaviro, a kind of *affect*, a kind of arousal.[34]

The excess of the *giallo* is also a function of its hyperbolic style. The *giallo*'s stylistic excess is evident in its saturated and jarringly contrasted color schemes, its hyperbolic use of film sound and music accompaniment, its elaborate, even flamboyant composition within the frame and in montage, and its unwieldy, frequently unresolved narrative form. But Thompson is correct to also read stylistic excess as a function of form and spectatorship; that is, excess is also a matter of a particular kind of viewing and a particular disposition toward a film style. She argues that "repeated viewings of a film are likely to increase the excessive potentials of a scene's components; as we become familiar with the narrative (or other principle of progression), the innate interest of the composition, the visual aspects of the décor, or the structure of the musical accompaniment, may begin to come forward and capture more of our attention."[35] In repeated viewings of the *giallo*, the viewer is gradually accommodated not to a gratuitous style but to stylistic excess as an intensification of the fragment.

Argento's stylistic fragments are amplified through their relatively loose placement within a rationalizing order, whether that order is a series of shots, an extended set-piece segment, or a narrative act within the whole. This is not to say that there is no formal schema underpinning the compositional choices in Argento's films; on the contrary, compositional elements are emphatically schematized within the set piece, but the schema reveals a potentially infinite array of fragments of the kind Bellour recognizes as foundational to Hitchcock's style. In Argento, the irrational fragment forms a basis from which other fragments materialize, each destabilizing and intensifying the frame, montage, narrative patterns, and soundscape. We see this excessive fragment in one of the early murder sequences in Argento's neobaroque masterpiece, *Suspiria*. The set piece is explicitly marked (as are all set pieces in the *giallo*) by a series of gratuitous signs: a wind that suddenly blasts open a set of windows; a garment hanging on a line buffeted by the wind; the Goblin music score that strikes a discordant note in its synthetic texture. These signs are gratuitous insofar as they do not point to an explicit rationale for the action of the sequence. Rather, the formulaic nature of the set piece is itself a gratuity, amplified by a set of gratuitous signs. Such signs within the *giallo* set piece rarely point to anything. These are affection images rather than action images.[36] As fragments, fleeting, disconnected from a continuous or coherent pattern, and ultimately irrational as a whole, such markings constitute images of sensation and sensory stimulation that plug the spectator into a "molecular assemblage with the body of the film."[37]

As the *Suspiria* set piece builds through systems of incremental excess, the stabbing motion of the killer's knife is itself staged as a set of fragments within the frame and between shots. Rather than the more conventional medium shot covering the scene of action, Argento cuts into a medium close-up to reveal a fetishistic angle on the knife and the ruptured body. It is clear at this point that the set piece is both a performance of excessive irrational violence and a rhythmic performance of montage cut to the increasingly dissonant patterns of the Goblin score. The set piece coheres around the murder act, but the act itself is a set of fragmentations within action. To return to Powell, the set piece functions as a generic action in the process of unraveling. The excess of the violation of the body is rendered almost comical. In a close-up of the wounded body, we see that the woman's chest cavity has been ripped open, with the heart beating at the base of the cavity. The knife then descends, captured in a close-up, and pierces the beating heart. It is a moment of excess that, in its violence, irrationality, and theatrical absurdity, functions as gratuitous action.

The *giallo* set piece is an elaborate stylistic performance, and perhaps most elaborate in Argento's films of the mid-to-late 1970s. Each action veers into irrationality in its jarring relation to a subsequent action or in its gratuitous distension of that action. Such excessive marks within the set piece destabilize the frame of vision and action for both character and spectator. Argento's use of the fragment as an overarching aesthetic figure, a kind of

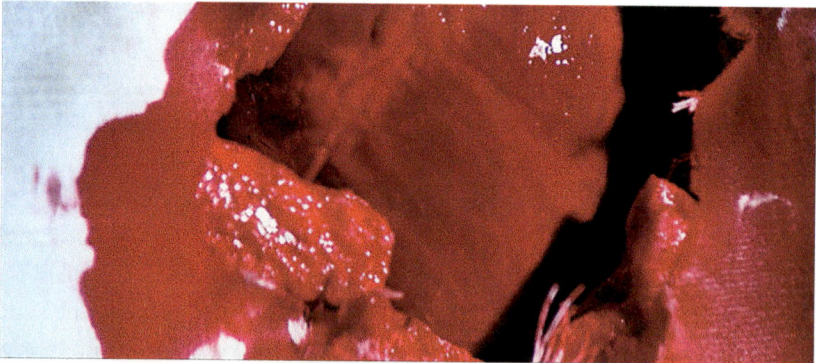

Figure 3.1 Gratuitous image and action: *Suspiria* (1977)

formal compositional building block, is equally sophisticated. This is a form of cinema that requires a highly specialized, and discretized, viewing. These are films in which set pieces exceed any semblance of a narrative, imagistic, or diegetic whole. In a different but not unrelated context, Eco famously described the cult text of cinema—a film such as *Casablanca*—as an intertextual and intra-textual assemblage.[38] Perhaps we might locate the *giallo* set piece here: as a discretized object, rationalized only within an infinitely deferred set of systemic relations. In subsequent chapters, I explore the fragmentation of the visual, aural, and narrative frame, but in this sequence in *Suspiria* we already see the *giallo*'s use of the affection image as the irrational motivation for action. If affect is a transgression of the whole, that is, if it is a rupture of containment, Argento's set pieces are a testament to the potential of cinema to register the shock of a gratuitous action as a perversely sublime spectacle.[39]

3.4. A Hitchcockian *Giallo* Sequence

Hitchcock released *The Birds* in 1963, the same year Mario Bava released his first *giallo*, *The Girl Who Knew Too Much*. The correspondence was clearly of greater significance and import for Bava than it would be for Hitchcock, and there is little evidence of *giallo* influence in Hitchcock's final films. And yet, in working through Hitchcock's cinema for this project, I wondered where one might trace the materialization of that momentary *giallo* tendency in an alternative color version of *Foreign Correspondent*. What became of that color montage and its striking stylistic excesses? My sense is that Hitchcock intensifies his aesthetic of the fragment in his later films, even while repressing a desire to see it overwhelm the screen and its spectator, as it would in *giallo* films such as Argento's *The Bird with the Crystal Plumage*, *Deep Red*, and *Suspiria*. One of Hitchcock's most interesting color montages occurs in a sequence in *The Birds*, released three years after *Psycho* and clearly continuing Hitchcock's own experimental approach to film montage. It is not a murder scene, but a scene of the discovery of a mutilated body, and it bears a curious resemblance to Hitchcock's vision of the color *Foreign Correspondent* murder scene.

The sequence in *The Birds* begins through a conventional setup: Lydia Brenner (Jessica Tandy) enters the Fawcett farmhouse and is surprised by the silence of the interior space and the disarray of the kitchen. Hitchcock covers her movement along a corridor from a low angle, effectively separating Lydia from the spectator. The next cut takes the spectator into the room, and we receive a medium shot of Lydia as she turns to survey the mess. The low angle is held, and while we are cut into the interior space, we remain bracketed off from the spectacle of violence; even prior to the discovery, Hitchcock seems intent on subduing the image of violence. The sequence now orchestrates a series of close shot reverse shots and profile shots involving Lydia, effectively suturing the spectator to her viewing position. We follow her gaze around the room and are cut into her point of view as her eyes fetch upon Fawcett's bloody legs, splayed out on the floor, visible only below the knees. It is worth noting here that the image bears some resemblance to the hypothetical image of feet in the *Foreign Correspondent* scene: "We pan down to the struggling feet." But whereas the feet in *Foreign Correspondent* "struggle" on action, presumably in close-up and held through the duration of the movement, Fawcett's feet are limp in their lifelessness. The image cuts from the feet to Lydia's eyes, which now pan down and to the right, and we receive the cut to a medium-long shot of Fawcett, seated-slumped on the floor, his eyes plucked out by birds.

It is a scene of shocking violence, and perhaps the most graphically violent sequence of Hitchcock's career. Yet the image of the mutilated body remains strangely muted, as does the way in which Hitchcock captures Lydia's reaction to the spectacle. She flees from the room, unable to let out the scream the spectator anticipates; there is a strange sense of theatricality or

Figure 3.2 Graphic violence: *The Birds* (1963)

even pantomime in Lydia's flight, which is very hard to fathom within the wider context of the film. At the moment of Lydia's sighting of Fawcett's body, Hitchcock focalizes the corpse through a series of jump cuts from medium-long shot to medium to close-up, each shot captured over silence.

The series of cuts moving into a tighter framing of the body is a magnification of the violent spectacle; in a literal sense, it takes us closer to the image of violence. And yet in another sense the jump cuts thoroughly distantiate the spectator from the action and from the reaction of Lydia. In its gross artifice, the jump cut is, as it was three years earlier in Godard's *Breathless*, a technique that had become associated with the film avant-garde and with the visibility of style that marked the French New Wave filmmakers. But here, oddly, in what is ostensibly a familiar set-up in a thriller, Hitchcock uses a set of jump cuts over screen silence as the reveal, the suspense film's "money shot," rendering the sequence somewhat unaffecting as visceral shock.

Subsequent to my reading of Hitchcock's description of the color *Foreign Correspondent* sequence, I could not help but wish for a very different coverage of Fawcett's mutilated corpse. I appreciate the ingenuity of the montage experiment that is the strangeness of a jump cut in a Hitchcock action sequence. I also appreciate the quotation of the jump cut as an experiment with film form that had gained traction in the aftermath of Godard's *Breathless*. But it is an intellectual montage more than a viscerally charged association of images; it is the distillation of an intellectual rather than affective image. In its stylistic affectation, the set of jump cuts display the mutilated corpse as a discrete fragment within a whole; the cuts literally segment what would otherwise be a continuous flow of the physical movement in the dolly of a camera or, less likely, a zoom of its lens. But in this disjointed series of cuts covering action, the sequence loses something of the affect of movement itself, and of the intensity of the fragment as part. Hitchcock's jump cuts play out as a form of muted continuity.[40] In *Foreign Correspondent*, covering a scripted murder sequence, Hitchcock would have "panned down to struggling feet"; he would have "[dollied] the camera up to and right into one of the tulips" in an excessive framing (perhaps even an extreme close-up) of the flower. And the crucial coda to the movement is a *splash* of blood, an action that brings an intensity to the frame, and turns what might be a less than interesting action image into an image of sensation. Such a coda, marked by a color saturation of the frame like an ink blot bleeding beyond its containment, might have been a moment of stunning intensity.

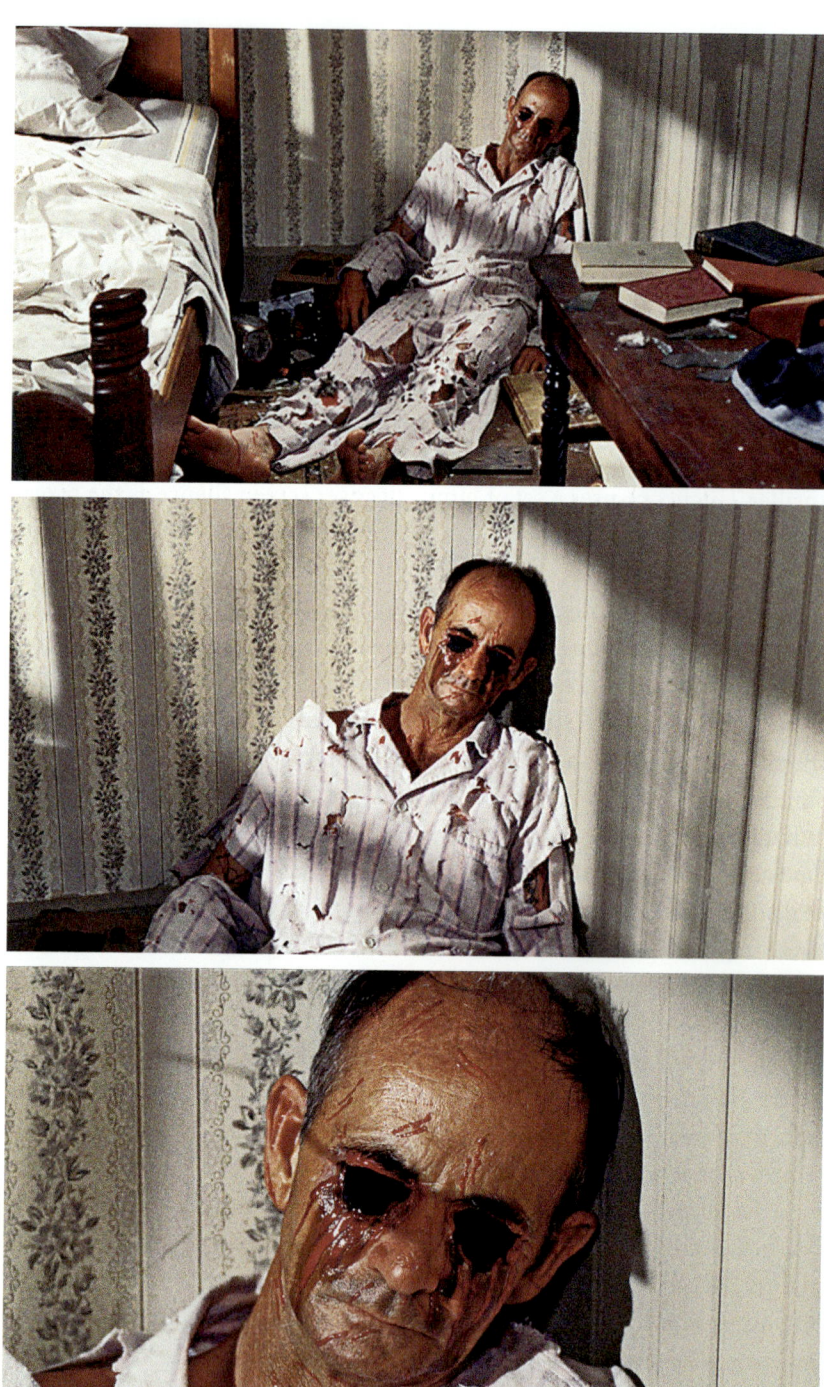

Figures 3.3–3.5 Muted action in the jump cut: *The Birds* (1963)

3.5. Fragments within Fragments: Imitation in De Palma's Odessa Steps Sequence

In a career of fantastically elaborate, gratuitous set pieces, De Palma's capacity for rendering a cinema of the fragment reaches a point of absurd exhibitionism in *The Untouchables*. If a set piece in Hitchcock or Argento can reflect what I have called an aesthetic of the fragment, in De Palma's Union Station sequence in *The Untouchables,* the fragment revels in its transgression of the whole, and it is all the more excessive and playful as a mode of imitation. As I will argue in the conclusion of this book, in the later films of De Palma the fragment tends toward an increasingly abstract relation to the whole. In this aesthetic, De Palma's most experimental films tend toward what I describe as a fractal narrative and image form, in which parts endlessly proliferate across an infinitely expanding system. If this is how Bellour perceives Hitchcock's elaborate formal systems, which I believe to be the case, De Palma's unique contribution to an aesthetic of the fragment is to ultimately privilege the part over the whole as a way of thinking about the composition of film images and narratives.

The Union Station sequence in *The Untouchables* is explicitly marked as the imitation of a prior set of film images: Capone's bookkeeper is to arrive at midnight, a narrative design that plays alongside Zimmerman's showdown at high noon, and then also Leone's quotation of *High Noon* (1952) in *Once Upon a Time in the West* (*C'era una Volte il West*, 1967). The set piece is also marked by a familiar formulaic buildup of suspense preceding the action, a contained location in which to stage the action, and at this point in late 1980s action cinema, the requisite gratuitous level of violence. The sequence announces itself as a performance of an American film genericity in which narrative and image signify "with a set of quotation marks that hover above it like an ironic halo."[41]

The extreme depth of field of the establishing shot of the exterior plays almost expressionistically, with high contrasts of light and dark and strong lines accentuating the vanishing point at screen right; such excessive visual cues render the shot gratuitous as a signifier of setting and gesture toward the stylistic excess that will mark the set piece as a whole.

Once inside the station, De Palma covers the space in a series of wide shots, setting up the spatial schematic that will organize the action. The break from the nonactive schematizing of space to the incitement of action occurs through a series of sound cues: the squeak of the wheels of a child's carriage, the crying of the child, and the absurd amplification of the child's lullaby on

Figure 3.6 Expressionist space: *The Untouchables* (1987)

the soundtrack that is unmarked as diegetic or nondiegetic sound. The spectator anticipates a transition—the irruption of action—throughout the four-minute duration of the sequence, but De Palma deliberately distends this incremental buildup of action, covering the points of view of Ness (Kevin Costner) and Stone (Andy Garcia), Ness's movement to assist the mother with the carriage, the child in its carriage, the entry point at the top of the staircase, and an assortment of figures inhabiting separate spatial segments within the station.

The set piece then breaks into a second movement, in effect producing a new fragment within the whole and subtending a new set of image and story relations. The split of the set piece is marked by a trumpet cue in the Morricone score. Morricone's sinister string tones accompany Ness's flight down the stairs to assist the mother. This new movement as fragment is organized around the central action of Ness, the mother, and the child ascending the staircase. The strings in the score play out a set of dissonant intervals, intensifying the spectator's anticipation of the irruption of action. As Ness reaches the top of the staircase, Capone's bookkeeper and his handlers pass by Ness, descending the staircase. Ness is then framed in a medium-long shot as he turns to the entry doors at the top of the staircase and recognizes one of Capone's henchmen. A series of shots on Ness and the henchman zoom in from long shot in a deep field to a Leonesque extreme close-up on the henchman's eyes.

It is at this point that the fragment again breaks from a syntax of the whole, inserting a further formal fragment that constitutes the most explicit act of imitation of De Palma's career.

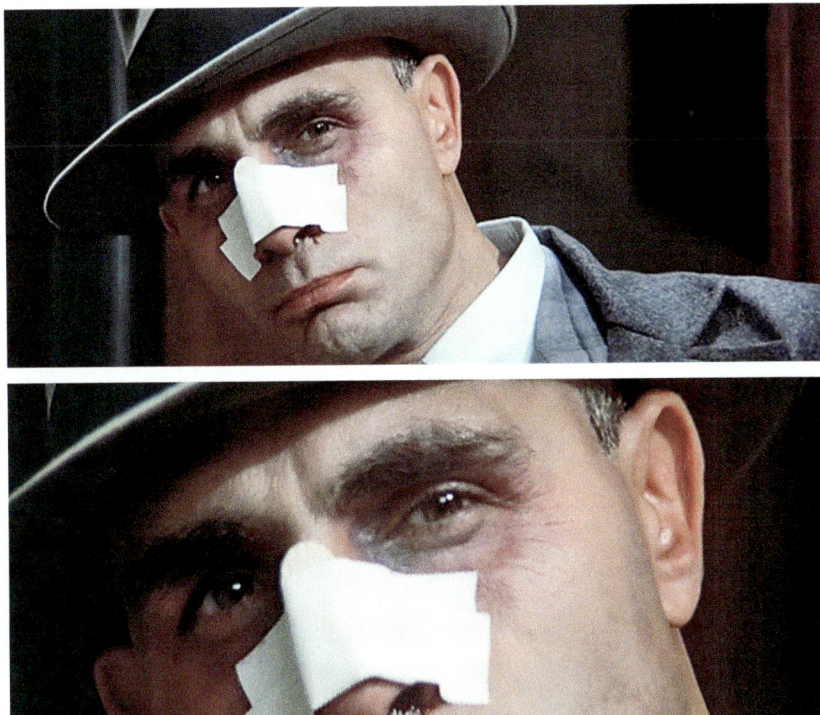

Figures 3.7–3.8 A Sergio Leone zoom: *The Untouchables* (1987)

In Eisenstein's famous sequence in which a child's carriage rolls down the Odessa Steps in *Battleship Potemkin* (*Bronenosets Potyomkin*, 1925), continuity in time is generally maintained across the jarring cutting. The spectator infers a basic temporal unity that renders the sequence realistic as a whole. But as a montage configuring diegetic space, Eisenstein's sequence is not so much discontinuous as noncontinuous; its editing regime uses the cut less as the communication of narrative action than as the catalyst for the formation of an emotional response to the action. For the spectator, the temporal flow is distended by a series of noncontinuous cuts, moving from the falling mother to the stroller to the wide shot of the steps, and then holding on a new spectator of the action, a woman that now stands in for the slain mother, who is herself slain in a graphic close-up.

Eisenstein's montage of 1:50 duration is a sequence of stunning emotional intensity. It coheres as a series in which fragments (Eisenstein's fifty-eight shots) configure an emotional whole, or what I would call an affective totality.

Figures 3.9–3.12 Eisenstein's noncontinuous cutting: *Battleship Potemkin* (1925)

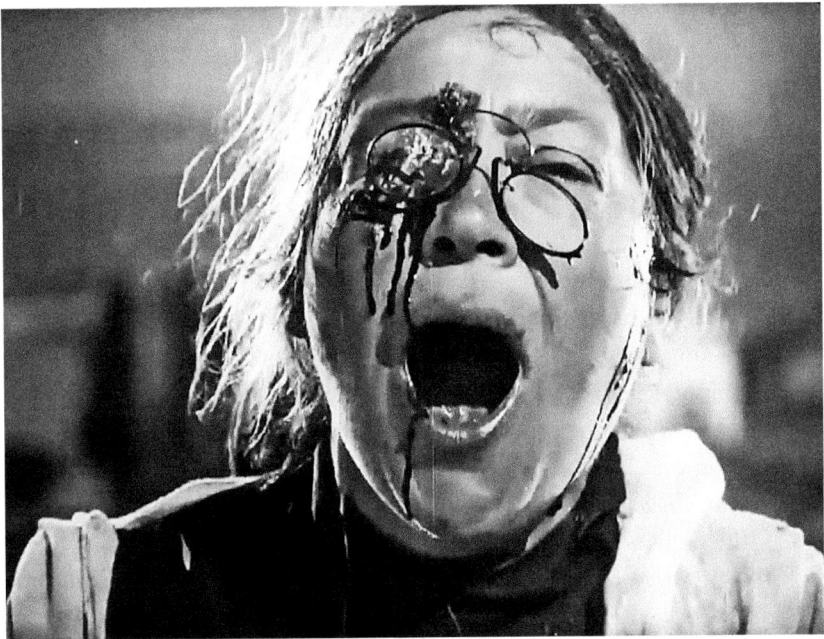

Figures 3.9–3.12 Continued

De Palma's imitation of Eisenstein's sequence begins with a hyperbolic visual cue: the Leonesque zoom into an extreme close-up on the henchman's eyes. The zoom also occurs over the slow-motion temporality that will cover the 1:40 duration of the sequence. The sequence maintains Eisenstein's temporal unity but reconstructs it in slow motion, clearly delineating the action along the previously established schematic of the Union Station interior. Morricone's strings cover the entirety of the action in rising and falling dissonant intervals, amplified over an otherwise reduced diegetic soundscape. De Palma's montage in slow motion emphasizes the clarity of temporal unity, restores spatial integrity within the frame, and plays out as an elaborately staged classical action set piece. And yet I would argue that this imitation of Eisenstein's action on the Odessa Steps is not what Deleuze calls "organic action in its entirety," that is, action as *whole*.[42] For me, De Palma's sequence breaks from a classical regime in its almost absurdly distended slow-motion image, which I read as a marker of excess. Like Hitchcock's crop duster menacing Roger Thornhill, in my reading of De Palma's imitation of Eisenstein, slow-motion functions as a gratuity "drained of all plausibility."[43]

In elaborate, extended slow-motion sequences in films such as *Carrie* (1976) and *Fury* (1978), but most emphatically in this sequence in *The Untouchables*, slow motion is not a mechanism for building suspense. One need only measure De Palma's slow-motion sequence against the almost unbearable suspense of Eisenstein's montage. Rather, distended slow motion in the De Palma set piece intensifies the duration of the fragment. It contains and hermetically seals the fragment in its curious temporality, breaking the set piece from the whole. The fragmentation in this new movement is twofold: on the one hand, the fragmentation is structural, splitting off from the previous movement and from the whole. But in its imitation of Eisenstein's famous montage experiment, which is the more provocative expression of the fragment, De Palma's authorial inscription is a mark of excess, and is staggeringly gratuitous. In Truffaut's words, De Palma's indulgence concocts a "fantasy of the absurd."[44] Less an acknowledgment or quotation of Eisenstein's work, the sequence is something like a reflexive insert of a fragment. But in a further transgression of the whole, the insert contaminates the whole as imitation, as self-conscious, reflexive gesture. It is this act of insertion that is the most emphatic transgression of Eisenstein's montage as whole. Staged within multiple lines of sight and action, slow motion enables the spectator to encounter the fragment in its distended, intensified duration. We might read this montage insert as a textual sample that emphasizes the exhibitionist or performative qualities intrinsic to imitation and yet proudly proclaims, "This is new."

In its capacity to proliferate and expand a set of systemic relations, the fragment attains a purity of form. It vibrates beneath and above the whole in its surfeit materiality. But then, De Palma's perverse redesign of Eisenstein's montage, now reschematized in Union Station, *distends* this materiality of the fragment; it slows it down and exhibits it, as if on display. The fragment thus enacts a double enunciation: it is both a quotation of Eisenstein's montage schema and, in imitation of that schema, its erasure.

4
The Fragmented Frame 1
Expression, Abstraction, Schematization

4.1. Frame as Fragment

I have argued that Hitchcock's cinema is anchored within an overarching classical style insofar as it is largely coherent as a narrative, visual, and aural art form. However, this classical style remains idiosyncratic and distinctive throughout his lengthy career. Following Calabrese in his reading of a neo-baroque aesthetic, I suggest that Hitchcock's style, even in its desire for communicativeness through story and character, "goes beyond limits or boundaries . . . to throw doubt upon an existing order."[1] And as Durgnat convincingly argues, "Hitchcock understood both schools . . . between montage kinetics and continuity flowings."[2] In this duality, Hitchcock's cinema remains something of a curiosity within the American classical cinema tradition.

In this chapter, I continue to analyze Hitchcock's pure cinematic style as a function of formal fragmentation within mise en scène and montage, now expressed in relation to the "quadrilateral cage"[3] of the film frame. But whereas the frame for Eisenstein is a limit value that seeks fulfilment in the whole, Hitchcock's frame as part is marked by a desire for segmentation and proliferation; it is both the manifestation of a closed system and an opening into what might present beyond the boundaries of the classical frame. The fragment is the part within the whole that, following Bellour, opens into an endlessly proliferating system of formal relationships. I find its most vivid expression in the composition of the frame in films such as *Shadow of a Doubt*, *Vertigo*, *North by Northwest*, *Psycho*, *The Birds*, and *Marnie*. Each of these Hitchcockian formal experiments is then brought to bear on the frame composition of the *giallo* and the cinema of Brian De Palma. I argue that the mechanics of the pure Hitchcockian frame are further complicated through a magnification and intensification of the frame as fragment in films such as Bava's *Blood and Black Lace*, *A Bay of Blood* (*Ecologia del delitto*, 1971), and *Lisa and the Devil*; Argento's *The Bird with the Crystal Plumage, Deep Red*, and *Suspiria*; Fulci's *Don't Torture a Duckling*; and De Palma's *Sisters, Obsession, Dressed to Kill, Blow Out, Body Double*, and *Carlito's Way*.

4.2. The Expressive Frame

The communicative frame privileges the content of its message, which in narrative cinema can take the form of story or character information, information on a setting or locale, or an informational cue contained in a prop placed strategically within the mise en scène. Its primary mode of address is communicative, and it takes as its primary addressee the cinematic spectator. For Peretz, the communicative frame is defined by "a logic of positions and places, and when submitted to it, we occupy, at least ideally, or as a teleological goal, a stable position of control toward communicated meanings."[4] We can align the communicative frame with the model of classical style discussed in the previous chapter. These aesthetic categories only function if communicative cues are relatively stable, coherent, and accessible. In the majority of films released within the Hollywood system during its classical and postclassical eras, communicative signs such an establishing shot over the French Riviera in *To Catch a Thief*, a close-up on a hand holding a key in *Notorious*, or the name of the Vanishing Lady imprinted on a window in a train compartment construct the relative stability of informational cues in mise en scène composition.

The expressive frame, on the other hand, suggests an emphasis on form, and thus a surplus of formal signifiers uncontained by or within communicative cues. While not precluding informational cues on story, character, and setting, the expressive frame also points somewhere else, and more precisely to a materiality of the frame that cannot be easily rationalized. If, as Martin suggests, a classical mise en scène "exists *to serve* the subject or story" in which "style expresses subject,"[5] the expressive frame will, in sometimes explicit and sometimes quite subtle moments, elide the principal informational materials of the mise en scène composition to draw attention to the form in which such materials are expressed. Even films most commonly associated with the classical cinema at times problematize this distinction between the communicative and expressive cinematic frames. Indeed, classical Hollywood style has always been more restless and adventurous than the designation of "classicism" suggests.[6] Perhaps this is because cinema is not a perfectly controlled aesthetic medium; a shot, a cut, or a mise en scène composition is subject to all manner of production contingencies that threaten the stability of classical form.

John Ford's *The Searchers* (1956) is in many ways a classical Hollywood western, and yet it announces its strange compositional rationale in a very early sequence. Ethan Edwards (John Wayne) approaches the Edwards homestead in one of the most famous long shots in Hollywood history. The shot communicates a great deal in terms of the iconography of setting, character (the lone figure that approaches in the distance carries a symbolic charge in the bodily shape and posture of John Wayne), and story. Yet Ford prefaces the opening onto the vista of Monument Valley by commencing the shot *inside* the home, framed by the open doorway.[7] The bright light of the exterior contrasts with the almost perfect black of the interior of the home, serving as a frame surrounding the image. In a fluid movement, the camera dollies from inside to outside, tracking the movement of Martha (Dorothy Jordan) as she views the slow approach of Ethan. Not unlike Hitchcock's reveal of a simulacral Greenwich Village in *Rear Window*, the spectator is attuned to the act of viewing itself in this explicit desire of the camera to reposition itself to see what lies within the frame. The duration of the dolly shot, as well as the striking contrast in light and dark in its hard-framed edges, establishes a dual-presentational mode in which the spectator engages the communicative materials of story as well as the expressive modality of an image aware of its compositional form. This dual-presentational mode accords with what Collins describes as cinema's "double referentiality."[8]

The establishing shot is, by definition, denotational: the image configures a deictic relation between the representation and the thing it is a representation of, establishing a time and place in the fullness of representation. But in the case of *The Searchers*, Ford's establishing shot ruptures a contained classicism to present a successful synchrony of communicative and expressive aesthetic modes. The camera instantiates a double-awareness of the diegetic world and its framed representation. Yet Ford is not as overt or playful in his use of the expressive frame as Hitchcock. To this synchrony of communicative and expressive modes, Hitchcock's films often add a layer of compositional reflexivity that explicitly points to the object of the frame within the mise en scène. A Hitchcock mise en scène and montage schema will often remind the spectator that the image is a formal composition. While Ford configures the vista of Monumental Valley as a framed image, there is nothing within that frame that points to its radical artifice within the diegetic world of the film; in a Ford western, the fullness of diegetic space is always clearly established for the spectator. But in Hitchcock, the framed view is attuned not merely to the compositional form of an image but to the mechanism that enacts that framing. In this context, Brigitte Peucker argues that "scenes of nature in Hitchcock's films are often heavily aestheticized."[9] Here I take Peucker to mean that even a casual shot in Hitchcock of an outdoor setting—for example, the exterior location shots of Newark, New Jersey, in the opening scenes of *Shadow of a Doubt*—is reflexively attuned to its status as artistic representation. An outdoor picnic setting in *To Catch a Thief*, with its framing of a profusion of sexual innuendo, is never merely that iconic setting. For Peucker, in Hitchcock's cinema, the foundational element of a classical realist style is subjected to a "spatial and ontological manipulation,"[10] and the brilliant move in her essay is to shift the focus from the ideal of the perfect continuity of the diegetic world to the ontological continuity between life and art.[11] I would add, however, that in my reading of the expressive frame that follows, the relation between art and life is less one of pure continuity, and certainly not the continuity in which cause (life) produces effect (art), but one in which life and art are exchangeable ontological forms.

Hitchcock will gesture time and again to this foundational ontological inversion in which the compositional form of a frame occludes, or at least obscures, the representation it contains. In the opening of *To Catch a Thief*, the spectator anticipates an establishing shot of the French Riviera, the film's exotic locale. In fact, we are provided with three exterior shots establishing location in the first sequence of the film, each functioning as a playful addendum to the film's inciting incident, the theft of jewels from the Intercontinental Carlton Cannes. The third and final establishing shot before the cut to the office of the *commissaire de police* depicts the impressive frontage of the hotel.

In tone and pacing, accompanied by a whimsical score by Lyn Murray, the opening sequence is more playful than one might imagine. The three establishing shots (as I've described them) are preceded by, and thus reflexively reproduce, four tourism posters that adorn the window of a local travel agent captured within the mise en scène of the film's opening credit sequence.

The image holds on this window for a significant duration, and the spectator's eyes are drawn toward the iconic Riviera scenery that will constitute the setting for the film. While a signifier of a time and place, the posters function also as an excessive, exhibitionistic second-order signification of that setting. The setting of the film, Hitchcock seems to suggest, is perpetually

Figure 4.1 Hitchcock's simulacrum setting: *To Catch a Thief* (1955)

enframed by a popular-cultural iconic signifier, and that signifier coheres most forcefully and elegantly within popular cinema. The Hitchcockian frame is thus at once a metonymic form—it stands in for a time and place—and a deictic signifier of the frame itself, pointing back to its compositional form within an iconographic lineage.

Hitchcock's use of the frame to signify more than its representational content has been widely recognized. In his detailed study of the significance of paintings in Hitchcock's films, Tom Gunning claims that "Hitchcock's mastery of cinematic framing beckons to us from nearly every shot of the film" and that he "used compositional frames to invoke the other arts, especially theatre and painting."[12] While I agree with many critics on this connection between Hitchcock's films and other art forms, Gunning's point seems particularly subtle. The act of invoking the other arts, as Gunning describes it, forges an ontological relation between one art form (for example, painting) and cinema. Hitchcock is not precisely drawing a relation as much as enacting an ontological transformation of the classical-realist basis of the cinematic image. If in the classical cinema the pro-filmic reality decants the diegetic reality of the film, in a cinema that exceeds the communicative regime of the image, the diegetic real effaces the pro-filmic reality as a preexisting form. This is to say that a framed image that makes explicit its framing radically destabilizes the relation between reality and its representation within a framed image. Gunning's reading of Madeleine Elster's viewing of Carlotta's portrait in *Vertigo* suggests as much: "There is more involved in this elegant scene than a detective noticing significant details. Through the dolly-in, the camera seems to sink into and open up the space of the painting, not only directing Scottie's (and our) attention, but seemingly confusing the space of observer and painting, of representation and reality."[13] And if this is the case, as Peucker suggests, the spectator must question his or her ontological relationship to even the most naturalistic frame in the Hitchcockian oeuvre.

4.3. Expression and Abstraction

Elder suggests that, in their efforts to realize a purely abstract film form in the mid-1920s, Hans Richter and Viking Eggeling produced visual forms that were "more strictly geometric—they are graphic forms reduced to rectilinear lines and simple curves (in Eggeling's case) or simple geometric forms bounded by straight lines (in Hans Richter's case)—and both artists hold the rhythms that govern the development and variation of these geometric forms to strict meters."[14] As Elder demonstrates, such early experimenters with film form understood that form to be founded on degrees of abstraction.[15] This decisive aesthetic leap derived from a basic paradox intrinsic to the filmic medium: artists such as Richter and Eggeling in Germany, but also Chomette and Dulac in France, understood that film offered a unique potential in its capacity for abstract form (geometric lines, as well spatial contrasts and continuities) produced through the machinic production of the film camera. If early modernist artists had been fascinated by cinema's automatic reproduction of the world, these artists intuited that the machinic apparatus offered an unprecedented capacity for formal, measured, regulated, and constructed abstraction.[16] The filmic medium was in this sense a pure producer of aesthetic form, and certainly Richter and Eggeling believed that "beyond all doubt the film [would] soon be taken over by the artists as a new field for their activity."[17]

Hitchcock's desire for abstraction within cinema's representational image is situated within larger currents of aesthetic practice and philosophical thinking on the abstract capacities of film form. My notion of abstraction in this context is twofold: I suggest that the spatiotemporal frame of pure cinema abstracts from the "real." Aesthetic realism desires organic wholeness, completion, and the logical relation of formal elements within the whole.[18] The abstract frame thus pulls away from the ideal of the realist film image. Second, and perhaps the more provocative movement, abstraction refers to a disengagement with the fullness of the representational image. This is a form of abstraction that depicts the constitutive elements of form: shape, line, pattern, color, tone—and, in the particular case of the film image, movement—*within* the regime of representation. There are the "purely" abstract films of Richter, which only employ "geometrical figures in motion organized into patterns."[19] But it is clear that Hitchcock's experimentation with film form occurred within the narrative, image, and sound mechanics of the representative film image. While the line between a representational and abstract art is not always clear,[20] we can say that, in the case of Hitchcock's films, abstraction, even in its emphasis on the constituents of form, always points to preexisting representational figures. In cinema's automatic production of the image, therefore, I conceptualize abstraction as a function of a spatial and temporal fragmentation, which in Hitchcock is a result of a particular kind of mise en scène and montage schema.

In Hitchcock, the film frame is not a window but a partial abstraction from the representational image that is simultaneously mapped onto the representational image. A chase sequence in a Hitchcock film meets the demands of story, character, and thematic development, but the formal properties of such sequences commonly exceed the dimensions of the representational image. The elaborate chase sequence through the British Museum in *Blackmail* (1929) and the chase across San Francisco rooftops that opens *Vertigo* are clearly motivated by the necessity of story, yet each is elaborate in its own way in its emphasis on the compositional complexity of shape and movement within the frame. In each sequence, Hitchcock articulates the potential of the abstract cinematic frame within the rationalizing principles of a classical style. Thus, Hitchcock can claim a monopoly on the "suspense film," yet at the same time speak about the formal aestheticism of the film frame in ways that are strikingly similar to artists of the pure cinema tradition. Consider this exchange between Hitchcock and Truffaut on the subject of *Psycho*:

TRUFFAUT: I must say that the architectural contrast between the vertical house and the horizontal motel is quite pleasing to the eye.
HITCHCOCK: Definitely, that's our composition: a vertical block and a horizontal block.[21]

While the artists that embraced the potential of an abstract cinema were explicit on the formal and phenomenological properties of this abstraction, Hitchcock's discussion of composition seems somewhat superficial. What is contained in the contrast between a horizontal and vertical axis? And yet, in another sense, the intimation of the film frame as a compositional form is a significant departure from the dominant classical paradigm. Imposing a horizontal/vertical contrast within the frame contaminates the organic whole of the pro-filmic environment. Truffaut is therefore correct to remark on this curiosity of the composition within the frame: on closer examination, the house of *Psycho* is shot as a vertical composition *against* the horizontal composition of the Bates motel.

Hitchcock's concession that the two dominant spatial planes of the film—the house and motel—represent a compositional contrast in line, shape, and

Figures 4.2–4.3 Axial composition: *Psycho* (1960)

of story is thus fairly conventional with its focalization of a principal character.[34] However, in compositional terms, the construction of the visual frame is interesting. The pan of the cityscape is captured on the horizontal, which stabilizes the frame. The shot of the city street is held in expansive vertical depth, providing a strong visual contrast with the horizontal pan of the previous shot; the contrast in scale and angle provides its own stabilizing perceptual logic within the frame. The next cut, however, is to a curious angle on the tenement building that houses Charlie in a medium long shot, followed by a tighter, equally canted angle (now from the obverse position) of the window of Charlie's room. While clearly signifying an off-kilter diegetic space (housing its sinister occupant), the angle unsettles the previous classically oriented set of frames. Further, the canting of the frame draws attention to the novelty of the frame itself in its transgression of an aesthetic norm.

After a fairly lengthy expositional sequence (common in Hitchcock's cinema of this period), Charlie discovers that men have been inquiring after him. Guilty of a crime, he flees the motel in a sequence that comprises the first explicit action movement of the film. What follows is an excellent example of a Hitchcockian action sequence orchestrated within a schematic frame. The pursuit begins as Charlie walks casually past the two men, who pretend not to notice him. We then cut to a long shot of Charlie as he recedes into the background of the frame, establishing a strong vertical axis that spatially connects Charlie to his pursuers. This vertical frame begins a play of geographic line and scale in a series of segmented frames within the frame. The entire pursuit is captured in a high angle shot atop a building, observing Charlie and his pursuers below in what appears to be two deserted parking lots cut through by a narrow laneway. The frame is explicitly centered in its geometric division, yet the interior of the frame accents diagonal lines running from top left to bottom right. The initial vertical frame is now reconstructed as a more complex set of geometric divisions. The action sequence central to the narrative development will play out within this schematic; it is an action sequence in which setting is abstracted into a confluence of shapes and lines traversed by moving figures. The entry point to this frame depicts Charlie in long shot cutting through the center of the space, further emphasizing the geometric division between the upper and lower segments. The shot is held from this angle as the pursuers enter the frame. The geometric logic of the frame is now intensified in the splitting of the two pursuers. In narrative terms, the pursuers simply part ways to cover more ground, but in compositional terms, which I am suggesting is of equal importance to Hitchcock's

Figures 4.8–4.9 The transgressive frame: *Shadow of a Doubt* (1943)

Figure 4.10–4.13 Geometric form in line and movement: *Shadow of a Doubt* (1943)

Figures 4.10-4.13 Continued

choreographing of the action, the splitting of the pursuers enacts a further division of the schematic.

Hitchcock's formal logic of counterpoint previously discussed in relation to *Psycho* explains the next cut and shot, which depict a vertically oriented frame, weighted from bottom left to top right, functioning as the geometric complement to the previous image. While in the previous frame bodies moved from right to left, one pursuer now moves from left to right in the top segment of the frame, accentuating the verticality of the space. The figure is again minuscule against the gigantic scale and canting of the buildings. The shot holds as the second pursuer moves into the frame from bottom left, completing the vertical composition as the two figures meet in the center of the frame. The camera holds, depicting the frustration of the pursuers, before panning aggressively to the left to reveal Charlie atop the building, presumably occupying the viewing position of the initial shot, watching his pursuers; a whimsical clarinet sound cue accentuates the "theatrical machinations" of the reveal and the sequence as a whole.[35] The sequence is less notable for its development of suspense (which is also diminished by the coda brought by the comedic sound cue) than for its play with the cinematic frame as a series of geometric forms in relation and in movement.

As Pomerance notes, Hitchcock had been fascinated with topographies of all kinds throughout his life, confessing an obsession in his adolescence with "trains, schedules, and the organization of movement in great cities."[36] It seems to me that this fascination was also with the elemental components of things, or the parts of aesthetic form. The film frame was no different. Throughout his film career, from the early amateur cinema of the silent era to the later experiments with image and sound composition,[37] Hitchcock's films inquire into the capacity of the cinematic frame to abstract from the representational constraints of a diegesis. One of the most startling experiments with the geometric frame occurs in *Blackmail* during the British Museum chase sequence. Not unlike the chase sequence in *Shadow of a Doubt*, in *Blackmail* the frame tends toward abstract geometric form such that the conclusion of the sequence depicts a jarring, almost Escher-like geometric configuration.

The influence of the German expressionists (and certainly Murnau) is writ large over this sequence in *Blackmail*. And yet the Escher association is also apt because it is an image that draws attention to its transgression of representational form. If, as Liz argues, "it was Hitchcock's ... obsessive dedication to make artifice conquer nature,"[38] in my reading, the schematic frame is not

Figure 4.14 Optical abstraction: *Blackmail* (1929)

precisely artifice but a formal abstraction, which is all the more intriguing as an aesthetic rationale within a mainstream cinema tradition.

If we reconsider the Hitchcockian frame as a schematic, we can challenge the dominant reading of these films that emphasize the logic of classical visual and aural style underpinning the development of narrative action. Returning to a film like *North by Northwest*, I am struck by the schematic structure of its form. In visual terms, the famous crop duster scene or the Mount Rushmore backdrop schematize a diegetic world rather than bring it out in an organic wholeness. If the establishing shot of the Mount Rushmore sequence is an assemblage of spatiotemporal component parts, we can we view the film as a schematic whole, attendant to its compositional parts. In her excellent study of *North by Northwest*, against the more conventional reading of the crop duster sequence as the staging of narrative action, Peucker reads the Hitchcock frame as a challenge to traditional perspectival forms of representation. She suggests that "Mount Rushmore features the most obvious convergence of nature and art.... In *North by Northwest*, release from the perspectival system occurs in the aestheticized spaces of nature."[39] Peucker is working through a formulation offered by Jameson of "spaces organized by a language," but she takes the notion of an aestheticized space further to suggest that "in the pinewood setting, as in Cézanne, we find an oscillation between a cubist three-dimensionality suggested by depth of field and the flattening of space produced by an emphasis on line.... And the earlier cornfield sequence contains frames which have a nearly abstract feel, despite the presence of Cary Grant as Roger Thornhill incongruous in their midst."[40] I would argue that what Peucker calls an "abstract feel" in fact sets an aesthetic foundation to the film as a whole, attendant to compositional form and to the potential of abstraction from the diegetic "spaces of nature."

In a major narrative turning point in *North by Northwest*, Thornhill is implicated in the murder of a diplomat in the United Nations Building in New York.[41] The sequence opens with a stunning low-angle depth of field shot of the building.

The building was famously designed in the International Style, with its emphasis on surfaces and angles and with a relative lack of ostentatious decoration.[42] The low angle of the shot displays the building encompassing the entirety of the frame. It is thus more than merely an establishing shot, particularly in its resemblance to the schematic image of the CIT Building in the film's credit sequence.[43] The cut to the interior again focalizes the

Figure 4.15 The United Nations Building, New York City: *North by Northwest* (1959)

Figure 4.16 Schematized space through matte composition: *North by Northwest* (1959)

aestheticization of form through an expressive low angle: in an expansive depth of field, Thornhill is a minuscule figure lost within an array of modernist lines, angles, colors, and shapes.

This is again one of Hitchcock's magnificent matte configurations, schematizing space as an abstract composition. After the principal action occurs in the building, Thornhill flees and is captured in a painted matte of an extreme high angle view of the building and its exterior. In its saturated color (focalized in the vibrant yellow of a line of taxi cabs and the blue of the water feature), modernist swirls, and hard line edges, Thornhill's flight as action sequence materializes as an abstract visual configuration.

The abstraction of Thornhill's flight (which is now a movement mapped onto a schematic frame) builds upon the Saul Bass–designed credit sequence over the CIT Building. The levels to which this credit sequence displays the cinematic image as abstraction are astonishing. The image begins as a green field cut through with diagonal lines from bottom left to top right. This is not a building but a shape constituted out of lines, angles, spaces, and color. The abstract image then materializes as a building, but even in this material form, it displays the abstraction of a reflected image composited onto the sleek surface of the glass.

Hitchcock seems drawn to the capacity of the image to signify its aesthetic autonomy; the image must signify itself first to activate the aesthetic

106 THE MECHANICS OF PURE CINEMA

Figure 4.17 Modernist line, pattern, and color: *North by Northwest* (1959)

Figure 4.18 Abstraction in glass: *North by Northwest* (1959)

disposition required of an abstract work. In its desire to abstract from the narrative design of the frame, and then to abstract even further from its representational allure, *North by Northwest* engages both the abstract field of the schematic frame in the CIT and United Nations buildings and the sustained movement and rhythm generated by the bodies traversing the frame. In this way, Hitchcock's desire for an abstract form of expression gestured toward a pure cinematic frame founded on scale, shape, form, color (or black and white contrast), line, and movement. In these examples, an establishing shot always signals its double referentiality, layering a spatial schematic over the flow of narrative action. Quoting Annette Michelson on the cinema of René Clair (who I have argued was a key touchstone for Hitchcock's formulation of a pure cinema style), Pomerance suggests that "cinema 'offers not merely a general, panoramic view of the landscape, but . . . a machine for the generation of infinite compositional variations.'"[44] As I argue in subsequent chapters, it is this schematizing of space and movement as potential that will set a foundation for an intensified mechanics of the frame in the cinema of the *giallo* and De Palma.

5
Intensified Schematics
Bava, Argento, and De Palma's *Body Double*

5.1. The Schematic Frame in the *Giallo*

The schematic frame abounds in the films of Mario Bava and Dario Argento, but where Hitchcock must deploy abstract composition judiciously, these filmmakers celebrate the schematic abstraction of the film frame as the foundation of a self-conscious aestheticism. In the *giallo*, the composition of the frame negates the organic wholeness of representative space and instead makes explicit the patterned relations within space itself. The diegetic world of the film is examined through the camera's lens as an assemblage of component parts, each potentially an abstract form.

The influence of Hitchcock's schematic frame is writ large on one of Bava's most influential films, *A Bay of Blood*. As I've previously argued, Bava's *The Girl Who Knew Too Much* demonstrated the filmmaker's desire to understand and develop a Hitchcockian genre and visual film style. In *A Bay of Blood*, the principal action of the opening set piece contrasts languid panning shots of the titular bay at dusk with the interior of an impressive, ornately decorated bayside mansion. The wide establishing shot of the mansion cuts into an extreme close-up on the spokes of a wheelchair: the cut is sudden and the perspective so tight that the image remains unfocused for several seconds. In this initial cut, Bava demonstrates montage less as a regime of spatial continuity than rhythmic, affective counterpoint: line, shape, scale, and perspective function within a logic of spatial contrast. But neither is Bava's cut an example of Eisenstein's dialectical montage, in which the part, in association, formulates the whole. In the *giallo* set piece, Bava's images, like Hitchcock's, privilege the interstitial play of the fragment within the whole. In the case of a single jarring cut to an unfocused visual field, montage displays the abstraction of form across the two shots.

Bava's camera fixates on objects in stasis or movement as discrete components of the frame: the close-up of the circular movement of the wheel

The Art of Pure Cinema. Bruce Isaacs, Oxford University Press (2020). © Oxford University Press.
DOI: 10.1093/oso/9780190889951.001.0001

Figure 5.1 Compositional segmentation: *A Bay of Blood* (1971)

in slow rotation, a hand on the wheel, the display of red polish on the nails, the pan down to a close-up of black leather boots. What is the function of these images? What are they supposed to signify? Against a traditional mise en scène founded upon narrative and dramatic exposition, such images fix upon the schematic of form within the frame. After the succession of unconventional, irrational close-ups,[1] the image cuts to a long shot of the deep space of an ornate sitting room.

This space-as-whole is fashioned through an assemblage of frames within frames: the image emphasizes separate spatial segments through diagonals on the left of the frame, the proud rectangular structures of a door and ceiling-high window frame in the deep background of the shot, the hard edges of a fireplace on the right of the frame, and a couch and chair in the right third of the frame that fashion a series of further angled divisions. The wheelchair in mid-ground provides a degree of stability; however, I would argue that the depth of field renders this stabilizing effect almost negligible.

Bava now introduces the character of Countess Federica (Isa Miranda), the occupant of the wheelchair, in a very strange and arresting close-up frontal shot. It is arresting precisely because it is neither a medium close-up, a denotational image of an identity or figure, nor a close-up, a psychological image of greater intensity. Very much like Hitchcock's liminal close-up of Babs on the staircase in *Frenzy*, this shot is not part of a classical film style; it is not exhausted as a communicative sign, but instead registers an affect

Figure 5.2 Intensified close-up: *A Bay of Blood* (1971)

Figure 5.3 Simulated classical perspective: *A Bay of Blood* (1971)

founded upon the intensity of a (partially) abstract figure.[2] The unconventional scale of this view further destabilizes the composition of the sequence. Bava then cuts from the close-up to the most striking geometric frame of the composition: an expansive depth of field shot of the room, with the object of the wheelchair now miniscule in the background.

The shot is presented as the anticipation of the coda of the sequence—the abrupt killing of the countess—but it is clearly not an establishing shot of a diegetic space. In its emphasis on a vertically elongated space, the frame

Figure 5.4 Replicated figures in reflection: *A Bay of Blood* (1971)

draws attention to a cinematic simulation of classical perspective. In spite of the ontological basis of its photographic media, the image appears to be an explicitly painterly composition. The reverse shot captures the countess's face through the framed quadrants of a windowpane, further obscured by a film of rain washing over the surface. The image now tightens in an expressive zoom, followed by a series of impressionistic extreme close-ups in various degrees of focus. The shot immediately preceding the death is a fast zoom into a mirrored reflection of the countess, and then an equally fast zoom out, displaying a reframed image that perhaps gestures to the scene of Madeleine's "confession" in front of a mirror in *Vertigo*.

On the one hand, this sequence covers a major plot point, the murder of the Countess Federica. The interior of the mansion could be construed as a location interior, a setting, which of course it is. But I am suggesting that Bava's mise en scène and montage pattern demonstrates an explicit address of the schematic frame that derives from Hitchcock. It is quite difficult to capture in words (and image stills) the strangeness of this set piece in *A Bay of Blood*. In the sequence, Bava seems to intensify the affect of the figure *as fragment*, which vibrates within the compositional whole, effectively charging the frame with what Shaviro calls a "mysterious power."[3] Shots in various scale and spatial relation seem unmoved by a relation to the whole. In this sense, each shot is an excess of contained, paradigmatic classical form. Indeed, throughout the film, Bava demonstrates that the schematic frame is a break from the regime of the narrative image. These are images—a medium

Figure 5.5 Geometric partitioning: *Blood and Black Lace* (1964)

close-up of a figure that seems almost apparitional, or the zoom into an extreme close-up on a visage prior to death—founded upon the intensification of the fragment and its effect on the sensorium of the spectator.

In *Blood and Black Lace*, Bava's interiors of the fashion-house setting demonstrate what Met suggests is an "aestheticized representation of physical aggression and sadistic acts."[4] The murder plot is a foil for the staging of increasingly elaborate set pieces contained within expressive compositional frames. This is the film in which Bava unwittingly constructs a compositional iconography of the *giallo* that would influence Argento and Fulci, but also, as I have argued, the cinema of De Palma. In the set piece murder in the antique store, perhaps the most elaborate of the film, Bava opens with a Murnauesque expressionist streetscape: we can see the image cut starkly with a series of vertical lines anchoring two discrete spaces within the frame. The segmented frame is further accented through the heightened, expressionist contrast of the blue and green color tone. The store is covered in a set of focal points anchored along directional lines and movement; objects partition geometric frames within the frame.

Bava's expressive use of color throughout the sequence draws attention to color as a formal compositional element. This is color as the excess of representation, which constitutes another formal abstraction from the representative image. Like Hitchcock in films such as *Vertigo* and *Marnie*, Bava uses color as a compositional element to intensify the sensorial capacity of the frame. Color is both an eruption of repressed desire within the narrative (a symbolic signification) and, in its more provocative function, an irrational mark within the frame, intensified in the striking contrast with greens and blues.

Bava's abstract aesthetic form is realized most sophisticatedly in what is loosely a surrealist film, *Lisa and the Devil*. While the film has several examples of stylistic innovation,[5] its more significant achievement is to reconstruct the *giallo* as a work of philosophical abstraction. The *giallo* is principally a formulaic genre form. It bears the hallmarks of the classical detective story: an amateur detective investigates a series of gruesome murders, with each murder bringing the detective and killer into closer proximity. While the *giallo* is derived from the classical whodunit (referenced explicitly in Bava's *The Girl Who Knew Too Much*), the source of its pleasure for most spectators lies in its excessive and unbalanced narrative and image composition. Nevertheless, the causal chain connecting the threads of a classical plot is maintained. The *giallo* from Bava's *Blood and Black Lace* to Argento's *Deep Red* and *Opera* concludes on an elaborate unveiling of the killer. The actions of the story are thus rationalized by the denouement, a process that crudely conforms to classical narrative resolution.

However, *Lisa and the Devil* is a hallucinatory mélange of gothic horror and *giallo* tropes. There is, at least on a superficial level, a series of murders, and the eponymous heroine (Elke Summer) seems best placed to discover the identity of the murderer. But rather than an investigation rationalized through a causal narrative process, the film devolves into a series of surrealist expressions of liminal ontological spaces and times. One of Bava's strongest philosophical motifs—the inexorable process of a Nietzschean eternal return—envelopes the film in a pall of ambiguity unconventional for the genre. Having finally escaped the villa that constitutes the majority of the film's setting, Lisa boards a plane to return to the United States. However, she then discovers that the interior of the plane is merely another undefined ontological space from which she cannot escape. Heffernan accounts for the film's critical and commercial failure in such terms: it bears a "lack of narrative clarity and an indifference to dramatic suspense."[6] He further aligns this lack of clarity with an "art cinema leavened with graphic violence and sexual perversion"[7] In its curiously unclosed narrative structure, *Lisa and the Devil* is a philosophical inflection of the *giallo* film. It is therefore no less a meditation on the compositional form of cinema at the level of visual, narrative, and generic structure. If *Blood and Black Lace* is the more explicit meditation on the cinematic frame as fragment, *Lisa and the Devil* employs a more restrained visuality to expand the formal parameters of the genre form. I therefore read the film as a surrealist work for its narrative excesses that breach a classical causality. The excess of narrative communication, like the excess of the montage fragment, is an irrational irruption within the whole. It would require Argento in films such as *Suspiria* and *Inferno* to synthesize an abstract visual style and a surrealist narrative structure.

If Argento quite naturally and intuitively inherited the stylistics of the *giallo* from Bava (which is the orthodox reading of that relationship), he intensifies the schematization of the *giallo* frame. For Wood, "Argento's iconography as well as his narratives take *gialli* conventions to dark extremes."[8] Argento frames the opening set piece of *The Bird with the Crystal Plumage* within a two-tiered art gallery. It is significant that his first stylistic statement as director materializes within what Peucker calls an "aesthetic space." But whereas Hitchcock's spaces were for Peucker a conscious aestheticizing of the "spaces of nature," Argento's art gallery interior provides an intensification of aesthetic reflexivity; in Argento, the display of art and its aestheticized spaces (galleries, museums, theaters, concert halls, etc.) are reflexively modeled exhibitionist spaces. The aesthetic space of this opening sequence materializes in two interrelated ways: the materiality of art within the space calls attention to cinema as an art form, with its emphasis on the depiction of framed space; the frame is thus at once a containment of an artwork and a thematized schematic underpinning cinema's aesthetic form. Second, the iconography of gallery and museum spaces also signals Argento's desire to explore cinema as compositional form; in Argento, there is always a second-order signification of the image, attending to form, style, and the aesthetics of presentation. This desire to interrogate cinematic form will characterize Argento's idiosyncratic style for the greater part of his career.

The introduction of the protagonist, Sam Dalmas (Tony Musante), in *The Bird with the Crystal Plumage* is an explicit display of the abstract potential of the film frame. The twofold introduction begins with a series of lengthy, complex tracking shots through a museum space. Story exposition is overwhelmed by the sheer virtuosity of the series of camera moves; as Koven suggests, such ostentatious movements of the camera privilege form over the content of the *giallo* story.[9] The introduction to Dalmas occurs in two aesthetic spaces: after leaving the museum with his paycheck, we pick up Dalmas later that night strolling along a deserted street. The dark of the surroundings is punctured suddenly by the bright white interior of an art gallery across the street. In narrative terms, the art gallery set piece constitutes the inciting incident of the film: Dalmas witnesses the attempted murder of a woman that will catapult him into the investigation. It is a formulaic story and character pattern familiar to Italian audiences. But Argento's fascination with the visual film medium overwhelms the imperatives of narrative development. The frame proclaims its formal aestheticism in the expressive long shot held in an expansive depth of field. The action of the attempted murder is minuscule in scale in the deep background of the shot. The spectator is further distantiated from the narrative focus by a series of partitions within the field that segregate the action of the museum from an entry foyer (midground of the shot) and Dalmas (the viewing position). The configuration of the tripartite frame, not unlike the depth of field frame I examined in *The Lodger*, draws attention to the action as a viewing spectacle. However, the frame configures far more than an image to be viewed. The vertical lines emphasize the frame as a configuration of geometrically segmented divisions, or multiple frames within the cinematic frame. As Gunning suggests of this visual motif in Hitchcock, such frames "relate to Hitchcock's stylistic point of view."[10] In Argento's case, this stylistic predilection composes the frame more literally and emphatically as a schematic beneath the representative image. While Hitchcock's schematic frame constitutes an abstraction from the representational whole (the diegetic space), the representation is never entirely occluded. Hitchcock's schematic frames are liminal spaces: they display form as shape, line, pattern, color, tone, and movement and yet point *somewhere*. Such excesses in Hitchcock, in their transgression of a classical whole, are also fleeting and judicious. But in Argento, as we will come to see, the schematic is frequently rendered as emphatically visible as the diegetic representation.

The interior of the gallery in the mid-ground and background of the frame further segments the image, in effect composing something like a collage of images superimposed into what would be, in a conventional pictorial analysis, the organic whole of the frame. The image as pictorial wholeness is abstracted into an assemblage of component parts: the geometry of rectangles and squares (oriented both horizontally and vertically), suggesting an emphasis on line and shape; the modernist gallery space beyond, with its clinically white, minimalist interior, and its assortment of exotic artifacts discernible in the deep background. Together, the tripartite frame functions as a densely packed visual assemblage. The next cut is to a close-up on the woman, with the knife threatening her face; the diegetic sound is amplified on the soundtrack, and the viewing perspective of Dalmas, in reverse shot, is muted, further rendering the interior of the frame perceptually strange. In its curious silence, the image of action is presented as a spectacle for contemplation; Dalmas and the spectator, held from the image in the long shot, examine

Figures 5.6–5.8 A modernist pictorial-cinematic space: *The Bird with the Crystal Plumage* (1970)

both the contents of narrative (the diegetic signifier) and the constituents of form: lines and shapes in pattern and spatial relation. In his emphasis on the formal schematic, the sequence intensifies the affect of nonnarrative, and nonrepresentative, visual and aural materials.

Like Hitchcock, Argento reserves his most adventurous frame compositions for enclosed, architecturally complex spaces. In a later murder set piece in *The Bird with the Crystal Plumage*, he commences the sequence with a long overhead shot of a vehicle parked at a roadside. The point here is not merely to focalize the primary character but to establish a geometric logic within the frame: the overhead shot inscribes a vertical axis, excessive shot length and scale, and the contrast of the white car against a black background.

This geometric figuring of space within the frame is a point of entry into a far more complex and adventurous experiment with formal abstraction. In the shot of the entry into the hotel, the image discards the primary character and instead focalizes on the geometric structure of a staircase.

In the classical style, the spectator would anticipate the requisite match cut to establish the continuity of the movement of the principal character. In discarding the narrative focalization around the central character, we could say that Argento's fixation on the geometric composition is a continuity breach. We cut back to the main character to trace her movement within the sequence; she waits for an elevator. Argento again privileges objects within the frame, and then at a more elemental, schematic level the geometry of

Figure 5.9 Establishing shot on vertical axis: *The Bird with the Crystal Plumage* (1970)

Figure 5.10 Shapes and patterning: *The Bird with the Crystal Plumage* (1970)

line and shapes in relation. Even a communicative story cue—the shot of the elevator panel to signal the arrival of the elevator—challenges the functional symmetry of the frame. The shot of the panel is too close; it seems to fixate on the threat of the elevator that moves ever closer. The elevator, metonymically signified as a panel on a wall, functions as a primary axial point within the frame. The compositional rationale of the frame—lines, contrasts, intersections—carries within that rationale an affective charge, an intensity that builds incrementally within the frame.

Prior to the death scene, Argento provides several further renditions of the schematic frame, first as a static shot and then as a series of compositions of triangular frames within frames.

He concludes the study of geometric form within the frame with an expressive rotation of the frame: line, angle, shape, and form are now energized through the movement of the geometric configuration. This is an abstraction of the frame as modernist architectural form that will become almost a cliché in the neo-noir science fiction film of the 1990s and 2000s.[11] If we recall Dulac for a moment and her emphasis on the image as rhythmic form, we see in Argento an intriguing play of abstract movement images; abstraction is animated as a schematic in rotation. The viewpoint then returns to the character as she ascends the staircase. The movement is captured in a continuing spiral pattern, with the camera covering her action with its own circular traversal of the stairwell. The frame is now charged with an intensity derived from a fixation on form in movement.

The woman is murdered in the elevator, with a paneled mirror against the rear wall interior. The murderer wears a black leather coat and gloves. In

Figure 5.11 Rotational geometric form: *The Bird with the Crystal Plumage* (1970)

close-up, the murderer withdraws a straight razor from a pocket and opens it to reveal the blade to the woman. She screams. The montage of the murder now builds through a series of shot reverse shots of the stabbing of the razor, each reverse shot bloodier and more graphic, both as excess and as pattern. Color is thus also a matter of form; as Godard famously quipped, and as it applies to Argento's indulgence in this sequence, blood is first a mark—a rupture within the formal composition of the frame—before it is a representation.

This murder sequence is perhaps Argento's most aggressive and individualistic aesthetic statement in *The Bird with the Crystal Plumage*. It lays the groundwork for an experimental frame that would become increasingly aware of its abstract potential in the *giallo* films of the 1970s and 1980s. Such set piece compositions would influence De Palma's use of *giallo* film tropes in films such as *Sisters* and *Dressed to Kill*. Reflecting on Argento's elevator murder sequence in *The Bird with the Crystal Plumage*, I would argue that, in its starkest imagery of the body and the violence done upon it, De Palma's elevator murder scene in *Dressed to Kill* exemplifies the schematic (and fetishistic) frame that informs Argento's set piece. De Palma's sequence, while more explicitly imitating Hitchcock's shower scene in its narrative taxonomy, is nearer to an aesthetic sensibility that distends the image of violence as action (the violating razor blade) and graphic form (the wounded body). De Palma's sequence is for me nearer to a reflexive aestheticism of the frame in Argento's scene than Hitchcock's shower scene two decades earlier.

Mark Kermode argues that Argento "was to add an operatic and graphic style [to the Italian *giallo*] that was all his own."[12] Kermode is always a perceptive critic, and while he is no doubt referring to the graphic nature of the violence in the Argento *giallo*, I want to appropriate his notion of a graphic aestheticism more literally. In a basic sense, "graphism" focalizes form. The graphic emphasizes the part—the line, angle, segment, space, and shape, but also, and perhaps most explicitly in the *giallo*, the blot, the color bloom, the gloss, the stain, the drop of blood—over and against the organic whole of the representational field. Thus, the graphic nature of Argento's *giallo* refers not only to graphic images of sexual violence but also to a more elemental logic of the image that privileges the part over the whole, and abstraction over materialization within the film frame. If Argento explored the schematic frame with a degree of caution in *The Bird with the Crystal Plumage* (evinced in three set pieces), in films such as *Deep Red, Suspiria,* and *Opera,* the schematic frame takes on a baroque theatricality that demonstrates a performative, reflexive, playful sensibility unimaginable in a Hitchcockian film.

5.2. De Palma's LA Shopping Mall: Metacinematic Schematization

While Bava and Argento intensify the frame as an abstract aesthetic form, De Palma's mall scene in *Body Double* is a marvel of pure compositional experimentation. In De Palma's hands, graphic form is enriched through the affect of bodies (including the body of the apparatus) in constant movement. In this analysis, I want to read the generic space of the Los Angeles shopping mall in terms of the formal schematic properties De Palma brings to the cinematic frame. The mall for De Palma is an iconic sign, pointing to a form of (cinematic) spatial organization and movement within a multilayered geometric space. For De Palma, the mall (much like the train station) is an architectural schematic. Like Hitchcock's signaling of the raising of the simulacral curtain in *Rear Window*, De Palma constructs his set piece as the metacinematic projection of the film's protagonist, Jake Scully (Craig Wasson); indeed, I would argue that *Body Double* constitutes De Palma's most explicit meditation on the nature of cinematic referentiality.[13]

Appropriating the central plot motif in *Vertigo*, Scully follows Gloria Ravelle (Deborah Shelton), a woman he has spied on at night, on a trip to the local mall. Close-ups on Scully in his car are shot using a deliberately artificial and explicitly marked rear projection, drawing attention to the composited nature of the image; we view Scully's close-ups as if on a screen. De Palma conflates the image of a physical location (the interior of Scully's car) with a rear projection of the exterior of that location, thereby collapsing the ontological distinction between the cinematic image and the diegetic world it seeks to represent. De Palma thus reconstructs the diegesis as an abstract configuration of a body against a crudely unfocused background. If the line between real and artifice in a Hitchcockian rear projection shot remains somewhat ambiguous in a diegetic space such as the Marrakech market in *The Man Who Knew Too Much*, rear projection in *Body Double* is marked within the frame as a distinct ontological form.[14]

Herzog describes metacinema as a "re-presentation of a representation."[15] In an insightful discussion of *Inglourious Basterds*, he suggests that the film "doesn't just question whether a representation can ever be identical to the presentation itself, but whether it can ever be anything other than a re-presentation drawn from other representations."[16] For Herzog, these are politically and morally charged questions. But I want to take a step back from the politics of metacinematic histories to ask: What is the ontology of a metacinematic *image*, and how does this image differ from the classical image of the cinema? Bazin's image of reality at least in part derives its special properties from its indexical relationship to the real. What makes the moving image so intoxicating, and such a powerful representation, is that it captures the world in its movement, which is in a sense a more complete capture of the ontological properties of our perceptual experience. As spectators of moving image cinema rather than still photography, we feel differently about an image in movement, and this is principally but not solely because movement instantiates the phenomenal properties of time.

The metacinematic image, on the other hand, neither indexes nor addresses the real as the object of its re-presentational logic. The object that gives the metacinematic image its re-presentational motivation is itself a deferred image, or as I have suggested in the case of the medium close-up of Scully, a (rear) projection of an image. What, then, is the nature of the relationship between a re*screened* image and the world in movement it seeks to index? In the case of De Palma, I would argue that the metacinematic image cannot avoid marking the framed (and now projected) image with its ontological otherness.[17] On the most basic level, the metacinematic image reconstructs the diegetic space as a simulacral space, a set. But in film production, a set is a configuration of space designed to achieve a particular

Figure 5.12 Metacinematic composition through rear projection: *Body Double* (1984)

compositional rationale; it is designed to be controlled and manipulated. The metacinematic image thus stultifies Bazin's "unity of image in space and time"[18] and reconstructs the organic relations between objects within a diegetic space through a compositional rather than realist logic. The metacinematic image effectively reconstructs the diegesis as a determinate, hermetically contained set. In a metacinematic image, light, sound, movement, and time—*form itself*—are schematic properties within the frame.

In *Body Double*, De Palma's rear projection metacinematic cue marks the excess of the representation, instantiating a movement into a discrete set piece within the film. The sequence begins with the segmented frame of the rear projection close-up/reverse shot.

Upon entering the interior of the mall space, De Palma shifts from a classically oriented coverage of the action (a medium shot of the two principal figures within the frame) into an elaborate, measured zoom out to capture the multitiered space of the mall as a compositional whole.

The schematic frame of the establishing shot emphasizes the vertical axis of the space (an expansive two-tiered structure), marking a central tension around a diagonal line from bottom left to top right. The verticality of the frame is further intensified through a series of gigantic arched windows marking shop fronts, as well as vertical pillars stabilizing the two tiers. The abstract diagonal line in the center of the frame isolates an escalator occupied by the two principal figures within the frame.

Figure 5.13 Schematic establishing shot: *Body Double* (1984)

This schematic establishing shot is an explicit presentation of the architectural foundations of the action De Palma will now choreograph. It is therefore more than a presentation of diegetic space. In her excellent analysis of compositional space in Italian cinema, Wood writes: "Diagonal cinematic compositions can therefore simultaneously indicate the presence of a real world constituted in deep space ... and at the same time put a brake on the realism effect."[19] De Palma's frame very much resembles the Hitchcockian geometric frame in *Shadow of a Doubt* in which the figures increasingly become secondary to the architectural structure underpinning the composition. In De Palma, this diminution of the body of the character is all the more emphatic in the action of the zoom from close to wide shot. The shot therefore eschews the realist continuity of establishing place as setting, while the zoom functions as a constriction of compositional form, a literal framing. We will see this form of schematic throughout De Palma's oeuvre, and I will return at greater length to the mechanics of the schematic establishing shot (now as a split frame) in the next chapter.

After holding the schematic establishing shot for what seems an inordinate length of time, the image cuts to a dollying reverse shot anchored within Scully's point of view/proximity to Gloria. It is critical to note here that the point of view shot in this sequence is not congruous with a purely subjective shot. The point of view functions as the realization of character (Scully) as well as the materialization of lines of action within the space. There is an element of Hitchcockian voyeurism in the mechanics of this shot, and as I discussed in a previous chapter, critics derided the film for its overt imitation of Hitchcock. But as Douglas Keesey has recently argued, this kind of image in De Palma departs from the Hitchcockian voyeuristic subjective shot through its persistent "self-reflexivity."[20] De Palma's emphasis on the framing of compositional form and action through the schematic establishing shot draws attention to the construction of the frame itself, as both form and movement.

The sequence now plays out a conventional voyeuristic action as Scully surreptitiously views Gloria in a woman's changing room in a high-end boutique. But again, we must read voyeurism not only as the relation between active and passive observer but also as the orchestration of a schematic visual field within the frame. I am suggesting that we view the dramatic action (the act of voyeurism) as intrinsic to the visual coordinates of the schematic frame. Private and public lines of sight are orchestrated as lines of action within the frame, incrementally intensified through greater degrees of experimentation. Scully is depicted in a long shot gazing through the store window, but his line of sight/action is suddenly broken by a split-diopter image, suturing the line of sight and the object of the gaze into a single image.

In this sequence, De Palma seems to capture the wide shot of an architectural space (a shopping mall) as a schematic for potential lines of abstraction within the frame. All images, De Palma seems to suggest, are enframed in their compositional potential; all images signify as framed compositions with increasingly complex sets of relations between objects within the frame and in relation to the frame.

This sequence represents a stunning achievement in the schematizing of the film frame as shape, line, pattern, and movement. Scully's surveillance of Gloria concludes in a dizzying confluence of movement sequences through the mall: lines of action are constructed and effortlessly deconstructed as characters submit to the compositional play of the frame and the kinetic energy of a constantly moving camera. De Palma recounts his process for composing the sequence in the following way:

"The Rodeo Collection [a mall in Beverly Hills] had just recently opened and this was the first movie shot there. That again was first looking at a space and then sort of choreographing the action within the space and going to the space and taking hundreds and hundreds of still photographs so you know exactly how it's going to look like on film, what works visually, what doesn't

Figures 5.14–5.15 Diegesis as deconstructed architectural space: *Body Double* (1984)

work visually. And then very scrupulously laying it out in order to shoot all the shots in order to make the sequence work. It's literally almost a deconstruction of an architectural space, with various different points of view and various angles, and to me this is the essence of cinema. This is what cinema does that no other art form can do. And having done a lot of these kinds of sequences early in my career, this was the penultimate use of this type of visual storytelling. And it's a delight to watch to me to this day because it has a beauty and purity about it that's captivating."[21]

Aside from the language, which is strikingly familiar to the way in which Hitchcock discussed his notion of a pure cinema in conversation with Truffaut, I quote De Palma at length to demonstrate just how compositionally attuned he is to the mechanics of the cinematic frame as the "purity" of that art form. De Palma seeks to deconstruct the cinema of its trappings in story and character to reveal the essence of the form beneath: the materialization of schematic, abstractly rendered framed spaces animated by movement.

6
The Fragmented Frame 2

Segmentation

> The moment one considers a film in its totality, one runs up against the necessity of naming the units.
>
> Raymond Bellour

6.1. The Split Frame

A split frame is a split in the visual image; in its literal materialization of the montage fragment, it is a particularly emphatic, performative transgression of what Bazin called the ontology of the photographic image. As I've argued at various points in this book, for Bazin, cinema's overarching imperative, a matter of both aesthetic form and a phenomenological experience of the image, was to emphasize the authenticity of movement within the frame and between frames. Bazin is quite explicit on the subject of movement insofar as he intends that the frame should express fidelity to the movement intrinsic to human experience.[1] And it is important to note that in Bazin's realist model, even montage—which is in one sense a splitting of the image—must remain faithful to a phenomenal reality.

If the overarching myth of total cinema seeks the fullness of a realist image, what is a split frame in De Palma, and how might Bazin have reacted to this technical and aesthetic device? In conceptualizing the ontology of the split frame, I again want to find the seed of the De Palma innovation in Hitchcock. But then there are no split frames (or split-screen shots) in Hitchcock of the kind that proliferate with increasing rapidity in the films of De Palma in the 1970s and 1980s. Hitchcock clearly displays a fascination with geometric form within the frame, which I've tried to show in several examples across his oeuvre. Such geometries schematize the frame and render it as a partial, incomplete abstraction from the whole. Such fragments are most apparent when animated by movement, constituting the formal fragment as a discrete movement image. We see such images in Thornhill's flight from the United Nations Building in *North by Northwest* and in lines of sight and action in chase sequences in *Shadow of a Doubt* and *Blackmail*. But the sheer visibility of a split screen—in its transgression of the hermetic frame—is not something we see in Hitchcock, even during the most experimental stages of his career.

In the analysis that follows, I want to challenge this line of thinking to suggest that Hitchcock had indeed experimented with the split frame, and with increasing aesthetic and philosophical sophistication. Further, I will argue that Hitchcock's most emphatic realization of the schematic frame occurs within split-framed compositions in his films of the late 1950s and early 1960s. This position requires reorienting a conventional approach to two Hitchcockian images that have fascinated critics and viewers alike: the mirror image, or reflection, which we see as a visual and thematic motif in the director's work, and the point of view / subjective shot, and especially those subjective shots that emphasize the viewing circuit between subject and object.[2] In the case of the mirror reflection, I want to reread that image as a formal split within the film frame rather than a reflection that indexes an a priori original figure. In the case of the subjective shot and its viewing itinerary, I want to argue that such a viewpoint in Hitchcock configures more than subjectivity, and, following Peretz's analysis of the split cinematic frame, I argue that the subject/object split in a Hitchcock point of view shot displays "the pain of disintegration of [the] imperative for unity."[3] We tend to read the subjective shot of cinema as the identification between spectator and screen. I read it instead as an excess of identification, and a rupture of the physical and psychological space of the frame. The subjective shot in Hitchcock is, quite literally, a *split*. If De Palma explored the intuitive possibilities of the split frame as part of the ontology of the cinematic image, I suggest it was part of a larger project to understand Hitchcock's fascination with fragmentation—and with the splitting of the visual frame—within an evolving cinematic language.

I discern three compositional uses of the split frame in the work of Hitchcock, Argento, and De Palma. First, the split screen is a narrative conceit, clarifying lines of action brought into proximity, thereby intensifying the rhythmic alternation of parts of the story. This is the least interesting use of the split screen and enacts a basic narrative parallelism. One might say that it is a novel form of parallel montage, in which the cut no longer fuses one frame to the next in perfect continuity but enters into the frame itself. We see

Figure 6.1 Split screen as simultaneous action: *Four Flies on Grey Velvet* (1971)

this technique used in *The Thomas Crown Affair* (1968). In several sequences in this film, the split frame synchronizes various parallel lines of action. This is the technique's overarching purpose: to establish the contained temporal field of the story. As I have argued elsewhere, this novel "intensified continuity"[4] of the split screen is exemplified in the narrative structure and mapping of the network television show *24* (2001–2010).[5]

In Argento's *Four Flies on Grey Velvet* (*4 Mosche di Velluto Grigio*, 1971), a man dials a telephone and pauses expectantly. This pause then instantiates a splitting of the screen and the revelation of the parallel action on the other side of the line.

In his second feature, as in *The Bird with the Crystal Plumage* a year earlier, Argento demonstrates the desire to experiment compositionally. Yet it is a very muted form of experimentation. The split image is no more than a novel parallelism, demonstrating a measured transgression of the classical parameters of the cinematic image. To my mind, this use of the split screen in *Four Flies on Grey Velvet* is little more than a stylistic affectation. In a similar but far more adventurous use of the technique, De Palma covers the first murder sequence in *Sisters* as a parallel montage within the frame. It is not precisely the coverage of parallel action (though it could be viewed in this way) but parallel points of view: the right half of the frame shows the wounded body of a figure crawling toward a window, while the left half shows the reverse angle of the figure's hand as it signals through the window.

The emphasis in the split frame is on building tension within the sequence as a whole: De Palma collapses subjective and objective lines of sight, offering the spectator something like an omniscient coverage of the action.

130 THE MECHANICS OF PURE CINEMA

Figures 6.2–6.3 Split screen as narrative conceit: *Sisters* (1973)

Nevertheless, the emphasis in the action is oriented toward narrative: Will somebody see this murder from the street? Will the wounded man be able to reveal the identity of his murderer? In each of these examples, the narrative impetus overwhelms the potential of the split frame as an abstract compositional form. While these uses of the split frame demonstrate the filmmaker's desire to transgress a classical compositional norm (the frame as spatial and narrational whole), in its belonging to another frame, even an imaginative use of the split screen displays a compositional rationale anchored in

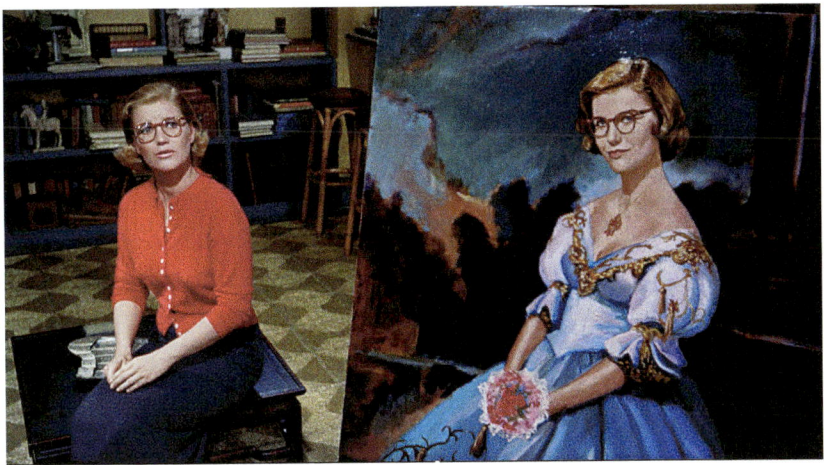

Figure 6.4 The split figure—Midge, Madeleine, Judy, Carlotta: *Vertigo* (1958)

narrative development. It is therefore of limited value in attempting to understand the split frame as a unique ontology of the cinematic image, that is, as an intensified fragment, or what Bellour calls "segmentation."

The split frame is far more provocative in its compositional intent when it diminishes the narrative pull of the image, drawing attention to the frame itself; the split frame is especially interesting when it actualizes the split as a formal element intrinsic to the composition. Peucker, for example, suggests that the moment that Scottie views the portrait of Midge as Carlotta Valdez is "almost a split-screen effect" in which "the line formed by the canvas bisects the film frame at a diagonal."[6]

But taking Peucker's lead, we might then consider an even more imaginative display of the split frame, also from *Vertigo*. Madeleine and Scottie perform a theatrical exchange of gazes in Ernie's restaurant. It seems that the point we should take from this performance is that the act of looking is duplicitous—of self (the subject) and of the other (the object of the gaze). How does Hitchcock realize this essential split in the act of looking? He splits the frame, dividing self from other and subject from object. The sequence begins as an exploration of the act of looking at an object—this is the erotic object of Madeleine Elster.[7] Kim Novak is accented within the frame in a flowing green dress. The sequence evolves through a series of increasingly complex and dense frames within frames. The famous circuitry of the gaze covered in a set of cuts between Madeleine and Scottie maintains a similar parallelism of perspective to that which we saw in the frame reverse frame of the murder in *Sisters*. Scottie looks at Madeleine; Madeleine "looks" at Scottie; and each gaze establishes at least a makeshift continuity within the visual field. But as I argued in my analysis of the introduction of the Lodger to Daisy, Hitchcock's mechanics of the gaze are rarely founded on an unproblematic spatial and psychological continuity. In the final movement of this sequence, the interior of Ernie's takes on the malleable qualities of the film set. The diegetic world begins to rupture, displaying its compositional form and materials. Madeleine pauses within a rectangular wooden frame that separates the seating area from the bar: in pausing, she is now inscribed within the composition as character *and figure*. The frontal shot (a portrait) reframes to compose a profile, again with the figure of Madeleine at a point of stasis. It seems critical that Madeleine is seen as a figure within a frame, unmoving and on display. In the final movement of the Ernie's restaurant sequence, we see a subtle materialization of the split frame: Madeleine as object of the gaze is split as she passes before a mirror. In the itinerary of the subjective gaze in this sequence, Madeleine emerges as a figure to be exhibited, and to be representationally composed within a viewing frame. The doubled figure is not self and other or substance and reflection, but rather *division and fragment*, the splitting of the whole into a radical ontology of the cinematic frame constituted in parts. Peretz is writing about the "excessive frame" in De Palma's *Blow Out*, but he may as well be writing about this splitting of the frame in *Vertigo*: "Excess does not have to do simply with the fact that there is a *plurality* of meanings or frames, a plurality of ways to *unify* . . . a situation but, rather, with an essential *multiplicity of fragments/frames*."[8]

The Ernie's restaurant sequence is an example of the potential of the film frame to spontaneously reframe, and therein to recomposite the organic, embodied character as an abstract figural form. In this sequence, Hitchcock achieves a philosophical disposition of the image founded on form as fragmentation, which materializes as a split of the image into constituent parts. *Vertigo* is Hitchcock's most confident depiction of action within an abstract cinematic frame, but we see this intuitive understanding of the capacity of the frame to split internally throughout his oeuvre. The motif of duplicity (including self-duplicity) and doubling is forcefully picked up in *Shadow of a Doubt*, a film that forms part of a larger philosophical exploration of the conflicted nature of identity. There are two simple split frames in that film that symbolize the split of identity in the film's protagonist, but which also foreground a compositional split within the frame. *Shadow of a Doubt*

Figures 6.5–6.7 Division and fragmentation—Madeleine: *Vertigo* (1958)

strikes me as one of the darkest films produced within the late classical era of Hollywood. It is a film in which the normative inscription of family and law is bludgeoned by an unremitting deviant presence within small town America. In the final sequence of the film (in which Uncle Charlie attempts to throw a teenage girl—his beloved niece—under a train), Uncle Charlie and Charlie (the niece) engage in a final confrontation. As if to augur the reversal in the plot that will shortly occur, Hitchcock uses an expressive split frame to separate the two Charlies within the image. The sequence as a whole emphasizes the verticality of the frame. Like De Palma's many spatial experiments with architectural spaces, in this sequence the train presents an opportunity to display a compartment in an expansive depth of field, anchoring the frame in the strong vertical axis.

The split in the frame is relatively muted and will be subsequently intensified in later films like *Vertigo* and *Marnie*. Yet in this single frame we can see an aesthetic disposition that privileges the display of the frame as fragment. The split in the frame is further intensified (and accented on screen) by movement in both segments: a boy moves horizontally across the deep background of screen left, defining the edges of that frame; the right segment

Figure 6.8 Segmented depth of field: *Shadow of a Doubt* (1943)

is intensified by Uncle Charlie's vertical movement from deep background to foreground. These split images are more than the collation of narrative information/action across two spaces; they are autonomous frames operating both independently and in concert.

The central set piece of *Marnie* occurs around a beautifully choreographed split frame sequence. While the action unfolds within a single frame, again, I want to read the frame not as a display of communicative materials (Marnie emptying the safe in screen right as the cleaner mops the floor in screen left) but as an abstraction of form in movement. The sequence as a whole is a configuration of unconventional shot scale, montage, and framing, but the critical movement occurs in a cut to a long shot as Marnie opens the lock of the safe. The expressive montage of close-ups and medium shots that precede this action now reveals the intent of the movement: the reveal of a split frame composition held in extraordinary duration (fifty-five soundless seconds) as Marnie commits her act of theft.

The geometric partitioning of the frame is of far greater interest than the narrational cue presented by the act itself. In fact, the emphasis on form overwhelms what would in a more conventional composition be the materials of narrative development: Marnie stealing the money and fleeing. The extreme depth of field; the oddly, very slightly canted low angle of the viewing position; and the emphatic partitioning of the frame by a load-bearing wall within the office all arrest the eye as a departure from what might be expected: the classical itinerary of the establishing shot and coverage of action. This frame demonstrates its fascination with schematic structure in its emphasis on vertical lines, including pillars from floor to ceiling and doors that loom unnaturally within the frame. But perhaps the most transgressive mark within the split frame is the image of the central figure within the action, Marnie, reduced to a minuscule shape in the deep background of the shot.

The shot concludes with a conventional cut to the protagonist as she moves back from the safe.

This apparently innocuous medium close-up achieves a great deal: it overwhelms the previous formal reflexivity of the frame with its conventional angle on the face, expression, and psychology of the principal figure within the action. The slightly soft focus on the visage of the woman returns the image to the more familiar itinerary of the classical gaze: we are again transfixed by the beautiful woman as erotic object. The medium close-up thus reestablishes the regime of the classical image, taking us further and deeper into the diegetic world and narrative action of the film. In spite of

136 THE MECHANICS OF PURE CINEMA

Figures 6.9–6.10 The split screen effect in excessive duration: *Marnie* (1964)

a wonderfully inventive experiment with the split frame, the frame as segmentation is ultimately occluded by its observance of a classical cinematic diegesis. The world of the film—which is to say, the world of the film encompassed within a film frame—remains for the spectator logical and organically intact. And yet, even if only for a brief sequence (fifty-five seconds in a film that well exceeds two hours' duration), the split frame of the office inscribes compositional space as line, shape, and segment rather than object, and the cinematic frame as abstract figuration rather than diegesis.

What is montage in this experimental sequence in *Marnie*, if not a split in the frame? Montage tends toward either a rationalization of continuity in

Figure 6.11 The classical scopophilic gaze: *Marnie* (1964)

the visual field, or a rationalization of noncontinuity. This montage composition tends toward at least the excess of continuity: it suggests more than it should and tantalizes the spectator with its abiding unease. Hitchcock's cuts are all the more arresting for breaching their communicative containment. As I have argued throughout this book, a pure cinema abstracts from the whole to compositionally address the relationship between its component parts. This particular engagement with the frame as compositional possibility is also a way of conceptualizing Hitchcockian montage as the endless proliferation of the process of segmentation. This is montage as the profusion of figures within an abstract compositional rationale: an angle in this shot animates a relation to a succeeding shot; a line fixes in an abstract relation to another line in a succeeding shot; a segment is split by a cut and sutured in a succeeding shot to form something like an imagistic collage; and so on. In the context of the split frame, we might say that the split in the seam of the frame is itself the basis of montage, no less than the split between two shots.

Hitchcock's purest split frame occurs beneath the fetishistic narrational impulse of the shower scene in *Psycho*.[9] Of the shower scene, Hitchcock said, "This is the action told in pieces of film. Expressing violence by the juxtaposition of the angles, and the pieces of film assembled."[10] This statement is the most acutely perceptive of Hitchcock's many attempts to articulate a pure cinema method. Here, pure cinema is not narration (the telling of story) or an intellectual montage (Eisenstein's "total film") but the revelation of action as juxtaposition. I'm sure Hitchcock would be satisfied with such a declaration, and it clearly displays its intellectual and stylistic debts to various currents in montage theory I've traced in this book. Yet in reflecting on how images form through juxtaposition, we can take Hitchcock's position further. Hitchcock's experimental montage in the shower scene in *Psycho* deconstructs the phenomenon of continuity itself. We encounter these images in aggressive, uncontainable movement as so many parts broken from the ideal of the compositional whole. Each image is thus a split, a spontaneous irruption within the visual frame. In his brilliantly detailed reading of the shower scene in *Psycho*, Philip Skerry suggests that "if one were to turn down the volume and just observe the metric rhythm, one would see a regularity of beat."[11] It's a fascinating point, although I am not convinced that the effect of this beat is merely to "match the increased heartbeat of its audience."[12] I agree with Skerry on the basis that each cut is a rhythmic form and force, and that, much as Dulac theorized in the 1920s, rhythm constitutes the basis of an abstract montage. Rhythm infuses each image and cut in *Psycho*'s shower scene with an abstract compositional rationale. If we engage the frames of the shower scene as whole, we see the shower scene not as a temporal *sequence* but as an abstract set of times, building rhythm, and, in that rhythm, sensation, in which angles and lines and shapes are juxtaposed. Such an image in *Psycho* would more effectively be described as a collage than montage, a position I will return to in an analysis of De Palma's *Femme Fatale* in the conclusion of this book.[13]

6.2. The Line Cross: Argento (and an aside to Bertolucci)

Hitchcock could have pushed the expressivity of the split frame so much further. The abstraction of a frame in mise en scène or montage—its intuitive capacity to split from within—is not precisely a process of reproduction (as it is in the representational image) or reflection (as it is in the conventional mirrored image), but a fracturing of the visual and sonic frame of cinema; the split frame within the cinematic screen is in this sense nearer to a fractal division. I have suggested that Hitchcock's split frame in films such as *Shadow of a Doubt*, *Vertigo*, and *Marnie* senses the possibility of the radical openness of the frame when broken from the itinerary of the whole. Yet each of these films ultimately subdues the affective transgression of the split to resettle the frame. *Vertigo*'s disturbing fragmented figure of Madeleine

Elster is rationalized as a deception staged by Gavin Elster; in the classical narrative style, Madeleine Elster *is* Judy Barton. *Marnie*'s split frame action sequence is conclusively reformed into the organic whole of the erotic image of the female in a soft-focus medium close-up. Uncle Charlie's split from his niece, in both symbolic and formal compositional terms, is sutured by the imperatives of a paradigmatic classicism. If Scottie's viewing of Midge's portrait is, as Peucker so persuasively argues, a "split screen effect," it would take filmmakers such as Argento and De Palma to actually split the frame.

As I argued at the beginning of this chapter, the split frame is an ontological break from the organic wholeness of the film image. The split frame cannot be made whole; it cannot be contained or rationalized. Its ontological basis lies precisely in this capacity to fragment. The split frame not only unsettles the organic whole of the image; it also marks the split itself—the fracture—as an abstract configuration. The ontology of such a frame troubles our most basic understanding of classical film form and its terminology. This is what makes De Palma's work so exciting and provocative. In the conclusion of his study of De Palma's cinema, Peretz suggests that "at the center of the De Palmian *oeuvre* . . . is a fundamental engagement with this horrifying and nightmarish dimension of the image, and we have associated this haunting horror cinematically with the discovery of the undergrounding movement of the camera, of the editing cut, of a multiplicity of perspectives with no unifying center, and with the discovery of the interrupted frame haunted by an internal outside."[14] I have traced De Palma's "haunted cinema" (by which I take Peretz to mean a cinema haunted by its incapacity to access the "whole," the ideal) to Hitchcock. Hitchcock materializes the part, the fragment, and, most emphatically, the split that will define De Palma's ontology of the cinematic image throughout his career. De Palma's films display a cinematic frame devoid of organic, determined relationships. Using Hitchcock's split frames as scaffolding for a deeper, more philosophically astute exploration, De Palma seems to move nearer to Dulac's fundamental principle of the cinematic image as the "relativity of images amongst themselves."[15] I take Dulac's notion of the image to be more than a shot, scene, or sequence; these are categories that facilitate a properly narrative medium. But a conception of the image as a pure element of cinema enables a more complex understanding of the "relativity of images" as an extension beyond our conventional understanding of montage. The split frame is, following Deleuze, a materialization of the part in relation to the whole, and of the image in its pure relativity.[16]

If we now read the split frame as a function of the image and its capacity for infinite relativization, we can identify the use of the split frame as part of a larger philosophical intervention. Hitchcock's most explicit split frame abstractions occur in the later experimental works, such as *Vertigo* and *Marnie*. A decade later, Argento explores the capacity of the schematic frame in films such as *The Bird with the Crystal Plumage* and *Four Flies on Grey Velvet* and, in his most adventurous compositional moments, explicitly marks the split in the frame; I offered an analysis of a scene in *Four Flies on Grey Velvet*. But if we reconceptualize the split not as a segmentation within the visual field but as a deeper, philosophically motivated "relativity of the image," we see that the split frame can be encoded in a formal contrivance as seemingly innocuous as a line cross.[17] In *The Bird with the Crystal Plumage*, Argento effectively splits the frame of a dialogue scene vertically without marking the split in a formal "split-screen" segmentation. Shot in an expansive depth of field, the image accents the vertical axis and the spatial segregation of the two figures.

This verticality is further emphasized by the movement of the woman from the deep background to the foreground of the shot; she holds momentarily in the foreground and then returns to the background in an equally measured movement. In what can only be described as a very strange departure from classical composition, Argento now cuts "across the line" to display the space from the reverse angle. While narrative continuity and character focalization is maintained through the dialogue that runs across the cut, the spectator feels the oddness of a cut that breaches classical continuity, and in a sense severs the organic whole of the frame. Argento's cut across the line conjures the same unsettling sensation of De Palma's split perspective shot in *Sisters*. The line cross is a materialization of a split within the organic whole of the frame.

Bernardo Bertolucci, with whom Argento worked on Sergio Leone's *Once Upon a Time in the West*, uses the line cross as an elegant (and far more expressive) split in the frame, symbolizing a larger thematic of social, political, and ideological fragmentation in the Fascist-era Italy of the film. In *The Conformist* (*Il Conformista*, 1970), one of Bertolucci's most visually arresting films, a sequence displays the home of Marcello's (Jean-Louis Trintignant) mother as a grossly distorted space; like so many of the authority figures of Fascist Italy, Marcello's mother is depicted as a grotesque. Bertolucci's frame therefore suitably displays a fracturing of the classical, harmonious frame. Marcello sits on his mother's bed as she recounts a vaguely incestuous

Figures 6.12–6.13 The line cross as spatial segmentation: *The Bird with the Crystal Plumage* (1970)

dream. After holding the two shot at some duration, Bertolucci suddenly cuts to the reverse angle as the dialogue continues, switching the position of the bodies on screen. This is certainly one of the strangest line crosses I've encountered; very little prompts this sudden reversal of the image. Unlike Argento's line cross in *The Bird with the Crystal Plumage*, Bertolucci explicitly marks the frame with this new compositional structure. But if Bertolucci wishes to draw attention to the transgressive nature of this frame, he now intensifies this transgression by crossing the line *on movement*. After a second highly visible line cross, Marcello's mother rises from the bed and walks to the background of the frame, toward an adjoining bathroom. The camera tracks this movement of Marcello's mother from left to right. As

Figures 6.14–6.17 Line cross segmentation on movement: *The Conformist* (1970)

Figures 6.14–6.17 Continued

both figure (Marcello's mother in the background) and camera (in the foreground) exit the room at screen right, Bertolucci's moving camera enacts a startling line cross. As the camera picks up Marcello's mother, now in the bathroom, the frame suddenly reverses its perspective without breaking the flow of the movement.

It's difficult to adequately describe the audacity of such an image in its transgression of a classical cinematic frame. Bertolucci seems to split the frame through juxtaposing compositional and affective continuity contained in the movement of the camera and the fracture of the frame itself through the line cross. The frame is suddenly a spatial inversion, a repositioned fragment within the whole, but the stylistic gesture is casual, almost playful. In my reading, such line crosses are not merely a breach of classical continuity but a spontaneous irruption of the image of framed space and therein instantiate a new set of image relations within the whole.

6.3. Intensifying the Split Frame: *Dressed to Kill*

De Palma realizes the potential of the split frame through increasingly complex, expressive split-screen compositions in his films of the 1980s. It is as if the intensity of the split increases with each experiment, emphatically marking the fault lines that separate action contained within a frame into its component parts. One of De Palma's signature split frame images occurs in *Dressed to Kill*. While it remains a split-screen composition functioning as parallel montage (or at least it appears this way), the space encompassing the split is now more complexly designed and densely populated. The earlier instrumental split frame of *Sisters* maintains a relative synchrony of the two perspectives; while that shot offers two perspectives of the same action, it is nevertheless perceived as whole. In *Dressed to Kill*, however, De Palma intensifies the split as demarcation. Each segment of the split is marked as a separate visual plane within the action, and each segment operates with its own compositional logic. Much like Hitchcock's approach to the rhythmic composition of montage in the shower scene, De Palma seems to set one segment of the split frame in a contrapuntal relation to the other, emphasizing spatial and rhythmic difference. In a cut to a split frame at a midpoint of *Dressed to Kill*, we see two images set side by side in a split-screen composition: the left frame depicts Dr. Elliott (Michael Caine) in his office; on the right, we see Bobbi, whom we assume to be a murderer.

Figure 6.18 Inciting segmentation: *Dressed to Kill* (1980)

The left frame displays the action in a medium shot as Elliott paces in his office; the right frame displays Bobbi in a close-up behind a pair of binoculars, spying on Liz Blake (Nancy Allen).

In this split frame composition, De Palma offers a complex itinerary of the cinematic gaze. Contrast in shot scale and depth of field and focus provide a visual interest. But more striking is the juxtaposition of the classical medium shot, which stabilizes the left segment of the frame, with the tighter voyeuristic angle of the right segment, which is a space of greater affective intensity. As a spectator, we inhabit both viewing itineraries simultaneously. I suggested earlier that the conventional use of a split frame composition encodes narrative parallelism: it ensures that we can rationalize the continuity of action across space. But while parallelism is clearly the compositional rationale of the split frame in *Sisters*, in this sequence in *Dressed to Kill*, the intent is to breach the anticipated spatiotemporal continuity of the organic frame, and in effect to split cinematic space into discrete spatial and temporal components. Criticism of *Dressed to Kill* (and more especially the negative criticism) questioned De Palma's use of the split frame in this sequence, suggesting that it constituted an unethical deception of the spectator. We learn in the denouement that Dr. Elliott and Bobbi are in fact the same person. I therefore take the point of such criticism: the split frame implies parallelism and therefore the simultaneity of action. It appears that Dr. Elliott's pacing in his office and Bobbi's spying on Liz Blake occur at the same time, and that the split screen is the explicit marker of simultaneity. But this is precisely why we need to reconceptualize the split frame as an abstract spatiotemporal formation rather than a measure of continuity within narrative action. In this instance, the image is not a deception simply because De Palma deploys the split frame to rupture the hermetic form of the classical frame. The "simultaneity" of the two segments is less a deception than the creative juxtaposition of spatiotemporal images. The relativity of the image in split frame now tends toward a relativity of the space and time intrinsic to the frame as whole.

De Palma maintains this split frame composition for an astonishing duration, developing three discrete though successively intensifying movements. We begin with the split between Dr. Elliott and Bobbi just discussed (forty seconds), then move directly into a second split frame composition between Dr. Elliott and Liz Blake (1:43), followed by a third split frame formation between Liz Blake and a television screen in Dr. Elliott's office (twenty seconds) (figures 6.19–6.20). The duration of the shot (though I am reluctant to use "shot" as a structural term) concludes on the most densely populated split frame of De Palma's career up to this point (figure 6.21). The preceding split frame compositions now materialize as a profusion of segmented frames within frames: Dr. Elliott sits in a chair in his office (the subjective point of view, frame 1); this (absent) subjective viewpoint materializes in a mirrored reflection, constituting a line cross and thus a rupture of the classical compositional field (Dr. Elliot in an armchair, the eye line constituting a line cross, frame 2); on the left of the screen, a third discrete frame is displayed on a television screen (a *Donohue* interview with a transgender woman, frame 3); on the far right of the screen, we see a rear shot of Liz Blake (the absent subject as mirrored reflection of frame 1) as she pins back her hair (frame 4); this "dirty" over-the-shoulder point of view is realized in a set of reflections in a tripartite mirror on the dressing table (frames 5 and 6); De Palma isn't done: Liz Blake watches the same *Donohue* interview on her television set (frame 7) in the deep background of the shot.

In a conventional analysis, this confluence of framed segments would be read as a single film shot. De Palma's sequence cannot be read in this way. The shot, even in Eisenstein, is a rationale for action. But in this signature De Palma split frame composition, the shot is overwhelmed by the pure relativity of the segment. This is what I take Bellour to mean by his notion of "segmentation," but in De Palma segmentation is nearer to a pure abstraction of form than a schematic for spatiotemporal action. We see here also the limitation of thinking through montage as a configuration of the whole. In such sequences, the intensity of the fragment overwhelms the montage *as whole*; the whole recedes beneath the intensity of the fragmentary gaze. The sheer virtuosity of this mode of cinematic perception recalls the complex

Figures 6.19–6.21 The pure relativity of the split frame: *Dressed to Kill* (1980)

visual itinerary I described in several Hitchcockian sequences, including the exchange of gazes in *The Lodger* and the split frame of Madeleine Elster as she leaves Ernie's restaurant in *Vertigo*. And yet Hitchcock's split frame could only suggest the abstract potential of the frame—its pure relativity—that De Palma realizes in this sequence.

Figure 6.22 The split diopter image: *The Untouchables* (1987)

6.4. A Purer Abstraction: The Split Diopter Image

The split frame would be compositionally enriched through De Palma's consistent deployment of the split diopter lens in his films of the 1970s and 1980s. A split diopter lens attaches to a primary camera lens, enabling the viewpoint to augment a primary spatial field with a secondary spatial field.

The unique effect created by this lens is to configure two distinct spatial compositions within the one shot, splitting the image into two spatial planes. While the split diopter image resembles the more conspicuous split frame effect previously discussed, the split diopter image is confined to manipulating the spatial composition within a single film frame. Unlike a more conventional split-screen composition, the split diopter image must be viewed from a single perspective. Thus, while the split-screen composition is conventionally used to advance the narrative in a particular way, the split diopter image explicitly draws attention to the spatial segmentation of the frame.

The split diopter lens is commonly used to extend the depth of field within a frame: "The split diopter lens simply permits focusing on a very close object on one side of the frame, while a distant subject is photographed normally through the uncovered portion of the prime lens."[18] The viewer cannot perceive the depth of field in its entirety, but in this use of the lens, complete and uninterrupted depth is inferred by the spectator. The inference of depth emphasizes the organic whole of the frame: in its composition, foreground and background are crudely sutured together, yet the split diopter erases the mark of the suture by creating "an *impression* of considerable depth."[19] The split diopter lens therefore was not only motivated by a desire for greater capacities of depth of field, but it was very quickly rationalized as merely one more tool in the filmmaker's kit to produce perceptual continuity within the visual field of the frame. For Ramaeker, the chief rationalization of the split diopter image as a conventional depth of field occurred by hiding the suture within the split field. The split in the lens projects a highly visible mark within the frame, in effect pointing to the artifice of the composition and the presence of the mark of the apparatus within the diegetic field. If the classical style is founded on the perceptual continuity and hermetic containment of the visual field, a breach of that field punctures not only the space as diegesis but the spectator's perceptual and psychological immersion within that field. In short, much as Hitchcock hid the cuts in the single-take coverage of the action in *Rope*, filmmakers intuitively experimented with ways to hide the mark of the split in the split diopter image. While the split diopter image is thus a stark negation of the perceptual "truth" of the representative image, as a configuration of the organic depth of field of the classical film image, the split as rupture within the whole must be subdued through the manipulation of the mise en scène composition of the primary frame. We see this desire to rationalize the split in Barry Levinson's *Rain Man* (1988). Charlie Babbitt (Tom Cruise) is set in a depth of field relation to Raymond Babbitt (Dustin Hoffman), his autistic brother. The split diopter field focalizes both characters within the frame simultaneously: Charlie's selfishness and arrogance and his skittishness in movement in the phone booth are contrasted with the serenity of Raymond's demeanor as he sits waiting in the deep background.

Figure 6.23 Split diopter segmentation as subjective delineation: *Rain Man* (1988)

The purpose of the shot is to contrive a relation between two characters, dividing the perceptual and psychological points of identification. The mark of the split is washed out within a vertical line of light at the edge of the boundary of the primary frame (the edge of the phone booth). It is a brilliant composition, but its motivation is clearly to emphasize story and character relation and to de-emphasize, or in fact entirely negate, the novelty of the visual composition and its transgression of a classical style. The technique in this instance is to mark subjectivity, both of the character complex of the story (Charlie and Raymond Babbitt) and of the spectator. I would call this a "natural field" split diopter image, in which the split field brings together two characters in radically separate depth planes. The erasure of the mark of the suture within the frame emphasizes the organic whole of the diegetic space. *Rain Man* is after all a road movie, and as such its generic tendency toward narrative closure and the resolution of conflict is founded on the perception of a classical diegetic frame.

Spielberg presents a more experimental use of the split diopter lens in *Jaws* in 1975. In the sequence of the second shark attack, Chief Martin Brody (Roy Scheider) sits on the beach looking for signs of the shark's appearance. As he is approached several times by locals, his gaze is compositionally split between the foreground of a conversation and the deep background of the ocean. The most imaginative composition of this split gaze is captured through a split diopter lens, compositing the figure of a man in close-up at frame right with the action in the ocean at screen left (the primary frame).

The contrivance of a primary and secondary depth of field creates an impossible depth cue. Unlike Levinson's use of the split diopter in what is a sequence charting narrative and character development, Spielberg emphatically marks the composition with the dividing line between the primary and secondary frames. Being a great admirer of Spielberg as a stylist, I would suggest that this is one of the most interesting compositions of Spielberg's films of the 1970s. For a filmmaker associated with an "invisible" compositional style, this split diopter image seems to me one of his most stylistically expressive (and transgressive) moments. And yet the motivation of this split diopter image is again not precisely formalist or compositional. Spielberg uses the split diopter to identify the spectator with Chief Brody's distracted and anxious gaze. Thus, while the technique is employed quite differently, I would argue that the primary function of Spielberg's split diopter image is again to express the subjectivity of the protagonist and spectator. The sequence concludes on a hyperbolic "*Vertigo* shot," in effect suturing the split

Figure 6.24 The split diopter image as untethered subjectivity: *Jaws* (1975)

gaze of the diopter image into the intensity of a point of view shot of almost comic (dis)proportion.[20]

If De Palma's split frame compositions reveal the potential of the frame as an abstract compositional form, his use of the split diopter is all the more transgressive of a classical representational style. In films such as *Obsession, Dressed to Kill, Blow Out, Body Double*, and *The Untouchables*, the split diopter image is less a composition founded on depth of field than a highly abstracted montage within the frame. In a sequence in *Obsession*, Robert Lasalle (John Lithgow) and Michael Courtland (Cliff Robertson) are in conversation in Lasalle's office. The depth of field within the office is compressed within a split diopter field: Lasalle in the left frame is held in a medium-long shot in deep focus, with the city visible in relative clarity in the deep-background vista through the office window.

Courtland is shot in profile in the right frame in a jarring close-up in shallow focus in which the background of the city is out of focus. On a thematic level, one could present a serviceable reading of this very strange composition: Lasalle commands the space with his confidence and arrogance, while Courtland's isolated profile in an extreme shallow focus suggests his entrapment within a fantasy. But if we remove ourselves from what is a turning point in the narrative to consider the visual character of the frame, the image takes on the disproportionate, almost irrational configuration of a surrealist composition. Courtland's profile dwarfs the frame in its disproportionality to Lasalle's full-body framing. The city that focalizes a realist depth of field in the left segment is an abstract figuration in the right. Yet the two images are sutured together and thus form one continuous image field. If

Figure 6.25 Irrational split frame composition: *Obsession* (1976)

we reject the dominant impulse to engage the split diopter field as a conventional split screen (a simulation of a classical edit), we encounter the image as a play on cinematic mise en scène and montage. The juxtaposition of an expansive depth of field with a shallow-focus close-up marks the suture line within the frame with striking clarity. How is the spectator to engage such an image in what is ostensibly an expositional sequence? The split diopter image in this frame also functions as a schematic composition, with each frame within the frame marked by the vertical columns of the office windows. As in Hitchcock's framing of set pieces in *Shadow of a Doubt*, *Vertigo*, and *Marnie*, in this shot in *Obsession*, the natural symmetry of the split is intensified by an aesthetic disposition toward geometric form.

In a later sequence in *Obsession*, De Palma appears to directly quote Hitchcock's rendering of the abstract geometric composition of the United Nations Building in *North by Northwest*. Returning to Lasalle's office, the shot commences with an abrupt upward tilt of the camera to cover the facade of a building exterior. While in its vertical movement, the camera pans left to right and continues upward to reveal the facade of a skyscraper. The aggressive vertical and horizontal movements destabilize the image; and, much like Hitchcock's coverage of the exterior of the United Nations Building, the movement of the camera does not configure an establishing shot as much as a geometrically segmented frame. De Palma then intensifies the abstraction of the frame. In cutting to the interior of the building, Lasalle's office is segmented within a split diopter field. While the mark of the suture is invisible (obscured by a vertical column in the window frame), De Palma's juxtaposition of a close-up (tending toward extreme close-up) and medium-long shot

Figure 6.26 Split diopter framing in depth of field: *Obsession* (1976)

emphasizes the compositional distortion of the interior space. The formal properties of lines segmenting the frame—line as form within the representational whole—produce distortions in scale between foreground (frame left) and background (frame right).

One of De Palma's most aggressive and playful uses of the split diopter image occurs in an early sequence of *Blow Out*. The film opens on a formulaic slasher scenario only to reveal that the film's protagonist, Jack Terry (John Travolta), is viewing the footage of a B-grade horror film. The film within a film immediately calls attention to compositional form, and in this case genre form, and *Blow Out* indeed constitutes one of De Palma's most sophisticated reflections on cinema as mediation. The opening sequence also explicitly quotes two other important textual sources: the opening and closing scenes of Argento's *Deep Red* and the opening point of view sequence of John Carpenter's *Halloween* (1978), which is itself a quotation of the opening sequence of *Deep Red*. The slasher film footage is followed by a credit sequence cut to highly amplified sound effects, signaling both a critical plot point of the film to follow (Jack is a sound recordist for a B-grade film producer) and the film's intention to depart from naturalistic compositional form.

The first post-credit sequence depicts Jack in a sound studio in a naturalistic split diopter image: Jack stands in the background of the shot while a television plays in sharp focus in the foreground; the split diopter seam is erased in the vertical axis of the left edge of the television frame, which conveniently runs the entirely length of the vertical axis. The split diopter image then cuts into a split-screen image, with the frame divided by an emphatic black line.

Figure 6.27 The split frame compositing parallel narratives: *Blow Out* (1981)

The split-screen is held as the two segments of the split frame unfold the narrative information required to make sense of Jack's sound recording job and the political context that will underpin the assassination at the core of the film's plot. Following this sequence, the image cuts to Jack standing on a bridge at night, recording "new wind" for the slasher film. De Palma covers Jack's position in a series of experimental angles, moving from extreme wide long shot to a medium close-up on Jack and his equipment. Each shift in scale, perspective, and angle is covered in the rhythm of a jump cut, suggesting a discretized set of images in geometric relation. The jump cut edits are then matched to the rhythmic croak of a frog on the bank of the river, captured in sharp close-up while framed in the right segment of a split diopter field (figure 6.28). The rhythmic croak on the soundtrack not only amplifies the soundscape intrinsic to the diegesis but also emphasizes the discretized nature of the spatial segments within the split diopter image. In contrast to the "naturalistic" split diopter image in Jack's studio, the close-up on the frog displays the schematic framework underpinning the composition.

It becomes clear that De Palma's intention is to compose the sequence as a montage experiment of increasingly discretized frames. The naturalistic split diopter image in Jack's studio is complicated in the compositional breach of the frog in the right frame of the split diopter image. However, that image remains somewhat naturalistic because of the relative obscurity of the split diopter seam, as well as the naturalistic scale of the frog in relation to the deep background of the space depicted in the left segment of the frame. But the next cut to a split diopter image crudely sutures Jack in long shot to an

Figure 6.28–6.29 Discretized sound and vision: *Blow Out* (1980)

extreme close-up on the eye of an owl previously heard on Jack's recording microphone.

The image inverts the naturalistic scale of the previous split diopter image in which the frog was composited in relative proportion to the background. In this split image, De Palma deliberately obscures the depth of field as continuity, rendering the two figures wildly disproportionate in scale. The split diopter image, De Palma seems to suggest, discretizes both the visual and sound image. The spectator thus inhabits two discrete frames set in contrapuntal relation, forming an environment in which perception is itself discretized through compositional form.

In collapsing the depth of field within the frame, the split diopter image decants separate cinematic frames and juxtaposes them into a set of new relations, and new potentialities.

De Palma's deployment of the split diopter frame in his films of the 1980s demonstrates an acute perception of the potential of this abstract cinematic frame. In these films, the split diopter image reveals the potential of the frame to *become more*, to signify in excess of what its content appears to offer. This is not an artificial cinema in the sense in which Bazin critiqued the German expressionist aesthetic[21] but a cinema assiduously attentive to the aesthetic and affective potential of film form. While De Palma's body of work is clearly not part of an American or European avant-garde filmmaking enterprise, its desire for a cinema of segmenting potential nonetheless partakes in some sense of Dulac's notion of the "relativity of images." As such, I see De Palma's use of the split diopter image as part of a much larger, and deeper, interrogation of the nature of cinematic form.

6.5. Abstract Movement: The Zoom

The zoom is a natural and intuitive outcome of the abstraction of filmic space. As a form of frame mobility, the zoom is less a representation of a pro-filmic reality than a reordering of the perceptual coordinates within the frame. In its cavalier attitude to the spatiotemporal field of the film, the zoom breaks from the fullness of representation and as such sees and perspectivizes in ways starkly different from the mobile framing of a dolly shot, a track, or a pan across a landscape. Such formal and technological interventions within the cinematic frame maintain a level of fidelity to the diegesis, both in what they show of an object (for example, a dolly from medium shot to close-up common in dialogue sequences in the classical Hollywood cinema) and in what they infer about cinematic space. The dolly, track, or pan maintains the integrity of space even as it construes a new viewing position and perspective. Thus, Hitchcock's elaborate crane movement in *Notorious*, while a striking stylistic experiment with movement and point of view, nonetheless conforms to a common visual perception of movement. The space—and its concomitant diegesis—remains intact.[22]

The zoom, on the other hand, is something quite different from more conventional forms of mobile framing. Popularized in the cinema of the 1960s, the zoom is less a spatiotemporal traversal than a re-perspectivization of the viewing.[23] It is, like the split-screen or split-diopter shot, an irruption within framed space, but unlike the frame, which segments, the zoom also distends space through movement within the image. This dual purpose of the zoom is critical to its operation: it offers both a new perspective (for example, a zoom into a close-up or a zoom out to a wide shot) and the sensation of movement and change (the movement itself occasioned by the shift in scale and distance within the frame). Thus, one can view what I would call an "establishing zoom" frequently used in the early sequences of Visconti's *Death in Venice* (1971), which is both a familiar marker of Visconti's visual style and an informational cue about place and character. However, in a Shaw Brothers kung fu genre film such as *The 36th Chamber of Shaolin* (1978), the rush zoom frequently emphasizes the affect of movement over the information cue contained in a change in viewing perspective. In its twofold capacity to reconstruct the frame, the zoom is potentially a radical cinematographic technique and is used sparingly and with great caution. It is therefore not surprising that, as Willeman has argued, "the zoom was a constant and rhetorical feature in films by the likes of Jesús Franco and Mario Bava."[24] Like Bava, Jesús Franco was a director at the head of the Spanish equivalent of the Italian *filone*, having produced and directed genre films such as *The Awful Dr. Orloff* (1962) and *Necronomicon* (1967). While spectators often misrecognize the effect of a dolly shot as a zoom, Willeman, quoting a study by Barbash and Taylor, offers a neat description of the distinction between the two formal techniques and their effect on the spectator: "Zooming into a person can never convey the same sensation as moving closer to the person. . . . If you zoom . . . the move feels unnatural and your spectators will sense (and share) your distance from the action. . . . If you zoom too much, you may destroy the spectator's suspension of disbelief in what they're seeing."[25] In this straightforward description of the function of the zoom, the zoom is aligned with an aesthetic founded on artifice. In a conventional cinema that privileges truth and authenticity, Willeman, working through Barbash and Taylor, cautions against the overuse of the zoom for fear it will distantiate the spectator from the integral unity of the diegesis and its subject matter.

This cautious use of the zoom is predicated on the zoom's function as informational cue. However, as Belton argues, the zoom also "abstracts [space] by flattening or elongating it. In effect, the zoom produces an ellipsis of space by both traversing and not traversing it."[26] It's unclear to me what Belton means by an "ellipsis of space," but it is clear from his description that the zoom abstracts from the pro-filmic space, therein reconstructing that space as a compositional form underlying the diegesis. In the terminology I've employed in this chapter, I would argue that the zoom constitutes a reframing of cinematic space that, in the words of Robin Wood, "[undermines] our sense of physical reality."[27] The commencement of the zoom not only re-perspectivizes the diegesis but also constructs within the frame a new perspective and movement itinerary. Against the dolly, the track, the pan, and the Steadicam, which I align with technologies that configure what Belton describes as "traditional notions of cinematic space,"[28] in its capacity for abstract movement within space, the zoom presents a unique potential for the cinema frame to spontaneously irrupt in excess of the diegetic world represented on screen.

Hitchcock's "*Vertigo* shot" is now legendary for its use of the zoom concurrently with a dolly movement of the camera to provide a new mode of spatial perception and temporal experience; the dolly zoom is said to contrive Scottie's experience of vertigo. For Hitchcock, the shot depicts the visual perception of "a man who's in an emotional crisis."[29] Yet while the shot was a stunningly original experiment with film form, it remained for Hitchcock a form of subjective, or point of view, cinematography. We can contrast Hitchcock's use of the zoom with almost any deployment of the zoom as a stylistic contrivance in the cinema of Bava, Argento, or De Palma. The critical distinction lies in the function of the zoom in the work of these filmmakers. If in Hitchcock, or indeed in the majority of films utilizing the zoom from the 1950s through the 1970s, the zoom remained a communicative cue rationalized within a diegetic world, in the cinema of Bava, Argento, and De Palma, the zoom explicitly reconstructs the diegesis as a compositional space subject to a spontaneous rupture in viewing perspective and framing. The dual function of informational cue and affective movement that characterizes the zoom shot is weighted dramatically toward the affect of movement and jarring perspectival change in this form of cinema, imbuing the frame with an intensity that is both performative in its exhibitionism and compositionally unsettling. In Bava's *Blood and Black Lace* and *Bay of Blood* or Argento's *Suspiria* and *Tenebrae*, the zoom corrupts the frame from within, displaying a diegetic space that is, as Belton suggests, "abstracted." In this abstraction from the diegetic world, the zoom displays an aesthetic disposition (of the filmmaker, but also of a genre such as the Italian *filone*, which adopted the zoom as a foundational cinematographic gesture) that foregrounds the image as compositional form.

6.6. Intensified Segmentation

The zoom is deployed in its fullest potential to corrupt the diegetic frame in Fulci's *Don't Torture a Duckling*. As an Italian director, Fulci operated on the periphery of *filone* production. If Bava and Argento had achieved recognition as major directors with early works (Bava's AIP released *Black Sunday* [1960] and Argento's *Bird with the Crystal Plumage* [1970]), Fulci's reputation was always as a lesser *filone* director.[30] Yet his peripheral status within the Italian film industry results in an oeuvre that not only is sensitive to the major currents of *filone* production of the 1970s and 1980s but is generally marked by a stylistic eccentricity even in the context of the *filone*'s excesses. *Don't Torture a Duckling*, Fulci's most acclaimed *giallo*, exemplifies the radical potential of the film frame as abstraction I have traced through Hitchcock, Bava, and Argento. In the following analysis, I read the Fulci set piece as intensified segmentation. This is to suggest not only that the segment is more visible as a structural component of the shot but that the segment is felt more intensively as a mode of affect.

Don't Torture a Duckling traces the formulaic narrative arc of a series of murders and a detective enlisted to solve the crimes. However, the iconography of rural Italy is an immediate departure from the urban setting of the *giallo* films of Bava and Argento. If, as Wood has argued, Argento's Italian cinema is a meditation on Italy's encounter with industrial and commercial modernity,[31] Fulci's meditation is on a localized tension between rural and cosmopolitan Italian identities. In its rural setting, one senses Fulci's desire to distance himself from the form of the *giallo* pioneered by Bava and Argento. Furthermore, as Church has argued, Fulci's cinema is more directly implicated in the *filone* as a transnational generic form, and one could speculate that Fulci's adoption of the *giallo* as a generic model incorporates both the Italian *gialli* of Bava and Argento (while affecting it through a unique stylistic register) and the American B-grade thriller emerging through AIP's output in the late 1960s and early 1970s.[32] One could further speculate that while De Palma's *Sisters* was released through AIP in 1973 and was clearly marked by a Hitchcockian influence, Fulci's experiments with image and sound seem a natural intermediary point of contact between Hitchcock and De Palma. If filmmakers such as Bava, Argento, and Fulci take the Hitchcockian desire for a pure cinema further, it is because these peripheral forms of cinema intuitively desired a more explicit transgression of aesthetic and ideological norms.

In an early sequence introducing the mysterious figure of the killer, Fulci draws on the compositional tropes of the *giallo* to situate the film within that genre. The frame segments through the action—a needle being inserted into the head of a doll—with increasingly jarring and destabilizing close-ups,

Figure 6.30 Fulci's segmented frame: *Don't Torture a Duckling* (1972)

dolly shots, zooms, and abrupt perspectival shifts through rack focusing. In the sequence that immediately follows, the unsettled frame in relative close-up is contrasted with a wide-angle geometric frame in the overhead shot of a staircase. Like Argento in the opening sequences of *The Bird with the Crystal Plumage*, Fulci emphasizes the flatness of the frame and the geometric vertical, horizontal, and diagonal axes. While the frame has a striking degree of depth, its profusion of angled frames within frames flattens the field and renders an abstract geometric configuration. The frame is held as a young boy ascends the spiral staircase; the abstract nature of the composition is now intensified by the counterclockwise rotation of the image.

The reflexive engagement with compositional form, in both wide and tight framing, is striking even in these introductory sequences.

As the narrative unfolds, it becomes clear that Fulci's set pieces will function as a series of performative compositional experiments. After the disappearance of another child in the village, police conduct an interview with the child's parents in what is a conventional exposition of story and character. The dialogue is covered in an innocuous set of shot reverse shots, although the focal split between foreground and background (that is, between the speakers) is more dramatic than in a conventional dialogue sequence. After a cut to an exterior scene in which the body of the boy is discovered in a forest (covered in a rush zoom), the image cuts again to a new dialogue sequence in a jarring split diopter frame.

The split diopter image functions as a coda to the more elaborately staged experiment with the frame. Each frame materializes as a break from the last, a fragmentation and destabilization of the frame as a whole. As in the

Figure 6.31 Reflexive depth of field composition: *Don't Torture a Duckling* (1972)

De Palma split diopter of the owl and Jack Terry, Fulci deliberately brings a close-up into an unsettling proximity with the deep background shot in the left field of the split diopter image. If the previous regime of relatively standard shot reverse shots had settled the visual frame, the cut to this split diopter image reminds us that Fulci's frame constitutes an infinite potential of spatial segmentation. The split diopter frame opens the sequence into a regime of stunning abstract patterns and movements. None of the angles utilized within this sequence conform to the patterns of what I would consider a classical coverage of diegetic space. Even a depth of field two shot unsettles the spectator with its unconventional framing of bodies within the space.

In the sequence depicting the death of Maciara (Florinda Bolkan), Fulci uses the exterior of the village setting as a canvas upon which to compose a complex assemblage of visual patterns. The sequence is orchestrated as a confluence of gazes, each providing a perspectival center. Maciara walks into a shot in an expansive depth of field, held in deep focus. It is the classical Bazinian image of Renoir and Welles, but it is exhibited here with a heightened degree of self-reflexivity.

The frame is accented through the verticality of Maciara's movement through the field, with bodies in foreground, mid-ground, and deep background providing spatial points of reference. Fulci's two-shot frame in the next image is an orchestrated segmentation: it is not a split diopter image such as we see in De Palma's composition in Lasalle's office in *Obsession*, and yet it simulates the segmented frame of the split diopter image.

Figure 6.32 A simulated split diopter perspective: *Don't Torture a Duckling* (1972)

In the casualness of the reveal of the segment—a compositional division within the frame—one could say that segmentation in this montage is a dominant aesthetic rationale. The cut to the next frame instantiates a free play of spatial segmentation animated by unstable rush zooms. In one striking movement, Fulci holds in long shot on a window that closes, pans down on the diagonal, and then rush zooms into a medium close-up on Maciara. In this expressive movement, the apparatus traces a double segmentation: first, the pan on the diagonal establishes a split in the frame from top right to bottom left; second, the zoom abstracts the image from the diegetic space, rendering the composition as spatial fragment.

Bordwell has argued persuasively that "the ways in which today's films represent space overwhelmingly adhere to the premises of 'classical continuity.'"[33] I think this claim is for the most part true. I have argued elsewhere that for all the projected chaos of the cinema of contemporary action directors such as Michael Bay, I can only conclude that "psychological continuity" is maintained over and above spatial and temporal breaches of continuity.[34] I see continuity as an existential value within the evolution of the classical paradigm. And yet I cannot help but feel that Fulci's segmented frame is something very different from Bordwell's regime of intensified continuity. If Bordwell's spatiality remains continuous in the contemporary American cinema, Fulci's segmentation of film space is a break of continuity both as the ontology of the classical frame and as a political/economic system underpinning that aesthetic tradition. The segmented frame in Fulci (but equally, as I have argued, Bava, Argento, and De Palma) is founded upon the image as fragment rather than whole. This is a question not only of aesthetics but of the existential value and purpose of images to spectators. Fulci's framed space always gestures toward the potential relativity of images in montage. In another modality and language I will take up in the next chapter, I suggest that Fulci's style is founded upon a philosophical and aesthetic tendency toward dissonance over consonance and spatial segmentation over and above the replete image of the whole that constitutes a classical cinema.

In the conclusion to his article, Belton suggests that "the zoom is symptomatic of the evolution of the language of cinema since the New Wave,"[35] which accords with Salt's position on the zoom in more self-consciously stylistic modes of cinema.[36] In his phrasing, Belton places the zoom in opposition to Bazin's "myth of total cinema." I think it is correct to situate the zoom within this larger trajectory of the evolution of the image. Belton continues: "Spatially distorting and inherently self-conscious, the zoom reflects the disintegration of cinematic codes developed before the Second World War."[37] In this narrative, the innovation of filmmakers such as Bava, Argento, Fulci, and De Palma are natural points on an evolutionary track, each representing the potential of the zoom to abstract from the "cinematic codes" that had traditionally informed cinematographic spaces and time. But the zoom in the kinds of cinema that would proliferate in the peripheral films of the Italian *giallo* breaks from the Bazinian image in even more emphatic and impactful ways. In Bava and Argento, but perhaps most strikingly in Fulci's *Don't Torture a Duckling*,[38] the zoom represents the further disintegration of a classical cinematic frame. The zoom makes the segment *larger*; it sustains the play of the segment within frames, and between frames as montage. Where segmentation in montage is a marker of structural fragmentation, the zoom further distends the fragment; it makes the fragment something more emphatic, more intensely felt.

7
Music You Can Hear
Toward an Abstract Soundscape

7.1. Pure Sound and the Talkie

The analysis of the art of sound gains traction within film industries and discourse only with the advent of the talkies in the late 1920s.[1] This sudden and dramatic desire on the part of filmmakers to expand the artistry of the cinema through sound design and production fermented within the aesthetic and political context of European modernity I traced in chapter 1. In 1928, Eisenstein, Pudovkin, and Alexandrov declared, "The dream of a sound film has come true. . . . The whole world is talking about the silent thing that has learned to talk."[2] Of course, the cinema was never a silent artistic medium; it had always been animated by the sound of music in increasingly elaborate forms and styles.[3] And yet the inference one takes from Eisenstein et al.'s "dream of a sound film [that] has come true" is surely that *all* sound, including nondiegetic music accompaniment, had been irrevocably changed by speech, sound effects, and the general synchronization of visual and sound image forms. The question that arrested Eisenstein, Pudovkin, and Alexandrov, but equally René Clair, one of the great advocates of the modernist cinema movement, was: How could sound enhance the essential characteristics of the filmic medium? For Eisenstein, less so for Pudovkin, sound had to conform to the requirements of montage. Regardless of technological innovation, for Eisenstein, "The basic and only means that has brought the cinema to such a powerful and effective strength is MONTAGE."[4] For Clair, equally desiring of an expanded soundscape, film sound might more modestly register an "interpretation of noises."[5] In the late 1920s, the role sound was to play in the evolution of film art was not only unclear but widely contested.[6]

V. I. Pudovkin's influential tract "Asynchronism as a Principle of Sound Film" was first published in Russia in 1929 and then translated into English by Ivor Montagu.[7] It is unclear precisely when this translation became available, but Basil Wright and B. Vivian Vaughn, in dialogue in 1934, have the following exchange:

> W.: To begin with, what do the aesthetes say about sound film?
> VB.: A great deal. Firstly they crack up contrapuntal sound and sound imagery as grand artistic effects.[8]

Neither Wright nor Vivian Braun identify these "aesthetes," yet their dismissal of a particular understanding of counterpoint seems to reference the general disposition of Eisenstein, Podovkin, and Alexandrov, who proclaim, "ONLY A CONTRAPUNTAL USE of sound in relation to the visual montage piece will afford a new potentiality of montage development and perfection. . . . THE FIRST EXPERIMENTAL WORK WITH SOUND MUST BE DIRECTED ALONG THE LINE OF ITS DISTINCT NONSYNCHRONIZATION WITH THE VISUAL IMAGES. And only such an attack will give the necessary palpability which will later lead to the creation of an ORCHESTRAL COUNTERPOINT of visual and aural images."[9] Pudovkin, a year later and somewhat more restrained, writes, "It will be appreciated that this instance, where the sound plays the subjective part in the film, and the image the objective, is only one of many diverse ways in which the medium of sound film allows us to build a counterpoint, and I maintain that only by such counterpoint can primitive naturalism be surpassed."[10]

As I have argued throughout this book, Hitchcock appropriated various aesthetic ideas from the European avant-garde for use in his own films from at least as early as *The Lodger* in 1927. It stands to reason that Hitchcock, an astute and enthusiastic student of the cinema at this point in his career, would have encountered Pudovkin's tract on the uses of sound for an artistic film form. In an interview with Stephen Watts in 1934, Hitchcock echoes the general polemic against the emergence of visual image/sound synchronization: "The arrival of the talkies, as you know, temporarily killed action in pictures . . . but it did just as much damage to music. . . . Yet when it became possible to blend film and music together in an artistic entity the opportunity was overlooked."[11] This is a statement that resonates both with the Eisenstein, Pudovkin, Alexandrov collective and René Clair, who feared the loss of an experimental visual film form. Writing in 1929, Clair suggests that "the visual world at the birth of the cinema seemed to hold immeasurably richer promise."[12] In his striking conclusion, Clair's piece feels almost an elegy for the recent death of cinema: "[Cinema in the era of the talkie] has conquered the world of voices, but it has lost the world of dreams."[13] Hitchcock seems to explicitly adopt the positions of Pudovkin and Clair on the necessity of thinking about the formal potential of sound design and production. For each of these filmmakers, working in different industries, within different aesthetic forms, and to very different cultural ends, the presumption is that while speech temporarily killed action, an artistic approach to sound might renew cinema's commitment to the purity of action. Hitchcock's narrative of the emergence of the talkie seems to call for a philosophy of sound design and production that was always already part of the cinema, that had always been part of cinema's essential form. But what form would sound take within this new artistic medium?

Synchronized sound developed quickly into a formal system, and just as quickly into a mass entertainment several critics identified, ironically, as something other than cinema. For many filmmakers and critics, the talkies of the late 1920s were not cinema but an amalgam of theatre and sound recording.[14] The opposition to the talkies, which emerged well before the talkies were an American and European phenomenon, was anchored largely in its commitment to the naturalism inherent in matching sound to visual images. A sound that was captured at the moment of an event could only be a spatial and temporal match for that event and therefore signified its conclusive source. Sexton persuasively argues that it was precisely the arrival of synchronized sound production that promoted a shared philosophical and artistic disposition toward the potential of the sound image.[15] If in 1929 the silent and early sound cinema had been threatened with extinction—Clair lamented that "the talking film exists, and those skeptics who prophesy a short reign for it will die themselves long before it's over"[16]—at the point of the most impactful technological transformation in the history of the medium, French, German, and Russian avant-garde filmmakers were galvanized in their efforts to reinvent the cinema again in the era of sound production.

The philosophical and practical application of early sound film was complex and diverse. Sexton argues that such experimentation "can be connected to modernist experimentation in other areas, particularly those related to musical theory and composition."[17] This position reflects my own sense of the emergence of a pure cinema discourse from European modernist avant-garde currents that included painting, sculpture, and, perhaps most impactfully, music. As the image moves toward greater liberation from meaning and toward greater abstraction in compositional form, sound design and production and musical accompaniment become increasingly indistinguishable. Foundational to the avant-garde experimental use of sound was a break from image-sound synchronization and a potential liberation of the sound image from explicit channels of visual communication. While it remains unclear precisely how successful nonsynchronization was in early sound cinema, Kristin Thompson has traced several varied uses of counterpoint image and sound relations in a set of Russian films produced between 1930 and 1934.[18] Similarly, while not precisely counterpoint in the Eisensteinian fashion, Sexton reads a more generalized aesthetic of counterpoint as a possibility in a number of films of the late 1920s made outside of Russia. Hitchcock's *Blackmail* has been widely studied for its experimental use of sound, and Sexton's notion that the film employs sound "in a creative rather than merely naturalistic manner" suggests that it displays an image-sound relation beyond synchronization.[19] Approaching Clair's position on the potential of the sound image as "noise," which I take to be sound in its most abstracted form, Weis writes of the use of music in a sequence in Hitchcock's *Secret Agent* (1936): "Almost from the start, music is potentially noise."[20]

My position is that Hitchcock, like Eisenstein, or Pudovkin, or Clair, consciously adapted the new medium of the early sound film as a continuing experimentation with film form. Experimental sound design within the European avant-garde cinema explored nonnaturalistic soundscapes, asynchronic and contrapuntal relations between sound and image, and in some cases radically ambiguous or open sound images, whether such images were rooted in concrete sounds or increasingly complex, abstract musical accompaniment. It is natural to expect that in his early sound films Hitchcock would follow suit. In his desire for a pure cinema, sound was merely one further element of an artistic form with unlimited potential. This is to suggest that Hitchcock's experimentation with sound was a natural extension of his experimentation with the visual image in his silent films. The degree of complexity of sound experimentation would only increase in the era of the 1950s and early 1960s. In the analyses that follow, I argue that experimental sound design and sound production should be viewed as a part of Hitchcock's project to realize a pure cinema form. For Chion, writing about the early sound film of the late 1920s (and we could say this equally of the cinema of Hitchcock and his imitators), "What was then called sound film was the last phase in the perfection of silent cinema."[21] In his detailed examination of a sequence in *The Birds* as palimpsest, Chion suggests that "every true sound film such as *The Birds* (and all of Hitchcock's sound films) carries something of a silent film within."²² In this chapter, I would like to carry Chion's position further to incorporate also the sound composition of the *giallo* and the cinema of De Palma, which seem to me equally born of the formal sensibilities of a silent cinema, inventively layering a soundtrack in a radically open, palimpsestic relationship to the visual image. Chion concludes about Hitchcock's sound films, which he clearly aligns with an avant-garde practice of the late 1920s, "It is in this sense that we can call the sound cinema an art of palimpsest, where one layer covers another that seems to be trying to be heard—an art where a silent film continues to bellow, despite the gag order of sound imposed by talking pictures."²³

7.2. Expanded Contrapuntal Sound in Hitchcock

Hitchcock consistently adopts a method of counterpoint in sound design to intensify the spectator's experience. As Weis argues in her influential study, "[Hitchcock's] soundtrack is . . . distinctly contrapuntal to the visuals."²⁴ However, we should be careful here: a Hitchcockian counterpoint is not precisely an Eisensteinian counterpoint, just as Hitchcock's use of montage rarely matched Eisenstein's intellectual montage. Rather, a Hitchcockian counterpoint as I conceive of it is nearer to a sound image that works independently from the visual track while enhancing a synthesis of visual and sound design within the compositional whole. As I've previously suggested, in his discussion of Arbogast's death in *Psycho*, Hitchcock describes the compositional rationale as contrast: "The long shot and the close-up of the big head as the knife came down at him. It was like music, you see, the high shot with the violins, and suddenly the big head with the brass instruments clashing."²⁵ The visual composition unsettles the frame through the contrast in image scale, proportion, and relation. The sound composition emerges through a confluence of musical tracks, each independent, though not precisely situated in counterpoint. A piercing four-note string motif fills the frame with unease. This motif is then followed by a single note that hovers in the background. The single-note track then carries over an unconventional medium long shot of Arbogast, his figure oddly isolated in the frame. When Mother enters in the overhead shot, the familiar string motif erupts, overwhelming the frame and stunning the spectator with the intensity of the action. For Hitchcock, this expressive montage was a function of image and sound *in relation*: "It was like music, you see."

In conventional musical counterpoint, two independent melodic and rhythmic lines interrelate to form a whole.[26] A musical composition organized through counterpoint is often thought to contain greater depth, complexity, and subtlety. In his description of the image-sound relation "as music," Hitchcock seems to depart from Eisenstein et al.'s more instrumental notion of visual/sound counterpoint, or at least to expand on the model of counterpoint Eisenstein in particular seems to use interchangeably with cinematic montage. For Eisenstein, counterpoint in sound and image relation, serving the aegis of intellectual montage, should be dialectical; that is, the relationship should create a new concept of the whole. But in his own break from image-sound synchronization, Hitchcock seems to conceptualize the image-sound relation as musical counterpoint rather than dialectical montage. This is a form of counterpoint in which the part also breaks from the whole and, in Elder's words, "contend[s] against it."[27] Hitchcock's compositional counterpoint, unlike Eisenstein's, reveres the part—"the high shot with the violins, and suddenly the big head with the brass instruments clashing." It would not make sense for Hitchcock to engage in a purely dialectical image-sound nonsynchronization within a mass entertainment medium. In this sequence in *Psycho*, sound registers both as an autonomous sound image and as part of a filmic whole. While sound and image in concert gesture uncertainly toward representation, in contending against the whole, the Hitchcockian contrapuntal relation builds vivid affective states, intensities, and large and small rhythmic sensations.

The autonomy of the sound image and its interrelationship with the visual image is perfectly illustrated in the opening sequence of *The Birds*. Melanie Daniels (Tippi Hedren) crosses a busy San Francisco street and enters Davidson's Pet Shop. As she walks across the street, the film holds in a single shot, all the while amplifying the sound of bird calls on the soundtrack; at this point the birds are unseen, and their sounds are therefore strange in the otherwise unremarkable street setting. Melanie's carefree movement is complimented by the sound of a wolf whistle interspersed with the rising sound of the birds; she pauses, turns, and smiles, presumably acknowledging the whistler. At this point, Melanie's sudden turn of the head prompts a cut (a reverse shot the spectator infers as Melanie's point of view) to a shot of the sky etched in shades of gray and black birds. It is a simple, economical introduction to the central character, the cosmopolitan, carefree setting of San Francisco, and the eponymous birds. Yet the compositional approach rejects a conventional synchrony in sound design. While providing much-needed narrative information, the sequence functions primarily to build atmosphere, excitement, and fear. This affective register is built through the amplification of the sound image over its supposed visual source. These sounds are clearly more than the sounds of the birds in the sky. The sounds exceed the visual signifiers in terms of the volume of the birds, the constancy of their sounds, and their gradually increasing amplitude on the soundtrack. In monophonic sound, as would have been the norm for a theatrical screening in 1963, the amplified soundscape would have been further intensified through its undifferentiated location within the visual frame. At the point of the cut, the wolf whistle presents a sound coda to Melanie's movement that matches her sudden stopping, turning, and gazing at the sky, at which point the sound of the birds is again amplified and reaches its point of crescendo. As Melanie turns toward Davidson's Pet Shop, presumably unconcerned by the birds, their sounds diminish in volume, constancy, and staccato texture. In this assemblage of a multitrack soundscape working independently from the visual image yet encompassing that visual field, sound is both a communicational cue and a rupture from the visual source. Aurality, like visuality, is a mark of excess.

Chion says something very similar about the mechanics of sound design in *Rear Window*. How does Hitchcock create a simulacral apartment building in Greenwich Village? In visual terms, he creates a pure cinematic relationship between subject and object. But it is the sound design that glues the whole and solidifies its compositional form. "We notice," says Chion, "that in terms of strict realism the sequence of all these sounds is quite improbable, for instead of overlapping and crowding each other, they follow each other so neatly.... Making full use of the audio-visual effect of *extension*, Hitchcock freely opens out and narrows in the courtyard sounds according to need."[28] In Hitchcock, the spectator infers an image-sound synchrony; this is sound in its most cautious enunciation, a sonic value added to predetermined visual content.[29] But the curious *affect* of the Hitchcockian sound image is derived through nonsynchronization and, further, a nonsynchronic counterpoint relation between sound and visual material. In his most radical sound compositions, Hitchcock demonstrates a reflexive experimental approach to the potential of the sound image as an autonomous object.

The Hitchcockian soundscape in these sequences in *Psycho* and *The Birds* represents an expanded contrapuntal film form. The sound breaks from the visual image, tracing an affective regime that in turn exceeds the content of the frame. We can situate Hitchcock's contrapuntal method within our larger discussion of the ontology of the segmented image. Image-sound synchronization infers a causal link between the visual image and its sound expression; that is, synchrony tells the spectator that the contents of the frame express the harmonious relations of the diegetic film world. But if sound exceeds this diegesis, if sound registers as an abstraction from the image-sound whole, the sound image is liberated from the diegesis. The unsettling issue then is that sound is no longer potentially nonsynchronous but necessarily nonsynchronous, and what then pushes composition to ever greater levels of formal experimentation is the way in which nonsynchronization is utilized to expand the formal potential of the frame. We know that sound is always already a referent.[30] But in a pure cinema mode, sound, much like the visual image, is potentially an abstract form broken from the concrete world of the diegesis. Before it is a representation of something else, sound can materialize as a pitch, a texture, a harmonic configuration, a dynamic range, and so on.

7.3. Hitchcock/Herrmann and De Palma/Donaggio: Imitation as Contrapuntal Form

If the music isn't heard, the viewer isn't moved.

Pino Donaggio

There are three sequences in *Dressed to Kill* that explicitly reconstruct sequences in Hitchcock films: the opening scene reworks *Psycho*'s shower scene as a sexual, and then violent, fantasy; Kate's (Angie Dickinson) slasher murder in an elevator explicitly imitates the formal montage regime of *Psycho*'s shower scene, though, as I argued earlier, this imitation is complicated by a more subtle imitation of the movement image of the Italian *giallo*; the third sequence is De Palma's most elaborate and multifaceted imitation of a classic Hitchcockian sequence, situated in a museum. Each sequence in De Palma represents a stylistically expressive set piece, taking the Hitchcockian sound and visual image as foundation and then reconstructing its compositional form and affective regime.

Madeleine Elster sits in the museum as if in a fugue, addressing the portrait of Carlotta Valdez. Her figure is seen from the point of view of Scottie, who remains unseen. Bernard Herrmann's score matches the furtiveness of Scottie's movement, layering a series of string pulses over the "Carlotta's but not Amanda, the space swells with undifferentiated sound sources in an uncontained aural expression of the violence that will ensue. Sound is less a signifier than a measure of intensity, a raw material within the frame for what Ndalianis calls "sensory encounters."[43] Visual and sound images intensify in concert, tightening the interior setting. Argento's framing matches this intensification, reframing the interior in graphic lines of intersection and convergence. The sequence concludes on perhaps the most absurd death sequence in *Deep Red* (if not in Argento's oeuvre), reveling in the hyperbolic staging of the set piece. If, as I have argued, the majority of Argento's set pieces display a stunning visual vernacular, this sequence demonstrates a similar disposition toward sound, in which a complex, multivalent, and increasingly dissonant and jarring soundscape exceeds the logic of signification.

In Argento, sound is frequently abstracted from conventional significatory fields. This is sound that tends toward a pure affect, or what Weis in another context calls "noise."[44] There is a long tradition of artists seeking the purity of sound within film form. Tarkovsky wrote eloquently of the purity of a cinematic soundscape as a transcendent field.[45] John Cage famously described the potential of a form of musical noise: "I believe that the use of noise to make music will continue and increase until we reach a music produced through the aid of electrical instruments which will make available for musical purposes any and all sounds that can be heard."[46] Like Cage, Argento's soundscapes, though contained by the medium of narrative cinema and its aesthetic complex, intuitively push sounds beyond their source and toward the potential of abstract sonic fields. Brophy describes the soundscape of *Suspiria*, perhaps Argento's most vivid and experimental film, as "audiovisual saturation . . . an hysterical unleashing of noise in libidinal, psychological and overall mind-bending modes . . . [that is] typically relentless, scathing and excessive."[47] In a similar vein, Mitchell describes the Argento-Goblin aesthetic as "sonic mayhem" and "sonic excess."[48] One key element of Argento's experiment with sound as a potentially abstract form is in the use of a sound image that transgresses the boundary between diegetic and nondiegetic fields, or between diegesis and the structure that mediates it. Shifting sounds between diegetic and nondiegetic fields is not exactly unheard of, but it is more common in genres of excess, such as horror and melodrama. In realist narrative films, a diegetic-nondiegetic crossing tends to be subtle; that is, it rarely exhibits itself as a stylistic conceit. We see a superb example of a subtle diegetic-nondiegetic crossing in the opening sequence of *The Godfather* (1972), in which Don Corleone dances with his daughter in a long shot. The pair move in perfect time with the famous Nino Rota waltz playing nondiegetically as accompaniment to the visual image. The Don and his daughter cannot hear this music, and yet their bodies move in 3/4 time to it. One senses a similar desire on the part of Hitchcock to push at the conventions of synchronized sound production design. In 1934, describing his method in *Waltzes from Vienna* (1934), Hitchcock recalls, "I arranged the cutting to match the rhythm of the music. . . . You must visualize the film moving in time with the music."[49] It might be a throwaway line, but it is also a provocative, somewhat counterintuitive approach to sound design in the era of image-sound synchronization.

The diegetic/nondiegetic threshold in the *giallo* is less a boundary than a liminal space to be freely explored. In the most cavalier, even gleeful moments in Argento, this liminal space expands to encompass diegesis and nondiegesis in something outrageously different, which is quite difficult to define and categorize in conventional cinematic terms. Part of what determines the ontology of such a space is *rhythm*: a visual image is imbued with a rhythmic character drawn from a sonic field. In several image-sound compositions in Argento, it is as if the visual image stretches into the soundtrack and extracts its rhythmic and harmonic sensibilities. In a particularly performative set piece late in *Deep Red*, the protagonist comes upon the house that is the point of origin of the mystery. In a classical cinema, the house should function as a site for narrative progression and resolution. Yet Argento seems more interested in the performative, playful aspects of sound and image in relation. A set of images display the house over a pulsing electronic bass beat; the beat is thick and emphatic over the series of cuts. The volume of the bass line and its insistence over a series of tight shots on the protagonist pulls the nondiegetic soundscape into the diegesis (from which sound is absent).

As the protagonist enters the house—breaking his way in with some force—the bass line shifts from a melodic line surrounding the I chord into the IV chord in a standard blues progression. At this point, it becomes clear that Argento is orchestrating the montage to a blues rhythmic and harmonic progression. The fact that it is a blues progression makes it all the more startling: in the formulaic structure of blues (the standard I–IV–V harmonic relation), the rhythmic and harmonic field of the bass line should be constricting. Yet in this sequence the set piece functions as a performance of a narrative revelation cut to a blues backing track. The critical crossing of the performance threshold from diegetic to nondiegetic sound field matches, on the beat, the crossing of the protagonist from the exterior to the interior of the house: the protagonist bursts through the door on beat one of the first transition to the IV chord. Now with the protagonist inside the house, the sequence evolves through a series of increasingly experimental visual compositions. Paralleling the complicating visual compositional forms, the bass line moves freely across the I–IV–V harmonic field, now expanded with a set of somewhat dissonant contrapuntal melodic sound cues. The sequence concludes suddenly on the revelation of an important clue that will take the narrative toward resolution, at which point the bass line drops from the track and the dissonant, disconcerting Goblin "Profondo Rosso" theme overwhelms the frame.

What is Argento doing here? My sense is that he is composing the set piece as a set of swelling rhythmic and harmonic progressions in which the blues bass line suffuses the visual image with a rhythmic and harmonic sensibility. We *feel* the movement of the bass line that animates the protagonist's movement through the house. This, again, is not sound as source but as affect, and in this diegetic-nondiegetic crossing, the function of the bass line seems predicated on rhythmic and harmonic relation as affective field. In its entirety, the sequence spans a duration of seven minutes, without dialogue, and with low-level diegetic sound effects. It is on one level a critical narrative turning point, but on another, the sequence is a performance piece that seems nearer to the genre of the music video. The set piece resolves as a multi-track synthetic convergence of harsh, grating, abstract sounds, like noise.[50]

The liminal space of diegetic/nondiegetic sound is a hallmark of the *giallo*. We see an equally imaginative transgression of diegetic and nondiegetic sound fields in Fulci's *Don't Torture a Duckling*. Indeed, Fulci seems to push the liminal sound space even further than Argento. In the set piece of Maciara's death, Fulci uses a diegetic/nondiegetic sound crossing to amplify the generic and performative aspects of the sequence. The movement opens in a neat aural quotation of Morricone's scores for Leone's westerns. As Maciara comes upon her assailants on the outskirts of the village, one of them leans into a parked car and turns on a radio. A blues-rock song ("Crazy," performed by Wes and the Airedales, 1969) blares out over the car, but in its volume on the soundscape, the sound extrudes from the diegetic source into what is a nondiegetic performative space. In this particularly sadistic sequence, much like Tarantino's use of "Stuck in the Middle with You" (Stealers Wheel, 1972) in the torture scene in *Reservoir Dogs* (1992), the song is a rhythmic accompaniment to a violent performance. This is violence and

Figure 7.1 Maciara's melodramatic death: *Don't Torture a Duckling* (1972)

sadism as spectacle. As Maciara is beaten, Fulci modulates the tone from sadistic violence to pathos with a track change on the car radio: whereas the grating blues rhythm of "Crazy" was energetic and dynamic (intensifying the act of violence), it gives over to a slow, melodic ballad in a minor key. In the coverage of the space with these music tracks, the sound image constantly breaks from its source, that is, the car radio. Indeed, the car is never again displayed as a sound "source" within the sequence. The amplified, unbroken soundtrack no longer crosses diegetic/nondiegetic soundscapes but now inhabits an expanded liminal space between the two. Against the more conventional sound cue that accompanies action, such liminal zones in *giallo* cinema are spaces of heightened sensation.[51] The conclusion to the sequence—Maciara's death in a raw close-up on the side of a road as the ballad finishes—is all the more affecting for its melodramatic, performative excess. In this set piece, one senses the importance of Fulci as an interlocutor in what is often deemed an instrumental intertextual exchange between the generic styles of Leone and Tarantino.

7.5. Toward a Pure Abstract Soundscape: Atonality in *Psycho*

Part of Hitchcock's training in the art of pure cinema derived from an interest in music and musical form. It should not surprise us that, as Schroeder has persuasively argued, "Hitchcock linked progress in filmmaking directly with music."[52] The Hitchcock-Herrmann collaboration has been examined extensively, and there seems to be a consensus that Herrmann did his best work with Hitchcock, which in turn was some of the best film scoring of the Hollywood era. Whether out of design or fortuity, Hitchcock's collaboration with Herrmann enabled the director to incorporate an approach to the film score that built on and significantly enriched a philosophy of pure visual form. If Hitchcock in some way remained committed to a pure visual cinema—that is, the silent-film aesthetic philosophy evident before the advent of the talkies—Herrmann's approach to film music evolved out of an interest in an expanding modernist musical compositional form and its capacity for harmonic and melodic experimentation. Cooper writes that Herrmann "reveled in the creative possibilities of music, refusing to restrict himself to a single mode of expression or technique."[53] But this sensibility was also fused with a philosophical disposition toward the function of music, whether in composition for performance or film scoring. In his celebratory article on the works of his close friend and mentor Charles Ives, Herrmann wrote: "Ives was developing thirty years ago a musical technique which today the moderns declare as their innovations. . . . In 1890, Ives was writing polytonality, which, in 1910, Milhaud introduced in popular garb. In 1902, he was producing poly-rhythms, atonality and tone clusters which many years later Stravinsky, Schoenberg, and Ornstein received credit for originating."[54] While Herrmann described himself as a neoromantic in compositional approach, nonetheless, he displays a keen interest in an evolving musical compositional form. And while Herrmann did not push atonality in composition in the way that Ives or Schoenberg might have, he clearly desired to explore the potential of musical form within the medium of cinema.

Herrmann's score for *Psycho*, so galvanizing as a complex soundscape, is now something of a popular cultural cliché.[55] In the context of a late classical Hollywood film, it remains a strikingly experimental score as the musical composition to what is ostensibly a slasher-thriller film. As several musicologists agree, Herrmann's use of ambiguous harmonic structures in earlier films such as *Vertigo* and *North by Northwest* speaks to the composer's more generalized tendency to depart from the settled harmonies familiar to the film spectator.[56] Of the harmonic structures in *Vertigo, North by Northwest,* and *Psycho*, Brown writes, "The very nature of these chords, with their simultaneously minor/major aura, immediately throws the viewer/listener off the rationalized centre of normal Western tonality into a more irrational, mythic domain in which oppositions have no implications that will be resolved by the passing of time but exist only as two equal poles of the same unity."⁵⁷ Brown's description of Herrmann's method, and particularly of this method in *Psycho*, sounds very much like Herrmann's description of atonal structures in the work of Ives or Schoenberg. In a similar vein, Donaggio, speaking about his own utilization of Herrmannesque harmonic structure in his De Palma scores, directly relates Herrmann's compositional method to a departure from a dominant Western harmonic system: "Students won't be studying Bernard Herrmann. They'll be studying Schoenberg, whom he took from to compose *Psycho*."⁵⁸

The penultimate sequence of *Psycho* reveals Mother speaking in internal monologue: "It's sad when a mother has to speak the words that condemn her own son"; she has presumably gained the ascendency over Norman's body. Husarik describes two major musical themes within *Psycho*—"Mother" and "Madness"—"represented by dissonance and atonality."⁵⁹ While all of *Psycho*'s score unsettles the spectator on some level, this tendency toward disharmony and fragmentation in Norman's subjectivity finds a more pointed, intensive musical expression the further the film progresses. For Husarik, Herrmann's score for *Psycho* increasingly tends toward destabilization and fragmentation: "At the beginning of the film Herrmann's cascades are triadic but, as the plot thickens, they evolve into chromatic or even atonal simultaneities."⁶⁰ This is a persuasive reading that is supported by a number of excellent detailed studies of Herrmann's score. However, I want to read form and function in the sequence less as a "thickening" of content than as a disassembling of the formal components that constitute classical narrative and its musical accompaniment. Herrmann's score over the revelation of Mother is deeply unsettling in its dissonance. Our ears search for a point of closure, or even rest, a tonal center from which to find some purchase for processing this dénouement. But it is precisely this tonal center that Herrmann withholds. The piece is less a "musical theme" in the traditional sense than a set of dissonant intervals that, in collusion with the spoken words of Mother in a direct address to camera, build to a stunning level of intensity.

In his examination of Western harmonic structure, Roger Scruton asks: "What happens to melody and harmony when tonality is abandoned? . . . The result remains controversial to this day."⁶¹ It seems to me that Herrmann's abandonment of tonality results in a remarkable film sequence that pushes the structure of visual, narrative, and aural form to breaking point. The outcome is an affect founded upon the rejection of an existential wholeness (whether of a classical visual composition, or narration, or of conventional harmonic and melodic musical forms) and a confrontation with the abiding absence that constitutes dissonance and atonality. What if, instead of listening to music as an accompaniment to a visual source, we encountered an image through the sensory schema of an atonal soundscape? In its abstraction from Western harmony, Herrmann's soundscape (and, within that soundscape, the affect of the image) takes on the quality of abstraction, of rootless noise.

Conclusion

The Fractal Image in De Palma's *Femme Fatale*

C.1. Fragments and Fractals

In closing this book, I want to reflect on what pure cinema is not: it is not a perfectly coherent, hermetic, self-sustaining formalism. Rather, the art of pure cinema seeks to invigorate form as the potential for philosophical and aesthetic change within the medium of moving images. The pure cinema I've attempted to trace through Hitchcock and his imitators seeks to intensify the unrestrained expressivity of the medium, to schematize form as the foundation of action, to make action a rhythmic configuration of visual and aural images, to break the frame from its representative (and diegetic) constraints, to make out of montage a pure relationality within and across the shot, and to display the image in its barest form, which is to say the *fragment*.

I have argued that pure cinema derives its aesthetic and philosophical vigor from the materiality of the fragment; this is the part that will not be contained or rationalized by the whole. The fragment is an unstable presence within the organizational system because it is not merely a part of something but a something-in-itself, which is then always a something else. The fragment exists as a surfeit materiality within the whole, and it is this materiality that provides the stimulus for change. But what is the nature of this material form in Hitchcock and his imitators? I have argued that the fragment manifests the division (a process of splitting) of the whole into a set of relational systems, with each system subtending a stratum of subsystems, which in turn subtend further subsystems, and so on to infinity. The process of dividing then facilitates a related process of differentiation within the structures of the image, which I have read through Bellour's notion of "alternation." The logic of division and differentiation—which is to say the logic of the fragment—is intrinsic to pure cinema. The effect of the fragment, in dividing and differentiating the frame, is to confront the spectator with an incomplete, and thus unrestrained, image. This is an image with a profoundly affective potential.

The Art of Pure Cinema. Bruce Isaacs, Oxford University Press (2020). © Oxford University Press.
DOI: 10.1093/oso/9780190889951.001.0001

Influenced by the philosophical and artistic dispositions of avant-garde artists—perhaps, most notably, Murnau, although I have sought to take the philosophy of the image to Dulac and the artists who sought to make of moving images a new philosophy of form and experience—Hitchcock sensed the potential of the image as fragment. But, as I have suggested, in even the most experimental sequences, the Hitchcockian fragment is restrained by the always visible relation of the part to the whole. In Hitchcock, therefore, the fragment is not a pure part; it is not what Deleuze calls difference in itself, which is the expression of something far more troubling for the spectator.[1] In films such as *Vertigo, The Birds,* and *Marnie,* we see the visual, aural, and narrative material that gestures toward its intrinsic incompletion. A red suppuration of the frame in *Marnie* is an expression of the fragment, as is a matte configuration of the Baltimore dockland in Marnie's visit to her childhood home. A split-screen effect in *The Lodger* or *Shadow of a Doubt* or *Marnie* ruptures the classical frame, and therein, the diegetic whole. But such experiments are fleeting departures from the logic of the whole that governed the classical style Hitchcock adopted from the mid-1920s. Even the pure fragment—which Truffaut insightfully called a gratuity—reveals itself momentarily, only to be rationalized within the dual and interrelated orders of representational images and classical narrative structures.

In the films of Bava, Argento, Fulci, and most emphatically De Palma, the fragment is realized through a deeper abstraction from representational form. The fragment is now literalized as the split within a frame that can no longer be sutured or made whole. In films such as *The Bird with the Crystal Plumage* and *Deep Red* or De Palma's *Dressed to Kill* and *The Untouchables,* the fragment cannot be reconciled to the whole, or indeed to any other determinate system. Rather, in the most ecstatic sequences (such as De Palma's imitation of Eisenstein's Odessa Steps montage), the fragment is made into a pure spectacle. And then, in these films, in addition to its visibility, the fragment is intensified through the affect of movement. We encounter such intensified movements (rather than intensified continuities) in the use of a pan and zoom in *Don't Torture a Duckling,* or in the extended slow motion of the concluding sequence of *Blow Out,* or in Bava's irrational montage in the opening set piece of *A Bay of Blood.* In such sequences, the fragment charges the image with its irrational excesses.

I have assembled Bava, Argento, Fulci, and De Palma as a cohort of Hitchcockian imitators. This desire to bear some similarity to the thrillers of Hitchcock was intrinsic to the design of the *giallo,* and the works of Bava, Argento, and Fulci take up a vernacular visuality I trace to Hitchcock.

CONCLUSION 187

Similarly, De Palma has made no secret of his career-long obsession with Hitchcock's films, and *Sisters* marks the first reflexive work of imitation as early as 1973. But I close this book with an analysis of De Palma's *Femme Fatale*, released in 2002, because it is De Palma (rather than Bava, Argento, and Fulci) who, in imitating Hitchcock, complicated and deepened the philosophical and artistic practice of a pure cinema of the fragment. De Palma's meditation on Hitchcock is thorough and comprehensive in its coverage, subtle in its engagement with the intricacies of form, and imaginative in its intensification of a pure cinematic style.

Femme Fatale, as its title playfully suggests, is a classic De Palma riff on the film noir genre. The image opens with the femme fatale of the title (Laure Ash, played by Rebecca Romijn) watching the final sequence of Billy Wilder's *Double Indemnity* (1946). We see Laure's alluring reflection in the black-and-white shot reverse shot dialogue playing on the TV screen.

But, then, this is not a reflection but a fragment laid over the representational image of the figures of Walter Ness (Fred MacMurray) and Phyllis Dietrichson (Barbara Stanwyk). This first image is both a fragment (the frame within the frame) and an opening into a proliferating set of systems. As Hagener suggests, the opening set piece "foregrounds [an] unending series of transpositions, transferences and translations."[2] On one level, *Femme Fatale* complicates the aesthetic of the fragment in terms of the complexity of the relational systems that constitute the whole. Even this opening sequence structured around the theft of jewels at the Cannes Film Festival is a dizzying concoction of images and sounds rhythmically cut to Ryuichi Sakamoto's playful imitation of Ravel's

Figure C.1 Intertextual fragments: *Femme Fatale* (2002)

Boléro. But this is not so remarkable an innovation; films like *Obsession*, *Body Double*, and *Mission: Impossible* (1996) proliferate storylines and image regimes with a gleeful exhibitionism. But *Femme Fatale* introduces a new ontology of the fragment. My sense is that if De Palma's films up until this point had experimented with the potential of the fragment within complex narrative and image systems, in *Femme Fatale* the fragment attains a purity of form, and in this form, a purity and elegance of expression. The fragment is now rationalized as the pure part within a system of evenly distributed parts, building variation and alternation into the fabric of the film at all levels of signification, from the microscopic image (a reflection on a television screen) to the image of monumental scale (a compositional collage that encompasses, like Baudrillard's simulacrum, the entirety of the representation). The fragment in *Femme Fatale* is therefore better described as a fractal image.

The notion of a fractal "is derived from the Latin word *frangere*, meaning to break or fragment."[3] But this is only part of the ontology of the fractal form. A fractal is also a part in relation to other parts, and this relationality is what gives the fractal form. The fractal is therefore an infinitely replicating pattern of shapes in relation to other shapes within the system. We could say that the fractal pattern is both a fragment and a whole in the same way that a melodic phrase is both a series of individual notes and, in terms of a pattern of intervals, a melodic whole. The fragment, as I have argued, materializes through a breach of containment; it is fundamentally irreconcilable with the whole. In this breach, the fragment is also a transgression. But in *Femme Fatale*, the fragment attains a clarity of structure and function within the whole. If the fragment of Bava and Argento, and indeed of De Palma's *Dressed to Kill*, *Body Double*, and *The Untouchables*, intensifies the Hitchcockian fragment as transgression of the limit of the whole, the fragment in *Femme Fatale* seems more assured of its purpose. It seems more settled in its autonomy, in its being *other*. In ontological terms, I would say that the fractal is a further expansion (and metamorphosis) of the fragment, constituting an inversion of the relation between the part and the whole, in which the whole is now rationalized by the individual (rather than aggregate) expression of the parts. The fractal is the pure expression of the whole as part.

C.2. Shapes and Patterns in the Notre Dame de la Croix Sequence

A fractal is a shape of infinite relations. In *Femme Fatale*, the fragment materializes as a fractal form, pointing outward while at the same time pointing inward, expanding infinitely in both directions. The fractal in *Femme Fatale* also expands in intricate new ways, engaging form more explicitly in relation to movement and time.

De Palma designs an elaborate fractal image for the first encounter of the film's two protagonists, Laure Ash and Nicholas Bardo (Antonio Banderas). This is a film in which such encounters are wildly improbable and yet never coincidental. Within the logic of the fractal, each segment is contingent on another. Laure and Nicholas exchange gazes at the film's nexus point—the steps of the Notre Dame de la Croix church. Like Hitchcock's staging of a pure cinematic relation in *Rear Window*, Laure stands on the steps while Nicholas photographs her. We open on a low-angle medium close-up on Laure, with Nicholas in deep background in the left of frame. It is not a split-screen composition, but the contrast in focus and color splits the frame down the middle. As Laure turns her head, the image focalizes Nicholas. We hold, maintaining the split frame, but slowly zoom in to center Nicholas within the frame. This movement is both a narrative focalization and the commencement of the segmentation of the space. A series of unremarkable shots display the central figures within the action to ensue: Nicholas, Laure, Veronica, and Racine. These are the only full frame images and cuts that approach a conventional continuity regime in a duration of 3:03. We then cut into the first split screen (Nicholas and Racine), followed by a cut to a second, more elaborate split-screen setting the points of view of Nicholas and Racine in relation within the frame. Laure sees Nicholas staring at her and yells, "Hey! What the fuck are you doing?" Before retreating into his apartment, Nicholas mutters, "Gotcha." Laure and Nicholas now move into separate segments within the space. She runs into a church, instantiating a third split-screen composition: the left frame follows Nicholas into his apartment while the right holds on Laure in the church's entrance. In the background of Nicholas's frame, we see what appears to be a large-scale photograph of the same space he has just photographed covering the entirety of one wall of the apartment. The dual action unfolds: Laure in the church in the right frame, Nicholas in the left, in his apartment, printing the photograph he has taken of Laure.

The sequence exemplifies the image as a fractal (and not purely fragmented) form. In its framing of the entirety of the action in split screen, there appears to be a logic to this spatiotemporal segmentation. Each frame is a densely populated, framed composition; each frame demonstrates significant compositional poise and complexity within the frame. The image cuts freely across these frames, recomposing the space through a series of subtle point-of-view variations. There is no classical logic of the image underpinning the sequence: images are, in ontological terms, segmented, and they remain so. De Palma resists reframing the whole, either as a full frame composition or as a wider shot of the action. The spectator is cut *into* the space, at eye level (which is both the eye of a character and the eye of the apparatus); the spectator is thus inserted into the perceptual regime of the fragment. The fragment is then intensified through the excessive duration of the split frame. In its framing of the space and action through multiplying split frames captured in both subjective and omniscient points of view, the image is formed through its intrinsic discretization. In the words of Adrian Martin and Cristina Álvarez López, this is De Palma's "cinematic [form of] vision."[4] But to take this notion further, it is a cinematic vision founded on shape and pattern as a fractal form.

C.3. Notre Dame de la Croix: Frame Breakdown

Frame 1: The shot opens in full screen, covering Laure and Nicholas in a split-screen composition enacted through focal length (figure C.2).

Figure C.2

Frame 2: A rack focalization of Nicholas in deep background. Foreground and background form a set of geometric figures within the frame (figure C.3).

Frame 3: A set of shots cover the viewpoints of the central figures within the action (figures C.4–C.5).

Figure C.3

Figures C.4–C.5

Frame 4: Nicholas and Racine in split-frame, undifferentiated point of view (POV) (figure C.6).

Frame 5: A cut to a reverse split frame: POVs of Nicholas and Racine. Jarring contrast between diagonal and frontal perspectives within the frame (figure C.7).

Frame 6: Nicholas in the left segment of the frame, approximate Laure POV; Racine's POV in the right (figure C.8).

Frame 7: Nicholas in the left segment of the frame; Racine in the right. Contrast in scale between long shot and close-up (figure C.9).

Frame 8: Return to Nicholas/Racine in dual perspective POV (figure C.10).

Figures C.6-C.7

Figures C.8–C.9

Figure C.10

Frame 9: Undifferentiated POV of Nicholas/Racine POV of Laure (figure C.11).

Frame 10: A cut from exterior to interior. Nicholas in his apartment in the left segment of the frame; Laure in the church in the right segment. Contrast between a close, densely populated frame with Laure in a sparse frame in deep background (figure C.12).

Frame 11: A second frame emerges within the left segment of the full frame: Nicholas's computer screen displays the digital image of Laure on the steps of the church. The right segment within the frame (Laure in the church) is held (figures C.13–C.15).

Figures C.11–C.12

Figures C.13-C.15

Frame 16: Return to frame 14: low angle on Laure in the left segment of the frame, extreme close-up of Racine's POV in the right segment (figure C.21).

Frame 17: Return to frame 15, holding. The couple then stands from the pew and moves toward the front of the church, providing a jarring dissonance on movement within the segmented depths of field (figure C.22).

Frame 18: Return to frame 16, holding (figure C.23).

Frame 19: A jarring cut to a new angle within an expanded tripartite split frame composition. In the left segment of the frame, an

Figures C.21–C.22

CONCLUSION 199

Figure C.23

over-the-shoulder POV of Nicholas (a return to his apartment interior), holding the photograph of Laure; on a closer examination, we see that the photograph is framed against a background of similar configuration. We realize that Nicholas holds the photo against the wall-sized photograph in his apartment. In the right segment, we see a matching over-the-shoulder POV of the couple as they approach Laure, seated in the back of the church. This reverse POV long shot is further segmented by a set of frames within frames in deep background (figure C.24).

Figure C.24

Frame 20: In the left segment of the frame, Nicholas gazes upon his photograph; the image forms a collage of multiple receding frames within the frame: Nicholas in foreground (over-the-shoulder POV), the photograph held in close-up in the mid-ground of the frame, the steps in a discretized assemblage of geometric shapes and patterns displayed in the wall-sized photograph in background. This radically discretized image is set to a measured movement in a slow zoom outward from the center of the image, Nicholas's photograph. In the right segment of the frame, Laure flees from the church (extreme long shot), moving across the same space Nicholas views in a static image in the left segment of the frame (figures C.25–C.28). As a whole, the image constitutes multiple shot scales and angles within the frame: an extreme close-up, a close-up, an undifferentiated background (Nicholas's left frame), an extreme long shot densely populated with objects in mid-ground (Laure's

Figures C.25–C.28

Figures C.25–C.28 Continued

flight down the steps of the church) and deep background (a delivery van that will become central to a later action).

This set piece in *Femme Fatale* reveals a collage of photographic forms set to two regimes of movement. Nicholas's photographic collage stands in for the projection of the ideal whole that can be only be rationalized through the itinerary of the fragment. The final image of the set piece approximates what Hitchcock attempted with the matte composition in *Marnie*: an ontology of the split frame. But the matte in early 1960s cinema was a tool for staging continuity in depth, and most spectators would have perceived it this way. De Palma's insert is therefore the greater affront to a traditional mode of perception. In its fractal logic, the spectator must inhabit the discretization of space and time, which is revealed through the logic of a discretized perception. This is not a frame that tends toward, or desires, the rationality of the whole. It is also not a mode of perception that can be reconstituted as an authoritative gaze.

In this sequence in *Femme Fatale*, we see a distinctive kind of looking that models a radical ontology of filmic form and perception. We could also extend this analysis, working through the idea of the image as fractal form, to the film as a whole, aligning frames in infinitely expanding systems of relationality across the entire work, then across De Palma's oeuvre, and then across the textual architecture the film invokes, including Wilder's *Double Indemnity* and the genre of film noir. But such an undertaking would be impossible within the confines of this analysis. We can merely say that this set piece is one further expansion and intensive complication of the fractal shape and pattern of the film, and that it opens the film to the potential of images in unrestricted shapes and patterns of association.

C.4. A Close-Up Without a Frame

Out of desperation, but also slightly on a whim, Laure Ash becomes Lily Watts (as Madeleine Elster became Judy Barton) and flees from the setting of Cannes and Paris. She boards a plane to the United States to commence a new life and is seated next to the future American ambassador, Bruce Watts (Peter Coyote), who will facilitate the completion of her identity transformation as an American citizen. In this narrative contrivance, De Palma embraces the potential of an open narrative form. Laure and Lily will remain the discretized fragments of a subjective wholeness, as Madeleine and Judy remain two parts of an unrealized subjectivity (if we read beyond the surface plot point of Elster's creation of Judy as a false identity).

Seated together in the plane, Lily and Watts fall in love in close-up. But in *Femme Fatale*, as in De Palma films more generally, the close-up of a face is always an excess of the subject; that is, De Palma is rarely interested in the pure function of character. The De Palma close-up is a spontaneous opening of the character (and actor) to the expression of the figure as an abstract form. Seated on the plane, Laure (now as Lily) and Watts engage in a dialogue. At

CONCLUSION 203

Figure C.29 Classical two-shot coverage: *Femme Fatale* (2002)

the commencement of the set piece, the coverage is conventional: Lily and Watts are held in a medium two shot that slowly dollies in as the characters begin to take an interest in each other.

It is a classical coverage founded on informational and narrative cues. However, as the dolly settles into a medium close-up frame (still in two shot), De Palma cuts into a series of very strange close-up shot reverse shots.

The close-up is strange because it is not purely the revelation of character. In its arresting play between the shot scales of close-up and extreme close-up, and in its disturbing proximity to the viewpoint of the spectator, this set of close-ups further composite Lily and Watts as figural forms within the fractal schema of the whole.

My sense is that these are not precisely, or fully determined, affection images, as Deleuze describes the close-up, though they share many of the affective qualities of the Deleuzian image. Deleuze describes the close-up in the following way: "As for the face itself, we will not say that the close-up deals with [*traite*] it or subjects it to some kind of treatment: there is no close-up *of* the face, the face is in-itself close-up, the close-up is by itself face, and both are affect, affection-image."[5] At its root I take affect to be an intensification of the image that pulls the spectator into the proximity of thought or feeling; these are Deleuze's two models of affection-image, one drawn from Griffiths (the image of thought) and one drawn from Eisenstein (the image of experience, or feeling). Deleuze distinguishes the function of the

Figures C.30–C.31 A figural form in close-up: *Femme Fatale* (2002)

"intensive" close-up (the image of experience, or feeling) as the instance in which "traits [of the face] break free from the outline, begin to work on their own account, and form an autonomous series which tends toward a limit or crosses a threshold."[6] De Palma's close-ups in this sequence, in their cavalier attitude to conventional shot scale and relation to the spectator, seem to partake of this crossing of a predetermined limit or threshold. Deleuze further suggests that the close-up does not fragment the object or the subjectivity inherent in that object, but that it "retains the . . . power to tear the image away from spatio-temporal coordinates in order to call forth the pure affect as the expressed."⁷

But not all close-ups are of the same shape or pattern in relation to a system of fragments. If we take the whole as a fractal system exemplified in Nicholas's collage composition, the close-up, in spite of its capacity for "pure affect," is also a fragment. But how can we reconcile this idea of the close-up and its capacity for pure expression with a fractal schema? While Deleuze's model of the close-up as affection image is vital to understanding the relationship between form and feeling within the film image, nonetheless, I would argue that not all close-ups tend with the same degree of certainty to the Deleuzian affection image. For example, in this exchange, the close-up is tighter, and thus in a sense more transfixing, on the figure of Lily; we are being introduced to Lily as if for the first time, not as a deception but as the spontaneous irruption of the figure within the character. Whether deliberate or fortuitous, there are points of light reflected in Lily's eyes that soften the focus on her face and suggest something beyond the character's visage. The lower frame of Lily's close-up is set over her bottom lip, accentuating the shape of her lips and generally tightening the focus on the affect of the lips and eyes within the face. We could certainly read the close-ups of both Lily and Watts as the expression of thought and feeling; as Deleuze suggests, "There is a great variety of close-ups of faces."⁸ And yet in these close-ups on Lily and Watts, I struggle to access the ecstasy of the close-up, which is to say the ecstasy of the close-up as a pure expression. My overwhelming sense is of a correspondence of figures that cannot be fixed in close-up at all.

We could ask: What are these close-ups *of*? Not character, because character in *Femme Fatale* is radically unsettled and incomplete. Not subjectivity, because the subject is essentially split across the field of the fragment; Lily/Laure is not the fragmented subject of a psychanalytic schema that seeks psychic wholeness. But neither are these close-ups a pure expression of thought, or emotion, or a state of being. There are depths within the pinpoints of light in Lily's eyes that are both a revelation and an obfuscation: a part and a whole of being. Perhaps we could say that these close-ups are of *figures*, always standing in for something else, always deferring the replete image of wholeness. If, as Deleuze suggests, the close-up is the pure image of affect, in De Palma the close-up is also a fragment, which is to say, the split image that rationalizes the whole. In fact, I would argue that, negotiating the part of Deleuze's position in which the close-up "[tears] the image away from spatio-temporal coordinates in order to call forth the pure affect as the expressed," the close-up cannot be broken from the itinerary of the fragment, which, as I have argued throughout this book, is vitally implicated in regimes of affect. This is to say that the close-up in *Femme Fatale* is, like the split frame, a *fractal image*, and one further opening into the fractal schema of the whole.

C.5. Pure Cinematic Vision: Gaze as Fragment

Seven years later, again in Paris, the image opens in a split frame of Nicholas, again situated on his balcony. In its thinly veiled imitation of Hitchcock's opening scene in *Rear Window*, De Palma's sequence plays out a tension between repetition and variation in the expansion of the fractal schema.

In the left segment of the frame, Nicholas sits on a chair in a medium long shot. In the right segment, he is shot from the same angle, but in a long shot slowly zooming out into an extreme long shot. The two segments, together, in their similarity and difference, instantiate a new regime of movement within the image. The left segment holds in the medium long shot as Nicholas takes a phone call; the angle and scale of the image remain the same for the duration of the shot. Shortly after the phone conversation commences in the left segment, the image in the right begins a slow, deep pan from Nicholas's apartment, covering approximately 180 degrees, and focalizes a conversation in front of a café in the extreme deep background of the shot. Upon setting its gaze on this conversation, the image in the right segment of the frame begins a slow zoom toward the conversation, holding the image of two women seated at the café. At this point, in the left segment of the frame, Nicholas's eyes are drawn to the conversation. He ends the phone conversation abruptly, stands from his seat, and in a state of excitement photographs the image, presumably matching the angle and scale of the right segment of the frame.

In my analysis of a desiring apparatus in *Frenzy*, I suggested that Hitchcock's achievement was to configure something like the autonomy of the filmic gaze. For Hitchcock, at the end of a long career of experimentation, this was a significant aesthetic and philosophical intervention into the language of cinematic form. In the sequence in which Babs is murdered off screen, the apparatus wishes to see beyond the door but is frustrated by vision's essential inadequacy. The gaze of Hitchcock's apparatus in that sequence is not an objective, impassive mode of perception. In that sequence, as in so many others across his films, Hitchcock sensed the potential of the fragmented gaze.

Figures C.32–C.37 The split gaze of the apparatus: *Femme Fatale* (2002)

Figure C.32–C.37 Continued

In De Palma's imitation of Hitchcock's pure cinematic vision, the split frame is both a coverage of two critical narrative segments of the film—Nicolas's phone call and the conversation of two women at a café—and a performance of the intrinsically split gaze of the cinematic apparatus. In this sequence, the apparatus is implicated in the regime of the fragment, which now achieves a stunning degree of autonomy from the representational image and its classical-realist cinematic frame. In the initial image of the split screen, the strange similarity in shot scale and angle of the two segments intensifies the affect of the fragment; the effect is something like the discontinuity of a jump cut contained within the one frame. But then the split achieves a new level of autonomy of the fragment. In every split frame I've examined in this book, the two images were set in clear relation to each other in terms of the coverage of action; in this way, even if tentative, the split fashioned a partial image of the whole. But in this split-screen composition in *Femme Fatale*, the split is a *split in itself*. In the capacity of the split to fragment the spatiotemporal regime across the two frames—that is, for one frame to move off from the other, as if unconcerned with the other's itinerary—the fragmented gaze materializes as a pure discretized vision. This split within the frame is no longer two parts of a whole (the left and right segments of the frame in predetermined relation) but a pure form of segmentation. And this is an image that troubles our most basic understanding of classical film form and its terminology.

C.6. De Palma's Final Statement on Method: The Infinite Image

The image zooms slowly out from a photograph constituted out of an infinite system of shapes and patterns.

The zoom is measured to Sakamoto's *Boléro* score, a reprise of the theme that underscored the opening heist sequence. The image is the revelation of the elements of form—the diegetic spaces and times disassembled into the image of the whole—and it seems that, in the final moments of *Femme Fatale*, De Palma is asking us to step back and contemplate the form of all things.

Describing the absolute-film movement headed by Richter and Eggeling in the 1920s, Elder writes: "The makers of absolute film proposed to avoid using the camera to reproduce the appearance of reality, and even to avoid reproducing movement. Instead they would create films from concrete forms, forms they would create by hand (using cut paper or cardboard, paints, and dyes)—forms that would lack any representational import; they would use the camera not to reproduce movement but to create a pure, artificial dynamic. Their films, then, would consist of abstract forms, whose movements would describe abstract shapes that have intriguing relations to one another."[9] I have attempted to situate De Palma within the lineage of such artists and their aesthetic and philosophical designs. The final image in *Femme Fatale* is also the image *of Femme Fatale*. Pure cinema materializes as a collage, painstakingly assembled by hand: like Richter and Eggeling, Nicholas has used concrete forms to erect the fragmented image of the whole. Representations are abstracted as geometric forms; characters materialize as figures: Laure and Veronica in an image fragment in the center left of the collage, seven years in the past, or Laure standing in front of the café near the top of the collage, now inhabiting the present. In Nicholas's construction of point of view, the gaze of the apparatus reveals the essential discretization of form. De Palma's diegesis is a pure abstraction.

The collage is De Palma's most resonant statement on method in a rich archive of such images across his films. The expression of form in so many elaborate set pieces is now distilled into the purity of a single image. It is at once a stunning composition—vibrant in the play of contrasts of color and light, cubist in its aesthetic sensibility—and a metaphor for De Palma's philosophy of pure cinema. In the films closest in spirit to what the avant-garde artists understood pure cinema to be—*Sisters, Obsession, Carrie, Dressed to Kill, Blow Out, Body Double, Raising Cain, Snake Eyes* (1998), *Femme Fatale,* and *Passion*—De Palma's image materializes as a pure fragment—a collage. In its materialization of the whole as the pure expression of the fragment, this is the kind of image that, in Tarkovsky's words, "stretches out to infinity, and leads to the absolute."[10]

Figures C.38–C.43 De Palma's infinite image: *Femme Fatale* (2002)

Figure C.38–C.43 Continued

Notes

Introduction

1. François Truffaut, *Hitchcock: The Revised Edition* (New York: Simon & Schuster, 1985), 214.
2. For a discussion of Hitchcock's "curtain-raising" effect, see William Rothman, *The "I" of the Camera: Essays in Film Criticism, History and Aesthetics* (Cambridge: Cambridge University Press, 2004), 222.
3. For a seminal reading charting *Rear Window*'s essential cinematicality, see Robert Stam and Roberta Pearson, "Hitchcock's *Rear Window*: Reflexivity and the Critique of Voyeurism," *Enclitic* 7.1 (1983), 136–145.
4. I agree with Rothman that Hitchcock, very early in his career, "announced his central concerns and declared a position—at once a philosophical one on the conditions of human existence and a critical one on the powers and limits of the medium and the art of film—to which he remained faithful for over fifty-five years." See William Rothman, *Hitchcock: The Murderous Gaze* (Cambridge, Mass.: Harvard University Press, 1982), 7.
5. Alfred Hitchcock, "Direction," in *Hitchcock on Hitchcock: Selected Writings and Interviews*, edited by Sidney Gottlieb (Berkeley: University of California Press, 1997), 255–256.
6. For example, see Alfred Hitchcock, "Lecture at Columbia University," in *Hitchcock on Hitchcock: Selected Writings and Interviews*, edited by Sidney Gottlieb (Berkeley: University of California Press, 1997), 269: "We have lost what has been—to me, at least—the biggest enjoyment in motion pictures, and that is action and movement."
7. Truffaut, *Hitchcock*, 61.
8. This position is articulated by David Sterritt, one of the most influential theorists of Hitchcockian cinema: "Hitchcock wanted images; he wanted pictures to do the talking." See Edwin Adrian Nieves, *Pure Cinema: An Analysis of Hitchcock Style* (video essay), *A Bitter Sweet Life* (blog):
    https://vimeo.com/144058644. For a discussion of the philosophical foundations of Hitchcock's visuality, see Philip J. Skerry, *Dark Energy: Hitchcock's Absolute Camera and the Physics of Cinematic Spacetime* (London: Bloomsbury, 2015).
9. In his otherwise superb examination of Hitchcock's shower scene in *Psycho*, Philip Skerry's notion of a pure cinema remains just as vague as Hitchcock's. While he goes to some length to study the visual mechanics of mise en scène and montage in many Hitchcock films (and to very productive ends), the conclusion is too often lacking in a theoretical analysis of pure cinema as method. To take one example from the book,

"Shot 19 is an amazing piece of cinematography and a perfect example of pure cinema." In this instance, in his extended discussion of *Spellbound* (1945), Skerry demonstrates the complexity of visual form, but the demonstration is less exacting about precisely what makes this use a "pure cinema" method, or, indeed, what distinguishes it as an artistic philosophy or practice. See Philip J. Skerry, *Psycho in the Shower: The History of Cinema's Most Famous Scene* (New York: Continuum, 2009), 201.

10. William Friedkin, in Nieves, *Pure Cinema*.
11. Martin Scorsese, in Nieves, *Pure Cinema*.
12. For an excellent study of Hitchcock's "imitators," see Thomas M. Leitch, "How to Steal from Hitchcock," in *After Hitchcock: Influence, Imitation, and Intertextuality*, edited by David Boyd and R. Barton Palmer (Austin: University of Texas Press, 2006), 251–270.
13. In a similar fashion, Chris Dumas argues that "De Palma picks up Hitchcock's interest in 'pure cinema' and refines it." See Chris Dumas, *Un-American Psycho: Brian De Palma and the Political Invisible* (Bristol, UK: Intellect, 2012), 58. The limitation of Dumas's study is that his focus is almost exclusively on the politics of De Palma's work and its reception in critical and scholarly writing. His engagement with form is therefore limited in the context of both Hitchcock and De Palma.
14. Bret Easton Ellis, "Unedited New York Times Quentin Tarantino Article," in *Bret Easton Ellis* (blog), October 29, 2015: http://breteastonellis.com/unedited-new-york-times-quentin-tarantino-article/.
15. Noah Baumbach and Jake Paltrow (directors), *De Palma*, 2015.
16. Owen Gleiberman, "Why I Can't Love Brian De Palma (Though I've Always Wished I Could)," *Variety*, June 26, 2016: http://variety.com/2016/film/columns/why-i-cant-love-brian-de-palma-1201803932/.
17. Brian De Palma, "Interviews: Brian De Palma in Conversation with Noah Baumbach," *Dressed to Kill* (Criterion Collection, 2015), DVD. In fact, De Palma has been saying much the same thing since the mid-1970s—see Robert E. Kapsis, *Hitchcock: The Making of a Reputation* (Chicago: University of Chicago Press, 1992), 198.
18. Adrian Martin and Cristina Álvarez López, "[De Palma's] VISION," *Mubi Notebook*, June 3, 2014: https://mubi.com/notebook/posts/de-palmas-vision.
19. In the broadest sense, the *giallo* refers to an Italian genre film industry and practice that emerged in the mid-1960s and gained popularity and aesthetic distinction throughout the 1970s. For an excellent analysis of the *giallo* as industrial and aesthetic form, see Mikel J. Koven, *La Dolce Morte: Vernacular Cinema and the Italian Giallo Film* (Lanham, Md.: Scarecrow, 2006).
20. Gleiberman, "Why I Can't Love Brian De Palma."
21. Gleiberman, "Why I Can't Love Brian De Palma."
22. Dmetri Kakmi, "The Key to De Palma's *Raising Cain*," *Senses of Cinema* 6 (May 2000): http://sensesofcinema.com/2000/brian-de-palma/raising/.
23. Phil Brown, "Brian De Palma Talks *Passion*, *The Untouchables* Prequel, *Capone Rising*, and his upcoming Jason Statham Movie at TIFF 2012," *Collider*, September 13, 2012: http://collider.com/brian-de-palma-passion-untouchables-prequel-capone-rising/.

24. Gérard Genette, *The Architext: An Introduction*, translated by Jane E. Lewin (Berkeley: University of California Press, 1992).
25. In cinema, we must consider "text" as all things that are part of an industry that organizes the material processes of production, aesthetic forms specific to the medium, but equally its exchanges with other mediatic forms, and the cultural ephemera that involves individuals such as directors and spectators. For a discussion of cinema's essential discursivity as industrial and cultural process, see Lúcia Nagib and Anne Jerslev, introduction to *Impure Cinema: Intermedial and Intercultural Approaches to Film* (London: I. B. Tauris, 2014), xviii–xxxi. For Barthes's seminal discussion of the essential freedom of textual form, see Roland Barthes, "From Work to Text," in *Image-Music-Text*, translated by Stephen Heath (London: Fontana, 1977), 155–164.
26. Genette, *Architect*, 81–82.
27. David Bordwell, *On the History of Film Style* (Cambridge, Mass.: Harvard University Press, 1997), 158.
28. I agree wholeheartedly with Richard Allen that any interpretation of Hitchcock's work must derive from a consideration of film poetics. However, I would further argue that poetics broadly conceived is a function of style. In my analyses of Hitchcock, I use the term "mechanics" to describe the way in which style materializes out of an engagement with the formal characteristics of the medium. See Richard Allen, *Hitchcock's Romantic Irony* (New York: Columbia University Press, 2007), xii–xiii.

Chapter 1

1. Ian Aitkin, *European Film Theory and Cinema: A Critical Introduction* (Bloomington: Indiana University Press, 2001), 78–87. For example, as early as 1912, YHCAM (an authorial pseudonym), writes, "The cinema spectacle is not a pale imitation of the theatre; it is a separate spectacle which corresponds to a new and very real Art, a special art which should be left to its own devices, with its own special authors and actors." YHCAM, "Cinematography," in Richard Abel, *French Film Theory and Criticism: A History/Anthology*, vol. 1, *1907–1929* (Princeton, N.J.: Princeton University Press, 1988), 69. For the classic statement on and defense of film's essential mechanical and phenomenological properties (and the artistic use thereof), see Rudolf Arnheim, *Film as Art* (Berkeley: University of California Press, 1957).
2. For a history of the emergence of early cinema out of the aesthetic and technological forms of other arts, see Giusy Pisano, "The Théâtrophone, an Anachronistic Hybrid Experiment or One of the First Immobile Traveler Devices?" in *A Companion to Early Cinema*, edited by André Gaudreault, Nicolas Dulac, and Santiago Hidalgo (Malden, Mass.: Wiley-Blackwell, 2012), 93.
3. John C. Tibbets, *The American Theatrical Film: Stages in Development* (Bowling Green, Ohio: Bowling Green State University Popular Press, 1985), 10–22.
4. For a general overview and historicization of modernism's emergence as a reaction to older aesthetic forms and political discourses, see Peter Childs, *Modernism* (New York: Routledge, 2016).

5. For an excellent analysis of the way in which modernist artists, critics, and intellectuals embraced the radical aesthetic and experiential potential of cinema, see R. Bruce Elder, *DADA, Surrealism, and the Cinematic Effect* (Toronto: Wilfred Laurier University Press, 2013).
6. Against what he calls an almost "hegemonic" position, Elder provides ample evidence that several strands of modernist art practice "embraced the new medium as the *ottima arte*, the 'top art,' that most truly exemplified modern, largely urban, life." See Elder, *DADA, Surrealism, and the Cinematic Effect*, 568.
7. Perhaps most famously, Dalí contributed the dream sequence to *Spellbound*, Hitchcock's film of 1945.
8. Susan Hayward, *Cinema Studies: The Key Concepts* (London: Routledge, 2000), 35. For an excellent, succinct analysis of the economic and aesthetic development of *cinéma pur* from the early 1920s, see Jan-Christopher Horak, "Discovering Pure Cinema: Avant-Garde Film in the '20s," *Afterimage* (Summer 1980), 3–9. We should note, however, that the notion of a pure visuality of the cinema finds its way into various currents of film theory and criticism well before the emergence of *cinéma pur*. See, for example, Marcel Gromaire, a French painter, writing in 1919: "The cinema is primarily *visual*. What will be the lyric plastic form of cinema, in short, its own proper language?" Marcel Gromaire, "A Painter's Ideas About the Cinema," translated by Stuart Liebman, in Richard Abel, *French Film Theory and Criticism: A History/Anthology*, vol. 1, *1907–1929* (Princeton, N.J.: Princeton University Press, 1988), 174–175. Gromaire is prescient in his projection of the potential of the new cinematic art. Sounding very much like the intellectuals and artists who comprised the *cinéma pur* movement, he further expounds: "Moving form is [cinema's] essential logic, the implacable intellectual basis constitutive of its nature as a work of art" (176).
9. Hayward, *Cinema Studies*, 35. Elder describes *Entr'acte* similarly as a cinema of "movement" within the frame and between frames. See Elder, *DADA, Surrealism, and the Cinematic Effect*, 198.
10. René Clair, "Pure Cinema and Commercial Cinema," translated by Stanley Appelbaum, in Richard Abel, *French Film Theory and Criticism: A History/Anthology*, vol. 1, *1907–1929* (Princeton, N.J.: Princeton University Press, 1988), 371.
11. In an evocative turn of phrase, Flitterman-Lewis describes *The Seashell and the Clergyman* as the "pure poetry of visual elements." See Sandy Flitterman-Lewis, *To Desire Differently: Feminism and the French Cinema* (New York: Columbia University Press, 1996), 118.
12. This is not to suggest that the cinema of Clair or Dulac was in some sense "unreal." On the contrary, and as I explore further, I concur with Maule that a filmmaker like Dulac engaged "cinema as the medium that allows a full expression of human emotions and experiences, as well as a direct rendition of reality." See Rosanna Maule, "The Importance of Being a Film Author: Germaine Dulac and Female Authorship," *Senses of Cinema* 23 (2002):

http://sensesofcinema.com/2002/feature-articles/dulac/. Clearly Dulac perceives the cinematic image as accessing reality in the purest sense, in spite of its potential to reject classical representative form.

13. Aitkin, *European Film Theory and Cinema*, 80.
14. For a concise analysis of *cinéma pur* as "abstract filmmaking," see Malcolm Turvey, *The Filming of Modern Life: European Avant-Garde Film of the 1920s* (Cambridge, Mass.: MIT Press, 2011), 47–56. For a seminal reading of Dulac's vision of the "expressive possibilities of the new medium," see Flitterman-Lewis, *To Desire Differently*, 47–48.
15. Germaine Dulac, "The Essence of the Cinema: The Visual Idea," translated by Robert Lamberton, in *The Avant-Garde Film: A Reader of Theory and Criticism*, edited by Adams Sitney (New York: New York University Press, 1978), 41.
16. Dulac, "The Essence of the Cinema," 41. Reflecting on Dulac's career through the 1920s, Williams suggests that "early twentieth-century France was dominated by an impulse of visual primacy . . . that was not independent from the advent of cinema." See Tami Michelle Williams, "The 'Silent' Arts: Modern Pantomime and the Making of an Art Cinema in the Belle Époque Paris: The Case of Georges Wague and Germaine Dulac," in *A Companion to Early Cinema*, edited by André Gaudreault, Nicolas Dulac, and Santiago Hidalgo (Malden, Mass.: Wiley-Blackwell, 2012), 103.
17. Germaine Dulac, "The Expressive Techniques of the Cinema," translated by Stuart Liebman, in Richard Abel, *French Film Theory and Criticism: A History/Anthology*, vol. 1, *1907–1929* (Princeton, N.J.: Princeton University Press, 1988), 305.
18. Tami Michelle Williams, "Beyond Impressions: The Life and Films of Germaine Dulac from Aesthetics to Politics," PhD diss. (University of California, Los Angeles, 2007), 28.
19. Flitterman-Lewis reads Dulac's pure cinema ethos as a fundamental transformation of the enunciative mode of the cinematic apparatus: "Dulac agitated for the creation of a 'pure cinema' whose resources and forms of expression would be specifically cinematic. She called for a visual poetics which emphasized the materiality of the cinematic signifier as against the conventions of narrative causality and visual continuity of the traditional commercial cinema." See Flitterman-Lewis, *To Desire Differently*, 26. In Flitterman-Lewis's account, then, a pure cinema style is also a political intervention.
20. Williams, *Beyond Impressions*, 168.
21. For an account of the European influence on Hitchcock's early cinema, see Sidney Gottlieb, "Early Hitchcock: The German Influence," in *Framing Hitchcock: Selected Essays from the Hitchcock Annual*, edited by Sidney Gottlieb and Christopher Brookhouse (Detroit: Wayne State University Press, 2002), 35–58. See also Charles Barr, "Hitchcock and Early Filmmakers," in *A Companion to Alfred Hitchcock*, edited by Thomas Leitch and Leland Poague (Chichester, UK: Wiley-Blackwell, 2014), 55–59.
22. Quoted in Lotte H. Eisner, *Murnau* (London: Secker & Warburg, 1973), 84. Eisner confirms the time frame of Murnau's writing.
23. Gottlieb, "Early Hitchcock," 42.
24. Alfred Hitchcock, "On Style," in *Hitchcock on Hitchcock: Selected Writings and Interviews*, edited by Sidney Gottlieb (Berkeley: University of California Press,

1997), 288. See also Robin Wood, "Retrospective," in *A Hitchcock Reader*, edited by Marshall Deutelbaum and Leland Poague (Chichester, UK: Wiley-Blackwell, 2009), 41.
25. Stephen Prince and Wayne E. Hensley, "The Kuleshov Effect: Recreating the Classic Experiment," *Cinema Journal* 31.2 (1992), 59–75.
26. Alfred Hitchcock, "The Kuleshov Effect," YouTube, October 22, 2012: https://www.youtube.com/watch?v=MCK53Lb4-pI.
27. A wipe is a form of transition from one shot to another in which the second shot emerges by traveling along the length of the preceding shot, usually from left to right. In this sequence, Hitchcock simulates a wipe through the opening of the door, thereby emphasizing the image of Madeleine as a revelation of some significance.
28. In Edward Branigan's close study of the function of point of view in this scene, he reads Scottie's gaze as a "continuing" point of view within the sequence as a whole; that is, Madeleine's image demonstrates Scottie's "heightened attention and growing obsession with Madeleine." Yet Branigan also acknowledges that Scottie's point of view is momentarily reflected in a mirror in a shot that incorporates one of Hitchcock's most explicit line-crosses. As a cinematic gaze, that is, as a viewing circuitry between Scottie and Madeleine, this way of seeing is irreducibly segmented, or split. See Edward Branigan, *Point of View in the Cinema: A Theory of Narration and Subjectivity in Classical Film* (Berlin: Mouton, 1984), 117–118.
29. Skerry, *Dark Energy*, xix.
30. Skerry, *Dark Energy*, 36.
31. For a historical account of the development of mise en scène as film form, see Adrian Martin, *Mise en Scène and Film Style: From Classical Hollywood to New Media Art* (Basingstoke, UK: Palgrave, 2014); see especially 47–57.
32. Donald Spoto, *The Art of Alfred Hitchcock: Fifty Years of His Motion Pictures* (New York: Random House, 1992), 9.
33. Truffaut, *Hitchcock*, 43–44.
34. Truffaut, *Hitchcock*, 44.
35. Truffaut, *Hitchcock*, 44.
36. Truffaut, *Hitchcock*, 49.
37. In his superb study of a Hitchcockian mise en scène and montage derived from musical concepts, David Schroeder suggests that this sequence achieves "an overall complexity in the counterpoint of motion similar to what composers achieve with counterpoint." See David Schroeder, *Hitchcock's Ear: Music and the Director's Art* (London: Continuum, 2012), 45. I return to the notion of visual and aural counterpoint in chapter 7.
38. Hitchcock suggested to Truffaut, "*The Lodger* is the first picture possibly influenced by my time in Germany." Truffaut, *Hitchcock,* 44.
39. Truffaut, *Hitchcock*, 46.
40. R. Wood, "Retrospective," 41.
41. For a lucid and precise reading of the ontology of Bazin's realist image, see Daniel Morgan, "Re-thinking Bazin: Ontology and Realist Aesthetics," *Critical Inquiry* 32.3 (2006), 443–481.

42. For her seminal reading of woman as refuse in *Frenzy*, see Tania Modleski, *The Women Who Knew Too Much: Hitchcock and Feminist Theory* (New York: Routledge, 2016), 107.
43. For an excellent study of the importance of Covent Garden to the film's larger meanings, see K. Brenna Wardell, "The Murderer in the Garden: Something Rotten in Hitchcock's *Frenzy*," in *Alfred Hitchcock*, edited by Douglas A. Cunningham (New York: Grey House, 2017), 173–191.
44. *Frenzy*, Hitchcock Collection (Universal Studios, 2001), DVD.
45. For two of many seminal discussions of the cinema's depiction of the "real," see André Bazin, "The Evolution of the Language of Cinema," in *What Is Cinema?*, vol. 1, translated by Hugh Gray (Berkeley: University of California Press, 1967), 23–40; and André Bazin, "An Aesthetic of Reality: Cinematic Realism and the Italian School of Liberation," in *What Is Cinema?*, vol. 2, translated by Hugh Gray (Berkeley: University of California Press, 1967), 16–40.
46. For his discussion of movement as "perpetual conversion," see Gilles Deleuze, *Cinema 1: The Movement Image*, translated by Hugh Tomlinson and Barbara Habberjam (Minneapolis: University of Minnesota Press, 2009), 20. Deleuze summarizes movement intrinsic to the shot in the following way: "The translation of the parts of a set which spreads out in space, the change of a whole which is transformed in duration."
47. See Bazin, "The Evolution of the Language of Cinema."
48. Luiza Liz, "Alfred Hitchcock and the Art of Pure Cinema," *Art Regard*, YouTube, February 17, 2017: https://www.youtube.com/watch?v=szmBC5rYEU8.
49. Truffaut, *Hitchcock*, 246.
50. Truffaut, *Hitchcock*, 276.
51. Barry Langford, *Film Genre: Hollywood and Beyond* (Edinburgh: Edinburgh University Press, 2005), 38.
52. Bazin, "An Aesthetic of Reality."
53. In Žižek's reading of *Vertigo*, he describes the physicality of the city as "overwhelmingly present." I would argue that this is more than a geographical presence; it is an excessive significatory presence based on locales, tourist attractions, and the cinematic iconography of the Hollywood film. See Slavoj Žižek, "*Vertigo*: The Drama of a Deceived Platonist," *Hitchcock Annual* 12 (2003–2004), 68.
54. I agree with Danks's superb analysis of the use of rear projection in Hitchcock's cinema. He concludes that the visual effect was part of a "broader combinatory and contrapuntal aesthetic found in his work." See Adrian Danks, "Being in Two Places at the Same Time: The Forgotten Geography of Rear Projection," in *B is for Bad Cinema: Aesthetics, Politics, and Cultural Value*, edited by Claire Perkins and Constantine Verevis (Albany: State University of New York Press, 2014), 68. I further develop the notion of a Hitchcockian contrapuntal aesthetic in chapter 7.
55. Michelle Piso, "Mark's *Marnie*," in *A Hitchcock Reader*, edited by Marshall Deutelbaum and Leland Poague (Chichester, UK: Wiley-Blackwell, 2009), 284.
56. André Bazin, "The Ontology of the Photographic Image," in *What Is Cinema?*, vol. 1, translated by Hugh Gray (Berkeley: University of California Press, 1967), 9–16. For a lucid reading of the symbolic content of the rear projection technique, see Maurice

Yacowar, "Hitchcock's Imagery and Art," in *A Hitchcock Reader*, edited by Marshall Deutelbaum and Leland Poague (Chichester, UK: Wiley-Blackwell, 2009), 25–34.
57. Piso, "Mark's *Marnie*," 284.
58. Truffaut, *Hitchcock*, 256.

Chapter 2

1. Leitch, "How to Steal from Hitchcock," 251.
2. Leitch, "How to Steal from Hitchcock," 269.
3. Leitch, "How to Steal from Hitchcock," 261–262.
4. For an analysis of the textual part as discretized object, see Umberto Eco, "*Casablanca*: Cult Movies and Intertextual Collage," in *The Cult Film Reader*, edited by Ernest Mathijs and Xavier Mendik (Maidenhead, UK: McGraw-Hill, 2008), 74.
5. Gilles Deleuze, *Cinema 2: The Time Image*, translated by Hugh Tomlinson and Barbara Habberjam (Minneapolis: University of Minnesota Press, 2009), 189.
6. André Bazin, "Cinematic Realism and the Italian School of Liberation," in *André Bazin and Italian Neorealism*, edited by Bert Cardullo (New York: Continuum, 2011), 33.
7. See, for example, Peter Bondanella, *A History of Italian Cinema* (New York: Continuum, 2009), 217–258. But it was also Bazin's championing of an aesthetic realism that influenced a generation of French filmmakers. See T. Jefferson Kline, "The French New Wave," in *European Cinema*, edited by Elizabeth Ezra (Oxford: Oxford University Press, 2004), 159–160.
8. John Orr, *Hitchcock and Twentieth Century Cinema* (London: Wallflower, 2005, 18.
9. David Bordwell, "The Art Cinema as a Mode of Film Practice," *Film Criticism* 4.1 (1979), 56–64.
10. Truffaut, *Hitchcock*, 103.
11. This is a film world that extrudes from a kind of "invisible" image and narrative style common to the classical Hollywood film. See David Bordwell, "Classical Narration," in David Bordwell, Kristin Thompson, and Janet Staiger, *The Classical Hollywood Cinema: Film Style and Mode of Production to 1960* (New York: Columbia University Press, 1985), 24–41.
12. Truffaut, *Hitchcock*, 194.
13. Raymond Durgnat, "Cat and Mouse Games," in *The Essential Raymond Durgnat*, edited by Henry K. Miller (London: British Film Institute, 2014), 33.
14. In his classic study of Hitchcock, Wood differentiates Hitchcock's popular cinema from the auteuristic, self-consciously aesthetic cinema of Bergman and Antonioni. While I take a slightly different position on the separate merits of Hitchcock and the European auteur cinema, my argument is that Hitchcock's acquiescence to a popular genre form is fundamental to the expression of a pure cinema style. See Robin Wood, *Hitchcock's Films Revisited* (New York: Columbia University Press, 2002), 58–59.
15. Mikel J. Koven, *La Dolce Morte*.

16. Donato Totaro, "A Genealogy of Italian Popular Cinema: the *Filone*," *Off-Screen* 15.11 (2011): http://offscreen.com/view/genealogy_filone.
17. Koven, *La Dolce Morte*, 3.
18. Koven, *La Dolce Morte*, 4.
19. Bondanella, *A History of Italian Cinema*, 310–313.
20. For a discussion of the intersection of Italian auteur and genre cinema, see Mary Wood, *Italian Cinema* (New York: Berg, 2005), 110–112.
21. Philippe Met, "'Knowing Too Much about Hitchcock: The Genesis of the Italian *Giallo*," in *After Hitchcock: Influence, Imitation, and Intertextuality*, edited by David Boyd and R. Barton Palmer (Austin: University of Texas Press, 2006), 202.
22. David Church, "One on Top of the Other: Lucio Fulci, Transnational Film Industries, and the Retrospective Construction of the Italian Horror Canon," *Quarterly Review of Film and Video* 32 (2014), 2.
23. Koven, *La Dolce Morte*, v.
24. Miriam Bratu Hansen, "The Mass Production of the Senses: Classical Cinema as Vernacular Modernism," *Modernism/Modernity* 6.2 (1999), 59–72.
25. Hansen, "Mass Production of the Senses," 71.
26. Hansen, "Mass Production of the Senses," 71.
27. Jeffrey Sconce, "Trashing the Academy: Taste, Excess and an Emerging Politics of Cinematic Style," *Screen* 36.4 (1995), 372.
28. See Alexia Kannas, "All the Colours of the Dark: Film Genre and the Italian *Giallo*," *Journal of Italian Cinema and Media Studies* 5.2 (2017), 175–179.
29. Sconce, "Trashing the Academy," *Screen*, 385.
30. Sconce, "Trashing the Academy," *Screen*, 392.
31. Jeffrey Sconce, "Trashing the Academy: Taste, Excess and an Emerging Politics of Cinematic Style," in *The Cult Film Reader*, edited by Ernest Mathijs and Xavier Mendik (Maidenhead, UK: McGraw-Hill, 2008), 113–114.
32. Adrian Martin, "A Walk through *Carlito's Way*," *LOLA* 4 (2013): http://www.lolajournal.com/4/carlito.html.
33. Eyal Peretz, *Becoming Visionary: Brian De Palma's Cinematic Education of the Senses* (Stanford, Calif.: Stanford University Press, 2008), 61.
34. For a colorful history of American auteurs of the 1960s and 1970s breaking the classical Hollywood mold, see Peter Biskind, *Easy Riders, Raging Bulls: How the Sex-Drugs-and-Rock 'n Roll Generation Saved Hollywood* (London: Bloomsbury, 1999).
35. Brian De Palma (interview), *Sisters* (Criterion Edition, 2000), DVD.
36. Leitch, "How to Steal from Hitchcock," 251.
37. De Palma interview, *Sisters*.
38. De Palma interview, *Sisters*.
39. Jon Lewis, *American Film: A History* (New York: Norton, 2008), 292.
40. For an excellent analysis of Spielberg as a blockbuster auteur, see Warren Buckland, *Directed by Steven Spielberg: Poetics of the Contemporary Hollywood Blockbuster* (New York: Continuum, 2006), 13–15.
41. Justin Wyatt, *High Concept: Movies and Marketing in Hollywood* (Austin: University of Texas Press, 1994).

Chapter 3

1. Hitchcock, "On Style," 288.
2. Sergei Eisenstein, "The Cinematographic Principle and the Ideogram," in *Film Form: Essays in Film Theory*, edited and translated by Jay Leyda (Orlando, Fla.: Harcourt, 1977), 37.
3. Eisenstein, "The Cinematographic Principle," 38.
4. Eisenstein, "The Cinematographic Principle," 39.
5. In his discussion of a "synthesis of fragments" in the aesthetic of the avant-garde, Turvey cites Lawder's discussion of Léger's *Ballet mécanique* (1923–1924): "Contrast is both the life-blood and the binding force of *Ballet mécanique*. The film is composed not from separate shots which link to each other as in most films, but from disparate ones which clash and collide." See Turvey, *Filming of Modern Life*, 57.
6. R. Bruce Elder, *Harmony and Dissent: Film and Avant-Garde Art Movements in the Early Twentieth Century* (Waterloo, Ont.: Wilfred Laurier, 2010), 281.
7. This seems to be Deleuze's position on Eisensteinian montage: "Eisenstein continually reminds us that montage is the whole of the film, the Idea. But why *should* the whole be the object of montage?" See Deleuze, *Cinema 1*, 29. For a more expansive discussion of the "caesura" within Eisensteinian montage, see 180–183.
8. Elder, *Harmony and Dissent*, 289.
9. Elder, *Harmony and Dissent*, 289.
10. For a reading of Hitchcock's cutting that appropriates the Soviet montage style, see Raymond Durgnat, *A Long, Hard Look at Psycho* (London: British Film Institute, 2010), 40.
11. Hitchcock, "On Style," 288.
12. See Allen, *Hitchcock's Romantic Irony*. In a more theoretically inflected application of theory to *Rear Window, Vertigo*, and *Marnie*, see Laura Mulvey, "Visual Pleasure and Narrative Cinema," in *Feminism and Film Theory*, edited by Constance Penley (New York: Routledge, 1988), 57–68.
13. Allen, *Hitchcock's Romantic Irony*, 146.
14. Žižek, "*Vertigo*," 67–82.
15. Raymond Bellour, "System of a Fragment (on *The Birds*)," in *The Analysis of Film*, edited by Constance Penley (Bloomington: Indiana University Press, 2001), 28. Elsewhere Bellour calls this formal patterning "the systematicity at the heart of the great American classicism." See Raymond Bellour, "To Alternate/To Narrate," in *Early Cinema: Space, Frame, Narrative*, edited by Thomas Elsaesser (London: British Film Institute, 1990), 360.
16. Deleuze, *Cinema 1*, 8.
17. Raymond Bellour, "A Bit of History," in *The Analysis of Film*, edited by Constance Penley (Bloomington: Indiana University Press, 2001), 3–4.
18. In his seminal study of the neo-baroque aesthetic in popular culture, Calabrese situates the emergence of a properly neo-baroque style in terms of the elevation of the significance of the "detail" or "fragment" in relation to the whole. See Omar Calabrese, *Neo-Baroque: A Sign of the Times*, translated by Charles Lambert (Princeton, N.J.: Princeton University Press, 1992), 68–74.

19. Kristin Thompson, *Storytelling in the New Hollywood: Understanding Classical Narrative Technique* (Cambridge, Mass.: Harvard University Press, 1999), 10.
20. R. Wood, *Hitchcock's Films Revisited*, 87.
21. Allen, *Hitchcock's Romantic Irony*, 146.
22. Allen, *Hitchcock's Romantic Irony*, 146.
23. Allen, *Hitchcock's Romantic Irony*, 145.
24. Truffaut, *Hitchcock,* 256.
25. Truffaut, *Hitchcock,* 256.
26. Raymond Bellour, "Symbolic Blockage (on *North by Northwest*)," in *The Analysis of Film*, edited by Constance Penley (Bloomington: Indiana University Press, 2001), 83.
27. Bellour, "Symbolic Blockage," 188.
28. Bellour, "Symbolic Blockage," 188.
29. Truffaut, *Hitchcock,* 256.
30. Truffaut, *Hitchcock,* 135.
31. Anna Powell, "A Touch of Terror: Dario Argento and Deleuze's Cinematic Sensorium," in *European Nightmares: Horror Cinema in Europe since 1945*, edited by Patricia Allmer, Emily Brick, and David Huxley (London: Wallflower, 2012), 168.
32. Kristin Thompson, "The Concept of Cinematic Excess," *Ciné-Tracts: A Journal of Film, Communications, Culture, and Politics* 2 (1977), 57.
33. Koven, *La Dolce Morte*, vi.
34. Steven Shaviro, *The Cinematic Body* (Minneapolis: University of Minnesota Press, 1994), 30.
35. Thompson, "The Concept of Cinematic Excess," 58.
36. The distinction between the action image and affection image is a matter of degree of what Deleuze calls "motoricity": "When a part of the body has had to sacrifice most of its motoricity in order to become the support for organs of reception, the principal feature of these will now only be tendencies to movement or micro-movements which are capable of entering into intensive series." See Deleuze, *Cinema 1*, 87.
37. Powell, "A Touch of Terror," 168.
38. Eco, "*Casablanca*," 67–75.
39. Koven, *La Dolce Morte*, 137–138.
40. My reading of this sequence and its violent coda in the set of jump cuts is thus in diametric opposition to the conclusion Sharff reaches in his close analysis of the same sequence. I agree with Sharff that the sequence is a bravura display of what he calls "kinesthetic" elements, that is, formal artistic elements derived from the medium of cinema. Sharff is correct to suggest that the set of jump cuts is a formal medium contrivance that is "not the way a person sees." But I disagree that Hitchcock's jump-cut reveal of the image of violence, aberrantly cutting from medium-long shot to close-up, "adds to the suspense." I've argued that the jump cut is always already marked by its avant-gardist lineage, that is, its contrivance of spectatorial distantiation, but I would further add that Hitchcock plays up the break from the traditional suspense montage of films such as *Vertigo* and *Psycho* by removing all sound from the montage, thereby intensifying the image of distantiation. See Stefan Sharff, *The Elements of Cinema: Toward a Theory of Cinesthetic Impact* (New York: Columbia University Press, 1982), 9–17.

41. Jim Collins, *Architectures of Excess: Cultural Life in the Information Age* (New York: Routledge, 1995), 148.
42. Deleuze, *Cinema 1*, 151.
43. Truffaut, *Hitchcock*, 256.
44. Truffaut, *Hitchcock*, 256.

Chapter 4

1. Calabrese, *Neo-Baroque*, 58.
2. Durgnat, *A Long Hard Look at* Psycho, 40.
3. Eisenstein, "The Cinematographic Principle and the Ideogram," 38.
4. Peretz, *Becoming Visionary*, 66.
5. Martin, *Mise en Scène and Film Style*, 22.
6. Tom Gunning, "Hitchcock and the Picture in the Frame," *New England Review* 28.3 (2007), 26.
7. For a superb analysis of this sequence as an expressive framing device, see David Kelly, "Narrative and Narration in John Ford's *The Searchers*," *Sydney Studies in English* 36 (2010), 170–172.
8. Jim Collins, "Genericity in the Nineties: Eclectic Irony and the New Sincerity," in *Film Theory Goes to the Movies*, edited by Jim Collins, Hilary Radner, and Ava Preacher Collins (New York: Routledge, 1993), 255.
9. Brigitte Peucker, "Aesthetic Space in Hitchcock," in *A Companion to Alfred Hitchcock*, edited by Thomas Leitch and Leland Poague (Chichester, UK: Wiley-Blackwell, 2011), 202.
10. Peucker, "Aesthetic Space in Hitchcock," 202.
11. Peucker, "Aesthetic Space in Hitchcock," 203.
12. Gunning, "Hitchcock and the Picture in the Frame," 14.
13. Gunning, "Hitchcock and the Picture in the Frame," 14.
14. Elder, *Harmony and Dissent*, 125.
15. Elder, *Harmony and Dissent*, 111–116.
16. Elder, *Harmony and Dissent*, 144–145.
17. Cited in Elder, *Harmony and Dissent*, 145.
18. As a useful foundational position, Tatarkiewicz argues that representational art represents "with the help of real shapes and not abstract signs. Reality is to them both a means and an end. That is why they are sometimes known as *realism*." See Wladyslaw Tatarkiewicz, "Abstract Art and Philosophy," *British Journal of Aesthetics* 2.3 (1962), 228.
19. Turvey, *The Filming of Modern Life,* 19.
20. Tatarkiewicz, "Abstract Art and Philosophy," 229–230.
21. Truffaut, *Hitchcock,* 269.
22. Elder, *Harmony and Dissent*, 145.
23. Truffaut, *Hitchcock*, 276.
24. Elder, *Harmony and Dissent*, 138.

25. Sean Cubitt, *The Cinema Effect* (Cambridge, Mass.: MIT Press, 2005), 192.
26. Murray Pomerance, "Some Hitchcockian Shots," in *A Companion to Alfred Hitchcock*, edited by Thomas Leitch and Leland Poague (Chichester, UK: Wiley-Blackwell, 2011), 240.
27. For a more general discussion of Hitchcock's topographical spaces, see Steven Jacobs, *The Wrong House: The Architecture of Alfred Hitchcock* (Rotterdam: 010, 2007), 46–47.
28. Pomerance, "Some Hitchcockian Shots," 242.
29. Pomerance, "Some Hitchcockian Shots," 241.
30. Pomerance, "Some Hitchcockian Shots," 241.
31. Martin, "A Walk through *Carlito's Way*."
32. In this sense, a schematic frame is also a formal *segmentation*, a notion I develop in subsequent chapters. Here I take my lead from Bellour's extensive examination of Hitchcock's cinema as an unclosed systemic classicism. For an overview of Bellour's notion of formal segmentation, see Hilary Radner and Alastair Fox, *Raymond Bellour: Cinema and the Moving Image* (Edinburgh: Edinburgh University Press, 2018), 12–15.
33. Pomerance, "Some Hitchcockian Shots," 242.
34. For an extended examination of the introduction of Uncle Charlie as the film's central character, see Rothman, *Hitchcock*, 181–183.
35. Bellour, "Symbolic Blockage," 83.
36. Pomerance, "Some Hitchcockian Shots," 240.
37. In his reflection on his career, Hitchcock clearly differentiates between an early "amateur" period and a period of sustained development and formal experimentation. See Truffaut, *Hitchcock*, 94.
38. Liz, "Alfred Hitchcock and the Art of Pure Cinema."
39. Peucker, "Aesthetic Space in Hitchcock," 208.
40. Peucker, "Aesthetic Space in Hitchcock," 209.
41. The lobby of the building was one of the stunning replicas of actual locations that mark Hitchcock's cinema. See Truffaut, *Hitchcock*, 252.
42. For an excellent study of the architectural contrast of "American open spaces" in the crop duster sequence and the "glass surfaces, sweeping plazas, marble masses, and elegant lobbies" of the United Nations Building, see Jacobs, *The Wrong House*, 299–300.
43. As Jacobs suggests, the opening credit sequence is an "abstract play of lines on a green surface" over the CIT Building in Manhattan. While the shot of the CIT Building has been erroneously identified as the United Nations Building of the later sequence, Hitchcock is clearly drawing a parallel between the CIT Building schematic and the setting for the elaborate action sequence that takes place in the United Nations Building. See Jacobs, *The Wrong House*, 299.
44. Annette Michelson, quoted in Pomerance, "Some Hitchcockian Shots," 240–241.

Chapter 5

1. In the classical style, a close-up is conventionally rationalized within a deterministic field of shot relations: long shot, medium shot, medium close-up, and so on.

Such shot scales help to build narrative continuity. In Bava's display of the scale proportions of the frame, the close-up is severed from a deterministic, unified spatial field, functioning instead as an irrational, excessive image. Such irrational compositions in the *giallo* are commonly utilized in elaborate murder set pieces, such as this opening to *A Bay of Blood*. For a comprehensive overview of the function of shot relation within various cinematic styles and contexts, see David Bordwell and Kristin Thompson, *Film Art: An Introduction*, 11th ed. (New York: McGraw Hill, 2017), 219–245.
2. In the strangeness of an encounter with this image, I seem to address a "figure" beneath the embodied form of the actor, or even the embodied form of the character. In this encounter, I conceptualize the figure beneath the diegetic figure as an abstraction. For this explanation of a sensorial encounter with this image in Bava, I found Adrian Martin's examination of the notion of "the figural" useful. See Adrian Martin, *Last Day Every Day: Figural Thinking from Auerbach to Agamben to Brenez* (Brooklyn: Punctum Books, 2012). In my sense of the "figural" nature of this image, Nicole Brenez's attempt to define the figure suggests a way of thinking through this abstraction within the frame: "The figure invents itself as the *force* of a representation, what forever remains to be constituted, that which, in the visible, tends to the Inexhaustible." Cited in Martin, *Last Day Every Day*, 7–8.
3. Shaviro, *The Cinematic Body*, 30.
4. Met, "Knowing Too Much about Hitchcock," 202.
5. See Kevin Heffernan, "Art House or House of Exorcism? The Changing Distribution and Reception Contexts of Mario Bava's *Lisa and the Devil*," in *Sleaze Artists: Cinema at the Margins of Taste, Style, and Politics*, edited by Jeffrey Sconce (Durham, N.C.: Duke University Press, 2007), 146.
6. Heffernan, "Art House or House of Exorcism," 152.
7. Heffernan, "Art House or House of Exorcism," 153.
8. M. Wood, *Italian Cinema*, 58.
9. Koven, *La Dolce Morte*, 123.
10. Gunning, "Hitchcock and the Picture in the Frame," 14.
11. Similar expressionist geometries function as schematic frames in films such as *Blade Runner* (1982), *Gattaca* (1997), and *The Matrix* (1999).
12. Leon Ferguson, *Dario Argento: An Eye for Horror* (Independent Film Channel, 2001).
13. For a discussion of De Palma's self-referentiality, see Dumas, *Un-American Psycho*, 61.
14. De Palma's rear-projection image is also facilitated by Scully's driving, covered in a tightly focused medium close-up. Jacobs argues that Hitchcock's images of driving (for example, in *Vertigo*) are a "perfect instrument of cinematic self-reflection." See Jacobs, *The Wrong House*, 45. In its intensifying of the ontological breach of the diegesis, De Palma's image is more visibly reflexive than is Hitchcock's, displaying the compositional frame as an assemblage of fragments.
15. Todd Herzog, "'What Shall the History Books Read?' The Debate Over Inglorious Basterds and the Limits of Representation," in *Quentin Tarantino's* Inglourious Basterds: *A Manipulation of Metacinema* (New York: Continuum, 2012), 278.
16. Herzog, "'What Shall the History Books Read?," 279.

17. In another sense, the framed "other" to the diegetic frame can be thought of as a further fragmentation of the cinematic frame as whole, and thus as an excess of representation. Peretz describes this relational excess as "the very being of the outside in the inside as a haunting it cannot contain." See Peretz, *Becoming Visionary*, 126.
18. Bazin, "The Evolution of the Language of Cinema," 35.
19. M. Wood, *Italian Cinema*, 184.
20. Douglas Keesey, *Brian De Palma's Split-Screen: A Life in Film* (Jackson: University of Mississippi Press, 2017), 178.
21. "Body Double: The Set Up—Featurette," in *Body Double* (Umbrella Entertainment, 2014), Blu-ray.

Chapter 6

1. André Bazin, "The Myth of Total Cinema," in *What is Cinema?* vol. 1, translated by Hugh Gray (Berkeley: University of California Press, 1967), 18–21.
2. For various kinds of analyses of these two forms of shot and montage relation, see Žižek, "*Vertigo*"; Mulvey, "Visual Pleasure and Narrative Cinema"; and Janet Bergstrom, "Alternation, Segmentation, Hypnosis: Interview with Raymond Bellour," *Camera Obscura* 3 (1979), 84. Bergstrom's engagement with Bellour's notion of alternation is a particular useful way of framing the subject-object relation underpinning the mirrored reflection and the point of view shot.
3. Peretz, *Becoming Visionary*, 125.
4. I tend to agree with Bordwell's position that the majority of Hollywood's post-classical experiments intensify traditional forms of aesthetic and spectatorial processes rather than breaking with the foundations of those traditions. The most common use of the split screen that gained popularity during this era would be an example of this intensified continuity. See David Bordwell, "Intensified Continuity: Visual Style in Contemporary American Film," *Film Quarterly* 55.3 (2002), 16–28.
5. Bruce Isaacs, *Toward a New Film Aesthetic* (New York: Continuum, 2008), 140–142. For an excellent analysis of the development of the split-screen technique in the 1960s and 1970s, see Malte Hagener, "The Aesthetics of Displays: How the Split Screen Remediates Other Media," *Refractory: A Journal of Entertainment Media* 14 (2008): http://refractory.unimelb.edu.au/2008/12/24/the-aesthetics-of-displays-how-the-split-screen-remediates-other-media-%E2%80%93-malte-hagener/.
6. Peucker, "Aesthetic Space in Hitchcock," 212. For a similar reading of a partitioned frame as a split-screen effect, see David Sterritt, *The Films of Alfred Hitchcock* (Cambridge: Cambridge University Press, 1993), 40–41. Sterritt reads the split screen as the "echo [of] the psychological state" of the main character in Hitchcock's *Blackmail*.
7. R. Wood, *Hitchcock's Films Revisited*, 111–112.
8. Peretz, *Becoming Visionary*, 128.
9. In Bellour's monumental studies of the "Hitchcockian system," even he grants *Psycho* a special place as a transgressive work: "[*Psycho*], in a sense, contravenes the classical

model of narrative—as well as that more singular model that is both an eccentric and exemplary version of it: the Hitchcockian system. Obviously, it does so, not in order to elude the system, but rather—through a greater degree of abstraction—to determine its regime(s)." See Raymond Bellour, "Psychosis, Neurosis, Perversion," translated by Nancy Huston, in *A Hitchcock Reader*, edited by Marshall Deutelbaum and Leland Poague (Malden, Mass.: Wiley-Blackwell, 2009), 341–342.

10. Hitchcock, "On Style," 288.
11. Skerry, Psycho *in the Shower*, 247.
12. Skerry, Psycho *in the Shower*, 247.
13. In discussion with Janet Leigh, Skerry offers the following perceptive remark: "What happens is that when Hitchcock starts to cut and edit that scene, it's like you're thrust into this very confined space and it becomes sort of an abstract space with all this terror happening." See Skerry, *Psycho in the Shower*, 20. While Skerry stops short of developing this notion of abstraction further, his approach to Hitchcockian montage as essentially an abstract, rhythmic form leads to some very productive conclusions.
14. Peretz, *Becoming Visionary*, 158.
15. Williams, *Germaine Dulac*, 143.
16. Deleuze, *Cinema 1*, 8.
17. For a clear and comprehensive overview of continuity editing and its breach through "crossing the line," see Bordwell and Thompson, *Film Art*, 230–233.
18. *American Cinematographer Manual* (1966), cited in Paul Ramaeker, "Notes on the Split-Field Diopter," *Film History* 19 (2007), 180.
19. Ramaeker, "Notes on the Split-Field Diopter," 181; my emphasis.
20. For a discussion of the visual mechanics of the second shark attack sequence in *Jaws*, see Buckland, *Directed by Steven Spielberg*, 95–99. I also engage in a more expansive analysis of this sequence, including Spielberg's "*Vertigo* shot," in *The Orientation of Future Cinema: Technology, Aesthetics, Spectacle* (New York: Bloomsbury, 2013), 183–190.
21. For an analysis of Bazin's complicated position on German expressionist aesthetics (and modernist aesthetics more generally), see Daniel Morgan, "Bazin's Modernism," *Paragraph* 36.1 (2013), 10–30.
22. For an image of the enormous crane contraption used in this shot in *Notorious*, see Truffaut, *Hitchcock*, 171. For a useful examination of the mechanics of that shot, see Bruce Mamer, *Film Production Technique: Creating the Accomplished Image*, 5th ed. (Belmont, Calif.: Wadsworth Cengage Learning, 2009), 14–15.
23. For an invaluable study of the evolution of the zoom lens, see Barry Salt, *Film Style and Technology: History and Analysis* (London: Starword, 1983), 333–335. Salt suggests that the modern use of the zoom was restricted to a more experimental European cinema until the European New Wave cinemas started to influence American film styles. The use of the zoom by filmmakers such as Bava and Argento quickly became synonymous with a second-tier genre film industry.
24. Paul Willeman, "The Zoom in Popular Cinema: A Question of Performance," *Inter-Asia Cultural Studies* 14.1 (2013), 106.
25. Willeman, "The Zoom in Popular Cinema," 106.
26. John Belton, "The Bionic Eye: Zoom Esthetics," *Cinéaste* 11.1 (1980–1981), 21.

27. Quoted in Belton, "The Bionic Eye," 25.
28. Belton, "The Bionic Eye," 21.
29. Truffaut, *Hitchcock*, 246.
30. Church, "One on Top of the Other," 2.
31. M. Wood, *Italian Cinema*, 56–60.
32. For an analysis of Fulci's transnational productions, see Church, "One on Top of the Other," 1–20.
33. Bordwell, "Intensified Continuity," 16.
34. Bruce Isaacs, "The Mechanics of Continuity in Michael Bay's *Transformer's* Franchise," *Senses of Cinema* 75 (June 2015): http://sensesofcinema.com/2015/michael-bay-dossier/michael-bay-transformers-continuity/.
35. Belton, "The Bionic Eye," 27.
36. Salt, *Film Style and Technology*, 335.
37. Belton, "The Bionic Eye," 27.
38. I have selected *Don't Torture a Duckling* as exemplary of Fulci's excessive *giallo* style, but those interested should also view *The Psychic* (1977), a film Tarantino quotes in *Kill Bill: Volume 1* (2003).

Chapter 7

1. Jamie Sexton, "Avant-Garde Film: Sound, Music and Avant-Garde Film Culture Before 1939," in *Sound and Music in Film and Visual Media: A Critical Overview*, edited by Graeme Harper, Ruth Doughty, and Jochen Eisentraut (London: Bloomsbury, 2009), 576.
2. S. M. Eisenstein, V. I. Pudovkin, and G. V. Alexandrov, "A Statement," in *Film Sound: Theory and Practice*, edited by Elisabeth Weis and John Belton (New York: Columbia University Press, 1985), 83.
3. James Wierzbicki, *Film Music: A History* (New York: Routledge, 2009), 13–28.
4. Eisenstein, Pudovkin, and Alexandrov, "A Statement," 83.
5. René Clair, "The Art of Sound," in *Film Sound: Theory and Practice*, edited by Elisabeth Weis and John Belton (New York: Columbia University Press, 1985), 93.
6. For a seminal reading of the evolution of film sound as an "unstable" object, see Rick Altman, *Silent Film Sound* (New York: Columbia University Press, 2004).
7. Elisabeth Weis and John Belton, "Classical Sound Theory," in *Film Sound: Theory and Practice*, edited by Elisabeth Weis and John Belton (New York: Columbia University Press, 1985), 77.
8. Basil Wright and B. Vivian Braun, "Manifesto: Dialogue on Sound," in *Film Sound: Theory and Practice*, edited by Elisabeth Weis and John Belton (New York: Columbia University Press, 1985), 96.
9. Eisenstein, Pudovkin, and Alexandrov, "A Statement," 84.
10. V. I. Pudovkin, "Asynchronism as a Principle," in *Film Sound: Theory and Practice*, edited by Elisabeth Weis and John Belton (New York: Columbia University Press, 1985), 91.

11. Stephen Watts, "Music in Film: An Interview with Stephen Watts," in *Hitchcock on Hitchcock: Selected Writings and Interviews*, edited by Sidney Gottlieb (Berkeley: University of California Press, 1995), 242.
12. Clair, "The Art of Sound," 93.
13. Clair, "The Art of Sound," 95.
14. Michel Chion, *Film, a Sound Art*, translated by Claudia Gorbman (New York: Columbia University Press, 2009), 36.
15. Sexton, "Avant-Garde Film," 576–577.
16. Clair, "The Art of Sound," 92.
17. Sexton, "Avant-Garde Film," 584.
18. Kristin Thompson, "Early Sound Counterpoint," *Yale French Studies* 60 (1980), 115–140.
19. Sexton, "Avant-Garde Film," 582.
20. Elisabeth Weis, *The Silent Scream: Alfred Hitchcock's Sound Track* (London: Associated University Presses, 1982), 65.
21. Chion, *Film, a Sound Art*, 36.
22. Chion, *Film, a Sound Art*, 171.
23. Chion, *Film, a Sound Art*, 171.
24. Weis, *The Silent Scream*, 19.
25. Truffaut, *Hitchcock*, 276.
26. Roger Scruton, "Rhythm, Melody, and Harmony" in *The Routledge Companion to Philosophy and Music*, edited by Theodore Gracyk and Andrew Kania (New York: Routledge, 2011), 31.
27. Elder, *Harmony and Dissent*, 289.
28. Chion, *Film, a Sound Art*, 286.
29. For Chion, the dominant aesthetic approach to sound design in film is to render sound invisible, the unquestioned source of the visual image that is "especially at work in the case of sound/image synchronization." See Michel Chion, *Audio-Vision: Sound on Screen* (New York: Columbia University Press, 1994), 5–9.
30. Stanley Cavell, *The World Viewed: Reflections on the Ontology of Film* (Cambridge, Mass.: Harvard University Press, 1979), 18–20.
31. David Cooper, *Bernard Herrmann's Vertigo: A Film Score Handbook* (Westport, CT.: Greenwood, 2001), 18–19. I use the term "cue" rather than "theme" to designate a shorter melodic piece; a cue can also function as a melodic fragment, whereas a theme tends to connote complete melodic movements.
32. Cooper, *Bernard Herrmann's Vertigo*, 19.
33. Cooper, *Bernard Herrmann's Vertigo*, 36.
34. Brian De Palma, "Interview," in *Dressed to Kill* (Criterion Collection, 2015), DVD.
35. Leitch, "How to Steal from Hitchcock," 257.
36. Lawrence O'Toole, "Donaggio Domani," *Film Comment*, September/October 1981, 18.
37. Pino Donaggio, "Interview," in *Dressed to Kill* (Criterion Collection, 2015), DVD
38. Donaggio, "Interview."
39. Chion, *Film, a Sound Art*, 286.
40. Shaviro, *The Cinematic Body*, 74.

41. Shaviro, *The Cinematic Body*, 114.
42. For an analysis of sound as a sensorial assault in the films of Argento, see Tony Mitchell, "Prog Rock, the Horror Film, and Sonic Excess: Dario Argento, Morricone and Goblin," in *Terror Tracks: Music, Sound and Horror Cinema*, edited by Philip Hayward (Oakville, Conn.: Equinox, 2008), 94–95.
43. Angela Ndalianis, *The Horror Sensorium: Media and the Senses* (Jefferson, N.C.: McFarland, 2012), 4.
44. Weis, *The Silent Scream*, 65.
45. Andrei Tarkovsky, *Sculpting in Time: Reflections on the Cinema*, translated by Kitty Hunter-Blair (London: Faber, 1989), 162.
46. Quoted in Alex Ross, *The Rest Is Noise: Listening to the Twentieth Century* (London: Picador, 2008), 398.
47. Quoted in Mitchell, "Prog Rock, the Horror Film, and Sonic Excess," 93.
48. Mitchell, "Prog Rock, the Horror Film, and Sonic Excess," 93–94.
49. Watts, "Music in Film," 244.
50. Hatch suggests that the Goblin aesthetic emerged in part out of the musique concrète movement of the 1940s, which consisted of the "manipulation and use of collected 'concrete' sounds made by items that were not specifically created for musical expression." See Craig Hatch, "The Horror of Progressive Rock: Goblin and Horror Soundtracks," in *Italian Horror Cinema*, edited by Stefano Baschiera and Russ Hunter (Edinburgh: Edinburgh University Press, 2016), 179–182.
51. For an excellent analysis of this sequence as exemplary of the technical and stylistic achievement of the *giallo*, see Koven, *La Dolce Morte*, 131–132.
52. Schroeder, *Hitchcock's Ear*, 2.
53. Cooper, *Bernard Herrmann's* Vertigo, 17.
54. Bernard Herrmann, "Charles Ives" (1997), Historical Archive, Bernard Herrmann Historical Society website: http://www.bernardherrmann.org/articles/archive-trend/.
55. James Wierzbicki, "Psycho-analysis: Form and Function in Bernard Herrmann's Music for Hitchcock's Masterpiece," in *Terror Tracks: Music, Sound and Horror Cinema* (Oakville, Conn.: Equinox, 2008), 17.
56. Royal S. Brown, "Herrmann, Hitchcock, and the Music of the Irrational," *Cinema Journal* 21.2 (Spring, 1982), 17.
57. R. Brown, "Hermann, Hitchcock, and the Music of the Irrational," 31.
58. O'Toole, "Donaggio Domani," 18.
59. Stephen Husarik, "Transformation of 'The Psycho Theme,'" *Interdisciplinary Humanities* 26.2 (2009), 146.
60. Husarik, "Transformation of 'The Psycho Theme,'" 150.
61. Scruton, "Rhythm, Melody, and Harmony," 36.

Chapter 8

1. Gilles Deleuze, *Difference and Repetition* (New York: Columbia University Press, 1994), 262–272. Deleuze also equates the "subordination of difference" to the

"requirements of finite or infinite representation" (264). In this model, difference, in its irreducibility, is a pure rather than relational phenomenon. I also want to thank Robert Sinnerbrink for steering me toward an ethics (and, indeed, metaphysics) of the fragment in the Continental philosophical tradition. Following Robert's prompt, while this has been a book about an aesthetic of the fragment in relation to moving image form, I want to claim a deeper ambition underpinning my study of the fragment in Hitchcock and his imitators, which I hope to realize in another work. In Simon Critchley's influential analysis of a space of representation in the aftermath of a metaphysics of the whole, following Schlegel, he writes: "The romantic model for the literary absolute, the genre par excellence for romantic expression"—which I equate to something like a pure aesthetics—"is the *fragment*. Now, the specificity of the fragment, its uniqueness, is that it is a form that is both complete and incomplete, both a whole and a part. It is a form that embodies interruption within itself. That is to say, the fragment fails." I would add, chasing Critchley's thought, the fragment fails only in its perpetual deferment of the whole. The ontological category I have continually fallen back on to describe the artistic disposition of Hitchcock and his imitators—the fragment, the part, the breach, the segment, the rent, the *split*—with such categories instantiating excess, disorder, and irrationality—shares an aesthetic and philosophical resonance with Critchley's poetic response to nihilism drawn from the poetry of Wallace Stevens, among other modernists. See Simon Critchley, *Very Little . . . Almost Nothing: Death, Philosophy, Literature* (London: Routledge, 2004), 123–124.
2. Malte Hagener, "Down the Rabbit Hole with Brian De Palma," in *La Galassia Casetti: Lettere di Amicizia, Stima, Provocazione*, edited by Ruggero Eugeni and Mariagrazia Fanci (Milan: Vita e Pensiero, 2017), 140.
3. Michael J. Ostwald and Josephine Vaughn, *The Fractal Dimension of Architecture* (Basel: Birkhäuser, 2016), 7.
4. Adrian Martin and Cristina Álvarez López, "[De Palma's] VISION."
5. Deleuze, *Cinema 1*, 88.
6. Deleuze, *Cinema 1*, 89.
7. Deleuze, *Cinema 1*, 96.
8. Deleuze, *Cinema 1*, 96.
9. Elder, *Harmony and Dissent*, 4–5.
10. Tarkovsky, *Sculpting in Time*, 104.

Bibliography

Aitkin, Ian. *European Film Theory and Cinema: A Critical Introduction*. Bloomington: Indiana University Press, 2001.

Allen, Richard. *Hitchcock's Romantic Irony*. New York: Columbia University Press, 2007.

Altman, Rick. *Silent Film Sound*. New York: Columbia University Press, 2004.

Arnheim, Rudolf. *Film as Art*. Berkeley: University of California Press, 1957.

Barr, Charles. "Hitchcock and Early Filmmakers." In *A Companion to Alfred Hitchcock*, edited by Thomas Leitch and Leland Poague. Chichester, UK: Wiley-Blackwell, 2014, 48–66.

Barthes, Roland. "From Work to Text." In *Image-Music-Text*, translated by Stephen Heath. London: Fontana, 1977, 155–164.

Bazin, André. "An Aesthetic of Reality: Cinematic Realism and the Italian School of Liberation." In *What Is Cinema?*, vol. 2, translated by Hugh Gray. Berkeley: University of California Press, 1967, 16–40.

Bazin, André. "Cinematic Realism and the Italian School of Liberation." In *André Bazin and Italian Neorealism*, edited by Bert Cardullo. New York: Continuum, 2011, 29–50.

Bazin, André. "The Evolution of the Language of Cinema." In *What Is Cinema?*, vol. 1, translated by Hugh Gray. Berkeley: University of California Press, 1967, 23–40.

Bazin, André. "The Myth of Total Cinema." In *What Is Cinema?*, vol. 1, translated by Hugh Gray. Berkeley: University of California Press, 1967, 18–21.

Bazin, André. "The Ontology of the Photographic Image." In *What Is Cinema?*, vol. 1, translated by Hugh Gray. Berkeley: University of California Press, 1967, 9–16.

Bellour, Raymond. "A Bit of History," translated by Mary Quaintance. In *The Analysis of Film*, edited by Constance Penley. Bloomington: Indiana University Press, 2001, 1–20.

Bellour, Raymond. "Psychosis, Neurosis, Perversion." In *A Hitchcock Reader*, edited by Marshall Deutelbaum and Leland Poague, translated by Nancy Huston. Malden, Mass.: Wiley-Blackwell, 2009, 341–360.

Bellour, Raymond. "Symbolic Blockage (on *North by Northwest*)," translated by Mary Quaintance. In *The Analysis of Film*, edited by Constance Penley. Bloomington: Indiana University Press, 2001, 77–192.

Bellour, Raymond. "System of a Fragment (on *The Birds*)," translated by Ben Brewster. In *The Analysis of Film*, edited by Constance Penley. Bloomington: Indiana University Press, 2001, 28–67.

Bellour, Raymond. "To Alternate/To Narrate." In *Early Cinema: Space, Frame, Narrative*, edited by Thomas Elsaesser. London: British Film Institute, 1990, 360–374.

Belton, John. "The Bionic Eye: Zoom Esthetics." *Cinéaste* 11, no. 1 (1980–1981): 20–27.

Bergstrom, Janet. "Alternation, Segmentation, Hypnosis: Interview with Raymond Bellour." *Camera Obscura* 3 (1979): 70–103.

Biskind, Peter. *Easy Riders, Raging Bulls: How the Sex-Drugs-and-Rock 'n Roll Generation Saved Hollywood*. London: Bloomsbury, 1999.

Bondanella, Peter. *A History of Italian Cinema*. New York: Continuum, 2009.

Bordwell, David. "The Art Cinema as a Mode of Film Practice." *Film Criticism* 4, no. 1 (1979): 56–64.

Bordwell, David. "Intensified Continuity: Visual Style in Contemporary American Film." *Film Quarterly* 55, no. 3 (2002): 16–28.

Bordwell, David. *On the History of Film Style*. Cambridge, Mass.: Harvard University Press, 1997.

Bordwell, David, and Kristin Thompson. *Film Art: An Introduction*, 11th ed. New York: McGraw-Hill, 2017.

Bordwell, David, Kristin Thompson, and Janet Staiger. *The Classical Hollywood Cinema: Film Style and Mode of Production to 1960*. New York: Columbia University Press, 1985.

Branigan, Edward. *Point of View in the Cinema: A Theory of Narration and Subjectivity in Classical Film*. Berlin;: Mouton, 1984.

Brown, Phil. "Brian De Palma Talks *Passion, The Untouchables* Prequel, *Capone Rising*, and his upcoming Jason Statham Movie at TIFF 2012." *Collider*, September 13, 2012. http://collider.com/brian-de-palma-passion-untouchables-prequel-capone-rising/.

Brown, Royal S. "Herrmann, Hitchcock, and the Music of the Irrational." *Cinema Journal* 21, no. 2 (Spring 1982): 14–49.

Buckland, Warren. *Directed by Steven Spielberg: Poetics of the Contemporary Hollywood Blockbuster*. New York: Continuum, 2006.

Calabrese, Omar. *Neo-Baroque: A Sign of the Times*, translated by Charles Lambert. Princeton, N.J.: Princeton University Press, 1992.

Cavell, Stanley. *The World Viewed: Reflections on the Ontology of Film*. Cambridge, Mass.: Harvard University Press, 1979.

Childs, Peter. *Modernism*. New York: Routledge, 2016.

Chion, Michel. *Audio-Vision: Sound on Screen*. New York: Columbia University Press, 1994.

Chion, Michel. *Film, a Sound Art*, translated by Claudia Gorbman. New York: Columbia University Press, 2009.

Church, David. "One on Top of the Other: Lucio Fulci, Transnational Film Industries, and the Retrospective Construction of the Italian Horror Canon." *Quarterly Review of Film and Video* 32, no. 1 (2014): 1–20.

Clair, René. "The Art of Sound." In *Film Sound: Theory and Practice*, edited by Elisabeth Weis and John Belton. New York: Columbia University Press, 1985, 92–95.

Clair, René. "Pure Cinema and Commercial Cinema," translated by Stanley Appelbaum. In Richard Abel, *French Film Theory and Criticism: A History/Anthology*. Vol. 1, *1907–1929*. Princeton, N.J.: Princeton University Press, 1988, 370–371.

Collins, Jim. *Architectures of Excess: Cultural Life in the Information Age*. New York: Routledge, 1995.

Collins, Jim. "Genericity in the Nineties: Eclectic Irony and the New Sincerity." In *Film Theory Goes to the Movies*, edited by Jim Collins, Hilary Radner, and Ava Preacher Collins. New York: Routledge, 1993, 242–264.

Cooper, David. *Bernard Herrmann's* Vertigo: *A Film Score Handbook*. Westport, Conn.: Greenwood, 2001.

Critchley, Simon. *Very Little . . . Almost Nothing: Death, Philosophy, Literature*. London: Routledge, 2004.

Cubitt, Sean. *The Cinema Effect*. Cambridge, Mass.: MIT Press, 2005.

Danks, Adrian. "Being in Two Places at the Same Time: The Forgotten Geography of Rear-Projection." In *B Is for Bad Cinema: Aesthetics, Politics, and Cultural Value*, edited by Claire Perkins and Constantine Verevis. Albany: SUNY Press, 2014, 65–84.
Deleuze, Gilles. *Cinema 1: The Movement Image*, translated by Hugh Tomlinson and Barbara Habberjam. Minneapolis: University of Minnesota Press, 2009.
Deleuze, Gilles. *Cinema 2: The Time Image*, translated by Hugh Tomlinson and Barbara Habberjam. Minneapolis: University of Minnesota Press, 2009.
Deleuze, Gilles. *Difference and Repetition*, translated by Paul Patton. New York: Columbia University Press, 1995.
De Palma, Brian. "Body Double: The Set Up—Featurette." *Body Double*. Umbrella Entertainment, 2014. Blu-ray.
De Palma, Brian. "Interviews: Brian De Palma in Conversation with Noah Baumbach." *Dressed to Kill*. Criterion Collection, 2015. DVD
Donaggio, Pino. "Interview." *Dressed to Kill*. Criterion Collection, 2015. DVD.
Dulac, Germaine. "The Essence of the Cinema: The Visual Idea," translated by Robert Lamberton. In *The Avant-Garde Film: A Reader of Theory and Criticism*, edited by P. Adams Sitney. New York: New York University Press, 1978, 36–42.
Dulac, Germaine. "The Expressive Techniques of the Cinema," translated by Stuart Liebman. In Richard Abel, *French Film Theory and Criticism: A History/Anthology* Vol. 1, *1907–1929*. Princeton, N.J.: Princeton University Press, 1988, 305–314.
Dumas, Chris. *Un-American Psycho: Brian De Palma and the Political Invisible*. Bristol, UK: Intellect, 2012.
Durgnat, Raymond. "Cat and Mouse Games." In *The Essential Raymond Durgnat*, edited by Henry K. Miller. London: British Film Institute, 2014, 31–34.
Durgnat, Raymond. *A Long, Hard Look at Psycho*. London: British Film Institute, 2010.
Eco, Umberto. "*Casablanca*: Cult Movies and Intertextual Collage." In *The Cult Film Reader*, edited by Ernest Mathijs and Xavier Mendik. Maidenhead, UK: McGraw-Hill, 2008, 67–75.
Eisenstein, Sergei. "The Cinematographic Principle and the Ideogram." In *Film Form: Essays in Film Theory*, edited and translated by Jay Leyda. Orlando, Fla.: Harcourt, 1977, 28–44.
Eisenstein, S. M., V. I. Pudovkin, and G. V. Alexandrov. "A Statement." In *Film Sound: Theory and Practice*, edited by Elisabeth Weis and John Belton. New York: Columbia University Press, 1985, 83–85.
Eisner, Lotte H. *Murnau*. London: Secker & Warburg, 1973.
Elder, R. Bruce. *DADA, Surrealism, and the Cinematic Effect*. Toronto: Wilfred Laurier University Press, 2013.
Elder, R. Bruce. *Harmony and Dissent: Film and Avant-Garde Art Movements in the Early Twentieth Century*. Waterloo, Ont.: Wilfred Laurier Press, 2010.
Ellis, Bret Easton. "Unedited New York Times Quentin Tarantino Article." *Bret Eston Ellis* (blog), October 29 2015. http://breteastonellis.com/unedited-new-york-times-quentin-tarantino-article/.
Flitterman-Lewis, Sandy. *To Desire Differently: Feminism and the French Cinema*. New York: Columbia University Press 1996.
Genette, Gérard. *The Architext: An Introduction*, translated by Jane E. Lewin. Berkeley: University of California Press, 1992.
Gleiberman, Owen. "Why I Can't Love Brian De Palma (Though I've Always Wished I Could)." *Variety*, June 26, 2016. http://variety.com/2016/film/columns/why-i-cant-love-brian-de-palma-1201803932/.

Gottlieb, Sidney. "Early Hitchcock: The German Influence." In *Framing Hitchcock: Selected Essays from the Hitchcock Annual*, edited by Sidney Gottlieb and Christopher Brookhouse. Detroit: Wayne State University Press, 2002, 35–58.

Gromaire, Marcel. "A Painter's Ideas About the Cinema," translated by Stuart Liebman. In Richard Abel, *French Film Theory and Criticism: A History/Anthology*. Vol. 1, *1907–1929*. Princeton, N.J.: Princeton University Press, 1988, 174–182.

Gunning, Tom. "Hitchcock and the Picture in the Frame." *New England Review* 28, no. 3 (2007): 14–31.

Hagener, Malte. "The Aesthetics of Displays: How the Split Screen Remediates Other Media." *Refractory: A Journal of Entertainment Media* 14 (2008): http://refractory.unimelb.edu.au/2008/12/24/the-aesthetics-of-displays-how-the-split-screen-remediates-other-media-%E2%80%93-malte-hagener/.

Hagener, Malte. "Down the Rabbit Hole with Brian De Palma," in *La Galassia Casetti: Lettere di Amicizia, Stima, Provocazione*, edited by Ruggero Eugeni and Mariagrazia Fanci. Milan: Vita e Pensiero, 2017, 140–142.

Hansen, Miriam Bratu. "The Mass Production of the Senses: Classical Cinema as Vernacular Modernism." *Modernism/Modernity* 6, no. 2 (1999): 59–71.

Hatch, Craig. "The Horror of Progressive Rock: Goblin and Horror Soundtracks." In *Italian Horror Cinema*, edited by Stefano Baschiera and Russ Hunter. Edinburgh: Edinburgh University Press, 2016, 175–190.

Hayward, Susan. *Cinema Studies: The Key Concepts*. London: Routledge, 2000.

Heffernan, Kevin. "Art House or House of Exorcism? The Changing Distribution and Reception Contexts of Mario Bava's *Lisa and the Devil*." In *Sleaze Artists: Cinema at the Margins of Taste, Style, and Politics*, edited by Jeffrey Sconce. Durham, N.C.: Duke University Press, 2007, 144–163.

Herrmann, Bernard. "Charles Ives" (1997). The Bernard Herrmann Historical Society Archives. http://www.bernardherrmann.org/articles/archive-trend/.

Herzog, Todd. "'What Shall the History Books Read?' The Debate Over Inglorious Basterds and the Limits of Representation." In *Quentin Tarantino's* Inglourious Basterds: *A Manipulation of Metacinema*, edited by Robert von Dassanowsky. New York: Continuum, 2012, 271–296.

Hitchcock, Alfred. "Direction." In *Hitchcock on Hitchcock: Selected Writings and Interviews*, edited by Sidney Gottlieb. Berkeley: University of California Press, 1995, 253–261.

Hitchcock, Alfred. "The Kuleshov Effect." YouTube, October 22, 2012. https://www.youtube.com/watch?v=MCK53Lb4-pI.

Hitchcock, Alfred. "Lecture at Columbia University." In *Hitchcock on Hitchcock: Selected Writings and Interviews*, edited by Sidney Gottlieb. Berkeley: University of California Press, 1995, 267–274.

Hitchcock, Alfred. "On Style." In *Hitchcock on Hitchcock: Selected Writings and Interviews*, edited by Sidney Gottlieb. Berkeley: University of California Press, 1997, 285–302.

Horak, Jan-Christopher. "Discovering Pure Cinema: Avant-Garde Film in the '20s." *Afterimage* (Summer 1980): 3–9.

Husarik, Stephen. "Transformation of 'The Psycho Theme.'" *Interdisciplinary Humanities* 26, no. 2 (2009): 144–158.

Isaacs, Bruce. "The Mechanics of Continuity in Michael Bay's *Transformer's* Franchise." *Senses of Cinema* 75 (June 2015). http://sensesofcinema.com/2015/michael-bay-dossier/michael-bay-transformers-continuity/.

Isaacs, Bruce. *The Orientation of Future Cinema: Technology, Aesthetics, Spectacle.* New York: Bloomsbury, 2013.
Isaacs, Bruce. *Toward a New Film Aesthetic.* New York: Continuum, 2008.
Jacobs, Steven. *The Wrong House: The Architecture of Alfred Hitchcock.* Rotterdam: 010, 2007.
Kakmi, Dmetri. "The Key to De Palma's *Raising Cain*." *Senses of Cinema* 6 (May, 2000). http://sensesofcinema.com/2000/brian-de-palma/raising/.
Kannas, Alexia. "All the Colours of the Dark: Film Genre and the Italian *Giallo*." *Journal of Italian Cinema and Media Studies* 5, no. 2 (2017): 173–190.
Kapsis, Robert E. *Hitchcock: The Making of a Reputation.* Chicago: University of Chicago Press, 1992.
Keesey, Douglas. *Brian De Palma's Split-Screen: A Life in Film.* Jackson: University of Mississippi Press, 2017.
Kelly, David. "Narrative and Narration in John Ford's *The Searchers*." *Sydney Studies in English* 36 (2010): 170–201.
Kline, T. Jefferson. "The French New Wave." In *European Cinema*, edited by Elisabeth Ezra. Oxford: Oxford University Press, 2004, 157–175.
Koven, Mikel J. *La Dolce Morte: Vernacular Cinema and the Italian Giallo Film.* Lanham, Md.: Scarecrow, 2006.
Langford, Barry. *Film Genre: Hollywood and Beyond.* Edinburgh: Edinburgh University Press, 2005.
Leitch, Thomas M. "How to Steal from Hitchcock." In *After Hitchcock: Influence, Imitation, and Intertextuality*, edited by David Boyd and R. Barton Palmer. Austin: University of Texas Press, 2006, 251–270.
Lewis, Jon. *American Film: A History.* New York: Norton, 2008.
Liz, Luiza. "Alfred Hitchcock and the Art of Pure Cinema." *Art Regard*, YouTube, February 17 2017. https://www.youtube.com/watch?v=szmBC5rYEU8.
Lowenstein, Adam. "The *Giallo*/Slasher Landscape: *Ecologia del Delitto*, *Friday the 13th* and Subtractive Spectatorship." In *Italian Horror Cinema*, edited by Stefano Baschiera and Russ Hunter. Edinburgh: Edinburgh University Press, 2017, 127–144.
Mamer, Bruce. *Film Production Technique: Creating the Accomplished Image*, 5th ed. Belmont, Calif.: Wadsworth Cengage Learning, 2009.
Martin, Adrian. *Last Day Every Day: Figural Thinking from Auerbach to Agamben to Brenez.* Brooklyn: Punctum, 2012.
Martin, Adrian. *Mise en Scène and Film Style: From Classical Hollywood to New Media Art.* Basingstoke, UK: Palgrave, 2014.
Martin, Adrian. "A Walk Through *Carlito's Way*." *LOLA* 4 (2013). http://www.lolajournal.com/4/carlito.html.
Martin, Adrian, and Cristina Álvarez López, "[De Palma's] VISION." *Mubi Notebook*, June 3, 2014. https://mubi.com/notebook/posts/de-palmas-vision.
Maule, Rosanna. "The Importance of Being a Film Author: Germaine Dulac and Female Authorship." *Senses of Cinema* 23 (2002). http://sensesofcinema.com/2002/feature-articles/dulac/.
Met, Philippe. "'Knowing Too Much' about Hitchcock: The Genesis of the Italian *Giallo*." In *After Hitchcock: Influence, Imitation, and Intertextuality*, edited by David Boyd and R. Barton Palmer. Austin: University of Texas Press, 2006, 195–214.
Mitchell, Tony. "Prog Rock, the Horror Film, and Sonic Excess: Dario Argento, Morricone and Goblin." In *Terror Tracks: Music, Sound and Horror Cinema*, edited by Philip Hayward. Oakville, Conn.: Equinox, 2008, 88–100.

Modleski, Tania. *The Women Who Knew Too Much: Hitchcock and Feminist Theory.* New York: Routledge, 2016.

Morgan, Daniel. "Bazin's Modernism." *Paragraph* 36, no. 1 (2013): 10–30.

Morgan, Daniel. "Rethinking Bazin: Ontology and Realist Aesthetics." In *Critical Inquiry* 32, no. 3 (2006): 443–481.

Mulvey, Laura. "Visual Pleasure and Narrative Cinema." In *Feminism and Film Theory*, edited by Constance Penley. New York: Routledge, 1988, 57–68.

Nagib, Lúcia and Anne Jerslev. "Introduction." In *Impure Cinema: Intermedial and Intercultural Approaches to Film*, edited by Lúcia Nagib and Anne Jerslev. London: I. B. Tauris, 2014, xviii–xxxi.

Ndalianis, Angela. *The Horror Sensorium: Media and the Senses.* Jefferson, N.C. McFarland, 2012.

Nieves, Edwin Adrian. "Pure Cinema: An Analysis of Hitchcock Style." *A Bitter Sweet Life* (blog), July 17, 2017. https://vimeo.com/144058644.

Orr, John. *Hitchcock and Twentieth Century Cinema.* London: Wallflower, 2005.

Ostwald, Michael J. and Josephine Vaughn. *The Fractal Dimension of Architecture.* Basel: Birhauser, 2016.

O'Toole, Lawrence. "Donaggio Domani." *Film Comment*, September/October 1981, 18.

Peretz, Eyal. *Becoming Visionary: Brian De Palma's Cinematic Education of the Senses.* Stanford, Calif.: Stanford University Press, 2008.

Peucker, Brigitte. "Aesthetic Space in Hitchcock." In *A Companion to Alfred Hitchcock*, edited by Thomas Leitch and Leland Poague. Chichester, UK: Wiley-Blackwell, 2011, 199–218.

Pisano, Giusy. "The Théâtrophone, an Anachronistic Hybrid Experiment or One of the First Immobile Traveler Devices?" In *A Companion to Early Cinema*, edited by André Gaudreault, Nicolas Dulac, and Santiago Hidalgo. Malden, Mass.: Wiley-Blackwell, 2012, 80–98.

Piso, Michelle. "Mark's *Marnie*." In *A Hitchcock Reader*, edited by Marshall Deutelbaum and Leland Poague. Chichester, UK: Wiley-Blackwell, 2009, 280–294.

Pomerance, Murray. "Some Hitchcockian Shots." In *A Companion to Alfred Hitchcock*, edited by Thomas Leitch and Leland Poague. Chichester, UK: Wiley-Blackwell, 2011, 237–252.

Powell, Anna. "A Touch of Terror: Dario Argento and Deleuze's Cinematic Sensorium." In *European Nightmares: Horror Cinema in Europe Since 1945*, edited by Patricia Allmer, Emily Brick, and David Huxley. London: Wallflower, 2012, 167–180.

Prince, Stephen, and Wayne E. Hensley. "The Kuleshov Effect: Recreating the Classic Experiment." *Cinema Journal* 31, no. 2 (1992): 59–75.

Pudovkin, V. I. "Asynchronism as a Principle." In *Film Sound: Theory and Practice*, edited by Elisabeth Weis and John Belton. New York: Columbia University Press, 1985, 86–91.

Radner, Hilary, and Alastair Fox. *Raymond Bellour: Cinema and the Moving Image.* Edinburgh: Edinburgh University Press, 2018.

Ramaeker, Paul. "Notes on the Split-Field Diopter." *Film History* 19 (2007): 179–198.

Ross, Alex. *The Rest Is Noise: Listening to the Twentieth Century.* London: Picador, 2008.

Rothman, William. *Hitchcock—The Murderous Gaze.* Cambridge, Mass.: Harvard University Press, 1982.

Rothman, William. *The "I" of the Camera: Essays in Film Criticism, History and Aesthetics.* Cambridge: Cambridge University Press, 2004.

Salt, Barry. *Film Style and Technology: History and Analysis.* London: Starword, 1983.

Sanjek, David. "Fans' Notes: The Horror Film Fanzine." In *The Cult Film Reader*, edited by Ernest Mathijs and Xavier Mendik. New York: McGraw-Hill, 2008, 419–428.

Schroeder, David. *Hitchcock's Ear: Music and the Director's Art*. London: Continuum, 2012.

Sconce, Jeffrey. "Trashing the Academy: Taste, Excess and an Emerging Politics of Cinematic Style." *Screen* 36, no. 4 (1995): 371–393.

Sconce, Jeffrey. "Trashing the Academy: Taste, Excess and an Emerging Politics of Cinematic Style." In *The Cult Film Reader*, edited by Ernest Mathijs and Xavier Mendik. Maidenhead, UK: McGraw-Hill, 2008, 100–118.

Scruton, Roger. "Rhythm, Melody, and Harmony." In *The Routledge Companion to Philosophy and Music*, edited by Theodore Gracyk and Andrew Kania. New York: Routledge, 2011, 24–37.

Sexton, Jamie. "Avant-Garde Film: Sound, Music and Avant-Garde Film Culture before 1939." In *Sound and Music in Film and Visual Media: A Critical Overview*, edited by Graeme Harper, Ruth Doughty, and Jochen Eisentraut. London: Bloomsbury, 2009, 574–587.

Sharff, Stefan. *The Elements of Cinema: Toward a Theory of Cinesthetic Impact*. New York: Columbia University Press, 1982.

Shaviro, Steven. *The Cinematic Body*. Minneapolis: University of Minnesota Press, 1994.

Skerry, Philip J. *Dark Energy: Hitchcock's Absolute Camera and the Physics of Cinematic Spacetime*. London: Bloomsbury, 2015.

Skerry, Philip J. *Psycho in the Shower: The History of Cinema's Most Famous Scene*. New York: Continuum, 2009.

Spoto, Donald. *The Art of Alfred Hitchcock: Fifty Years of His Motion Pictures*. New York: Random House, 1992.

Stam, Robert, and Roberta Pearson. "Hitchcock's *Rear Window*: Reflexivity and the Critique of Voyeurism." *Enclitic* 7, no. 1 (1983): 136–145.

Sterritt, David. *The Films of Alfred Hitchcock*. Cambridge: Cambridge University Press, 1993.

Tarkovsky, Andrei. *Sculpting in Time: Reflections on the Cinema*, translated by Kitty Hunter-Blair. London: Faber, 1989.

Tatarkiewicz, Wladyslaw. "Abstract Art and Philosophy." *British Journal of Aesthetics* 2, no. 3 (1962): 227–238.

Thompson, Kristin. "The Concept of Cinematic Excess." *Ciné-Tracts: A Journal of Film, Communications, Culture, and Politics* 2 (1977): 54–63.

Thompson, Kristin. "Early Sound Counterpoint." *Yale French Studies* 60 (1980): 115–140.

Thompson, Kristin. *Storytelling in the New Hollywood: Understanding Classical Narrative Technique*. Cambridge, MA: Harvard University Press, 1999.

Tibbets, John C. *The American Theatrical Film: Stages in Development*. Bowling Green, Ohio: Bowling Green State University Popular Press, 1985.

Totaro, Donato. "A Genealogy of Italian Popular Cinema: the *Filone*." *Off-Screen* 15, no. 11 (2011). http://offscreen.com/view/genealogy_filone.

Truffaut, François. *Hitchcock: The Revised Edition*. New York: Simon & Schuster, 1985.

Turvey, Malcolm. *The Filming of Modern Life: European Avant-Garde Film of the 1920s*. Cambridge, Mass.: MIT Press, 2011.

Wardell, K. Brenna. "The Murderer in the Garden: Something Rotten in Hitchcock's Frenzy." In *Alfred Hitchcock*, edited by Douglas A. Cunningham. New York: Grey House, 2017, 173–191.

Watts, Stephen. "Music in Film: An Interview with Stephen Watts." In *Hitchcock on Hitchcock: Selected Writings and Interviews*, edited by Sidney Gottlieb. Berkeley: University of California Press, 1995, 241–245.

Weis, Elisabeth, *The Silent Scream: Alfred Hitchcock's Sound Track*. London: Associated University Presses, 1982.

Weis, Elisabeth, and John Belton. "Classical Sound Theory." In *Film Sound: Theory and Practice*, edited by Elisabeth Weis and John Belton. New York: Columbia University Press, 1985, 75–82.

Wierzbicki, James. *Film Music: A History*. New York: Routledge, 2009.

Wierzbicki, James. "Psycho-analysis: Form and Function in Bernard Herrmann's Music for Hitchcock's Masterpiece." In *Terror Tracks: Music, Sound and Horror Cinema*. Oakville, Conn.: Equinox, 2008, 14–46.

Willeman, Paul. "The Zoom in Popular Cinema: A Question of Performance." *Inter-Asia Cultural Studies* 14, no. 1 (2013): 104–109.

Williams, Tami Michelle. "Beyond Impressions: The Life and Films of Germaine Dulac From Aesthetics to Politics." PhD diss., University of California, Los Angeles, 2007.

Williams, Tami Michelle. *Germaine Dulac: A Cinema of Sensations*. Urbana: University of Illinois Press, 2014.

Williams, Tami Michelle. "The 'Silent' Arts: Modern Pantomime and the Making of an Art Cinema in the Belle Époque Paris: The Case of Georges Wague and Germaine Dulac." In *A Companion to Early Cinema*, edited by André Gaudreault, Nicolas Dulac and Santiago Hidalgo. Malden, Mass.: Wiley-Blackwell, 2012, 99–118.

Wood, Mary P. *Italian Cinema*. New York: Berg, 2005.

Wood, Robin. *Hitchcock's Films Revisited*. New York: Columbia University Press, 2002.

Wood, Robin. "Retrospective." In *A Hitchcock Reader*, edited by Marshall Deutelbaum and Leland Poague. Chichester, UK: Wiley-Blackwell, 2009, 35–46.

Wright, Basil, and B. Vivian Braun. "Manifesto: Dialogue on Sound." In *Film Sound: Theory and Practice*, edited by Elisabeth Weis and John Belton. New York: Columbia University Press, 1985, 96–97.

Wyatt, Justin. *High Concept: Movies and Marketing in Hollywood*. Austin: University of Texas Press, 1994.

Yacowar, Maurice. "Hitchcock's Imagery and Art." In *A Hitchcock Reader*, edited by Marshall Deutelbaum and Leland Poague. Chichester, UK: Wiley-Blackwell, 2009, 25–34.

YHCAM. "Cinematography." In Richard Abel, *French Film Theory and Criticism: A History/Anthology* Vol. 1, *1907–1929*. Princeton, N.J.: Princeton University Press, 1988, 67–76.

Žižek, Slavoj. "*Vertigo*: The Drama of a Deceived Platonist." *Hitchcock Annual* 12 (2003–2004): 67–82.

Filmography

The 36th Chamber of Shaolin. Dir. Liu Chia Liang (1978).
8 1/2. Dir. Federico Fellini (1963).
Apocalypse Now. Dir. Francis Ford Coppola (1979).
L'Avventura. Dir. Michelangelo Antonioni (1960).
The Awful Dr. Orloff. Dir Jesus Franco (1962).
A Bay of Blood (*Ecologia del delitto*). Dir. Mario Bava (1971).
The Birds. Dir. Alfred Hitchcock (1963).
The Bird with the Crystal Plumage (*L'uccello dale piume di cristallo*). Dir. Dario Argento (1970).
Blackmail. Dir. Alfred Hitchcock (1929).
Blade Runner. Dir. Ridley Scott (1981).
Blood and Black Lace (*Sei donne per l'assassino*). Dir. Mario Bava (1964).
Blow Out. Dir. Brian De Palma (1981).
Blow Up. Dir. Michelangelo Antonioni (1966).
Body Double. Dir. Brian De Palma (1984).
Carlito's Way. Dir. Brian De Palma (1993).
Carrie. Dir. Brian De Palma (1976).
Un Chien Andolou (*The Andalusian Dog*). Dir. Luis Buñuel and Salvador Dalí (1929).
Citizen Kane. Dir. Orson Welles (1941).
The Conformist (*Il Conformista*). Dir. Bernardo Bertolucci (1970).
The Conversation. Dir. Francis Ford Coppola (1974).
Dario Argento: An Eye for Horror. Dir. Leon Ferguson (2000).
Death in Venice. Dir. Luchino Visconti (1971).
Deep Red (*Profondo Rosso*). Dir. Dario Argento (1975).
De Palma. Dir. Noah Baumbach and Jake Paltrow (2015).
Disque 927. Dir. Germaine Dulac (1928).
Don't Look Now. Dir. Nicholas Roeg (1973).
Don't Torture a Duckling (*Non si Sevizia Paperino*). Dir. Lucio Fulci (1972).
Dressed to Kill. Dir. Brian de Palma (1980).
Emak-Bakia. Dir. Man Ray (1926).
Foreign Correspondent. Dir. Alfred Hitchcock (1940).
The French Connection. Dir. William Friedkin (1971).
Frenzy. Dir. Alfred Hitchock (1972).
Friday the 13th. Dir. Sean S. Cunningham (1980).
Fury. Dir. Brian De Palma (1978).
Gattaca. Dir. Andrew Niccol (1997).
The Girl Who Knew Too Much (*La Ragazza che Sapeva Troppo*). Dir. Mario Bava (1963).
The Godfather. Dir. Francis Ford Coppola (1972).
Halloween. Dir. John Carpenter (1976).
Hatchet for the Honeymoon (*Il Rosso Segno Della Follia*). Dir. Mario Bava (1970).
High Noon. Dir. Fred Zinnemann (1952).

Inferno. Dir. Dario Argento (1980).
Kill Bill: Volume 1. Dir. Quentin Tarantino (2003).
Lisa and the Devil (*Lisa e il Diavolo*). Dir. Mario Bava (1973).
The Lodger. Dir. Alfred Hitchcock (1927).
Marnie. Dir. Alfred Hitchcock (1964).
The Man Who Knew Too Much. Dir. Alfred Hitchcock (1934).
The Man Who Knew Too Much. Dir. Alfred Hitchcock (1956).
Man With a Movie Camera. Dir. Dziga Vertov (1929).
The Matrix. Dir. The Wachowskis (1999).
Mean Streets. Dir. Martin Scorsese (1973).
Mission: Impossible. Dir. Brian De Palma (1996).
Murder a la Mod. Dir. Brian De Palma (1968).
Necronomicon. Dir. Jesus Franco (1967).
North by Northwest. Dir. Alfred Hitchcock (1959).
Nosferatu. Dir. F. W. Murnau (1922).
Obsession. Dir. Brian De Palma (1976).
Once Upon a Time in the West (*C'era una Volta il West*). Dir. Sergio Leone (1967).
Opera. Dir. Dario Argento (1987).
Passion. Dir. Brian De Palma (2012).
The Psychic. Dir. Lucio Fulci (1977).
Psycho. Dir. Alfred Hitchcock (1960).
Raging Bull. Dir. Martin Scorsese (1980).
Rain Man. Dir. Barry Levinson (1988).
Raising Cain. Dir. Brian De Palma (1992).
Rear Window. Dir. Alfred Hitchcock (1954).
Reservoir Dogs. Dir. Quentin Tarantino (1992).
Le Retour à la Raison. Dir. Man Ray (1923).
Rhythm 21. Dir. Hans Richter (1921).
Rhythm 23. Dir. Hans Richter (1923).
Rope. Dir. Alfred Hitchcock (1948).
The Searchers. Dir. John Ford (1956).
Secret Agent. Dir. Alfred Hitchcock (1936).
Shadow of a Doubt. Dir. Alfred Hitchcock (1943).
Sisters. Dir. Brian De Palma (1973).
Snake Eyes. Dir. Brian De Palma (1998).
Spellbound. Dir. Alfred Hitchcock (1945).
Strangers on a Train. Dir. Alfred Hitchcock (1950).
Suspiria. Dir. Dario Argento (1977).
Sunrise. Dir. F. W. Murnau (1925).
Taxi Driver. Dir. Martin Scorsese (1976).
Tenebrae. Dir. Dario Argento (1980).
Théme et Variations. Dir. Germaine Dulac (1928).
The Thomas Crown Affair. Dir. Norman Jewison (1968).
To Catch a Thief. Dir. Alfred Hitchcock (1955).
Topaz. Dir. Alfred Hitchcock (1969).
Torn Curtain. Dir. Alfred Hitchcock (1966).

The Untouchables. Dir. Brian De Palma (1987).
Vertigo. Dir. Alfred Hitchcock (1958).
Vivre Sa Vie. Dir. Jean-Luc Godard (1962).
Waltzes from Vienna. Dir. Alfred Hitchcock (1934).
The Wedding Party. Dir. Brian De Palma, Wilford Leach, and Cynthia Munroe (1969).

Index

Figures are indicated by *f* following the page number

For the benefit of digital users, indexed terms that span two pages (e.g., 52–53) may, on occasion, appear on only one of those pages.

absolute-film movement, 209–10
abstract aesthetic form, 113, 120
abstraction
   avant-garde cinema and, 92
   cinéma pur as, 17, 23, 40, 89–90
   expression and, 89–94
   in *Frenzy,* 40
   in the *giallo,* 108, 113, 120
   in *The Lodger,* 27–29, 40
   in *Marnie,* 39–40, 96–97, 135, 140
   in mise en scène or montage, 138–39
   in *North by Northwest,* 103–4, 105, 106*f*
   optical abstraction, 103*f*
   pure abstract soundscape in *Psycho,* 181–84
   schematic frame and, 30
   split diopter image and, 148–56
   in *Vertigo,* 27–29, 140
   the zoom and, 156–58
aesthetic modernism, 15–16
aesthetic realism
   Bazin's comment on, 43
   of Bergman, Godard, Fellini, Cassavetes, 43
   components of, 89–90
   influence on Italian New Wave cinemas, 43
aesthetic space, 114–15
affective counterpoint, 108
Aitkin, UU, 2
Alexandrov, G. V., 164, 165
Allen, Nancy, 145, 147*f*
Allen, Richard, 215n28
"alternation" notion of Bellour, 185
Altman, Robert, 94
Álvarez López, Adrian, 7–8

American International Pictures (AIP), 5–6, 46
American New Wave Cinema, 6–7
American vernacularism, of De Palma, 50–51
Animal Trilogy (Argento), 47
antimodernist stance, of Hitchock, 43–44
Antonioni, Michelangelo, 42–43
Apocalypse Now (Coppola), 6–7
Argento, Dario, 5. *See also specific films*
   abstract aesthetic form of, 120
   adventurous frame compositions of, 117
   aesthetic space and, 114–15
   aural excess in films of, 177–79
   Bava's influence on, 119*f*
   compositional choices by, 71–72
   the fragment in films of, 186
   geometric compositions of, 117–18
   giallo in films by, 71–73, 72*f*
   imitation of Hitchcock, 6, 186
   Inferno, 46–47
   Kermode's comment on, 120
   line cross and, 138–44
   on meeting Sergio Leone, 48
   Mitchell's study of, 231n42
   montages in films of, 71–72
   Opera, 47
   pure cinema mode of, 41–42
   schematic framing in films of, 108
   Tenebrae, 8–10
   use of the zoom, 158
   whole-part relation in films of, 69–70
   Wood's comments on, 114
art films, 43–44
"Asynchronism as a Principle of Sound Film" (Pudovkin), 164–65

aural counterpoint, 93f, 169, 218n37
avant-garde
    application of sound in films, 19
    influence on Hitchcock, 165–66, 186
    pure cinema and, 15–19
The Awful Dr. Orloff (Franco), 156–57
axial composition, 91f, 92

badfilm subgenre, 49–50
Battleship Potemkin (Bronenosets Potyomkin, Eisenstein), 79–83, 80f
Baumbach, Noah, 6–7
Bava, Mario. *See also specific films*
    abstract aesthetic form of, 113, 120
    compositional segmentation in films of, 109f
    the fragment in films of, 186
    Hatchet for the Honeymoon, 47
    Hitchcock's influence on, 5, 108
    imitation of Hitchcock, 186
    influence on Argento, De Palma, Fulci, 112
    Lisa and the Devil, 47
    montages in films by, 46–47
    pure cinema mode of, 41–42
    schematic framing in films of, 108–14, 120
    use of color as compositional element, 112
    use of the zoom, 158
    use use of the zoom, 158
    whole-part relation in films of, 69–70
A Bay of Blood (Bava), 5, 108, 158, 176
    compositional segmentation in, 109f
    "figure as fragment" in, 118f
    the fragment and, 186
    intensified close-up in, 110f
    replicated figures in reflection in, 111f
Bazin, André, 33–34
    comment on aesthetic realism, 43
    discussions of cinema's depication of the "real," 219n45
    metacinematic image and, 121
    myth of total cinema and, 163, 227n1
    ontology of realist image of, 218n41
    split frame and, 127–28, 155–56, 161
    text on rear projection technique, 219–20n56

beach-party musicals, 49–50
Bellour, Raymond, 1
    "alternation" notion of, 185
    analysis of Hitchcock's work, 64, 66–67, 77, 227–28n9
    formal segmentation notion of, 225n32
    on segmentation, 127, 129–31, 146–47
    studies of Hitchcock, 64–65, 71–72
Belmondo, Jean-Paul, 43
Belton, John, 156–58, 163
Bergman, Ingmar
    modernist aesthetic sensibility of, 43
    The Seventh Seal, 42
    Wild Strawberries, 42
birds-eye view, 94–97
The Birds (Hitchcock), 2, 5, 73
    Bellour's analysis of, 64
    birds-eye view in, 94–97
    Chion's analysis of, 167–68
    giallo sequence in, 73–75, 74f, 76f
    graphic violence in, 74f, 76f
    Hitchcockian gaze in, 21–22
    intrinsic incompletion in, 186
    modernist proclivity of, 43–44
    sound-image relationship in, 169–70
    topographic framing in, 95f, 95–97, 225n28
The Bird with the Crystal Plumage (L'uccello dale piume di cristallo) (Argento), 41–42
    aesthetic space in, 114–15
    aural excess in, 176
    the fragment and, 186
    framing in, 114, 119
    impact of aural excess, 176
    modernist pictorial-cinematic space in, 116f
    rotational geometric form in, 119f
    schematic framing in, 120
    shapes and patterning in, 118f
    vertical axis shot in, 117f
Blackmail (Hitchcock), 90, 102–3, 103f, 127–28, 166–67, 227n6
Black Sunday (La Manchera del Demonio) (Bava), 46
Blood and Black Lace (Sei donne per l'assassino) (Bava), 41–42, 46–47

compositional iconography of *giallo* in, 119*f*
geometric partitioning in, 112*f*
giallo in, 113
interior design in, 119*f*
use of the zoom in, 158
Blow Out (De Palma), 127
avant-garde and, 210
discretized sound/vision in, 155*f*
the fragment and, 186
Peretz's comment on, 131–32
slow motion sequence, 186–87
split diopter images in, 151, 153, 154*f*
Blow Up (Antonioni), 46–47
Body Double (De Palma), 8–10
deconstructed architectural space diegesis, 125*f*
schematic establishing shot in, 123*f*, 123
split frame in, 151
Bordwell, David, 227n4
Branigan, Edward, 218n28
Breathless (Truffaut and Godard), 42, 43–44, 75
Buckland, Warren, 221n40
Buñuel, Luis, 15–17, 27–29

Caine, Michael, 144, 145*f*, 147*f*
Calabrese, Omar, 84, 222n18
Cape Fear (Scorsese), 175–76
car chase montage, 4
Carlito's Way (De Palma)
elasticity of cinematic visuality in, 56–57
generic, tonal, rhythmic transition in, 56
Martin's structural analysis of, 50–51
schematic framing in, 51*f*, 55–56, 57*f*
split screen effect in, 21–22, 52
Carrie (De Palma), 175
Cassavetes, John, 43
Un Chien Andalou (The Andalusian dog) (Buñuel), 15–17, 27–29
Chion, Michel, 167–68, 170, 175–76, 230n29
Chomette, Henri, 16–17
cinéma pur. *See* pure cinema
Clair, René, 16–17, 105–7, 164, 165–68
classical style, 42–45, 64–66, 68, 84–86, 90, 111–12, 148–49, 186, 225–26n1
Collins, Jim, 86

communicative frame, 85
compositional counterpoint, 94, 169
compositional reflexivity, 86–87
compositional segmentation, 109*f*
Connery, Sean, 8–10, 53
contrapuntal sound, 168–75
The Conversation (Coppola), 6–7
Coppola, Francis Ford. *See also* *specific films*
art-house/New Wave sensibility of, 6–7
creation of American art cinema form, 53
Corman, Roger, 5–6, 46
Costner, Kevin, 53, 77–78
counterpoint
affective counterpoint, 108
aural counterpoint, 93*f*, 169, 218n37
compositional counterpoint, 94, 169
Eisensteinian counterpoint, 168
in Hitchcockian method, 102, 168
montage and, 92
musical counterpoint, 94, 169, 174–75
musical/orchestral counterpoint, 165, 169, 174–75
nonsynchronic counterpoint, 170
rhythmic counterpoint, 175–76
Schroeder's comment on, 218n37
spatial contrast and, 94
Thompson's study of, 166–67
use in sound design, 168
visual counterpoint, 93*f*, 169, 218n37
Wright's/Braun's dismissal of, 165
Coyote, Peter, 202
Cruise, Tom, 148–49, 149*f*
Cubitt, Sean, 94
cult films, 49–50, 220n4, 221n31

Dada, 15–16
Dalí, Salvador, 15–17, 27–29
Death in Venice (Visconti), 156–57
deconstructed architectural space diegesis, 125*f*
Deep Red (Argento)
the fragment and, 186
giallo in, 113
impact of aural excess, 177–78
schematic framing in, 120
split diopter images in, 153

Deleuze, Gilles, 42
  description of the close-up, 203–5
  description of the fragment, 186
  on "motoricity," 223n36
  position on Eisenstein's montage, 222n7
  split frame and, 139
  on the "subordination of difference," 231–32n1
De Palma, Brian, 5. *See also specific films*
  admiration for Spielberg, 53
  American New Wave Cinema and, 6–7
  American vernacularism of, 50–57
  Bava's influence on, 119*f*
  comments on *Sisters*, 52–53
  comparison with Hitchcock, 6–7
  description of pure cinema, 18
  Dumas's comment on, 214n13
  giallo and, 10, 119
  "haunted cinema" of, 139
  Hitchcock's imitation of, 41–42
  imitation of Eisenstein, 77–83
  imitation of Hitchcock, 7, 8–10, 41–42, 52–53, 119, 186, 209
  Keesey's comment on, 123–24
  metacinematic schematization by, 120–26
  montages in the films of, 7, 8–10, 82, 83
  Peretz's study of films of, 46–47
  pure cinema mode of, 41–42
  rear projection technique of, 120–22, 122*f*, 226n14
  segmentation and, 7–8, 145*f*
  shared vernacular visuality with Hitchcock, 48–49
  spatial experiments with architectural spaces, 131–32
  split diopter lens used by, 148, 151–56
  split frame and, 21–22, 127–29, 138–39, 140–47, 145*f*, 147*f*
depth of field frame, 114–15
dialectical montage, 108, 174–75
Dickinson, Angie, 8–10, 171
diegetic gaze, 26–27
diegetic sound (soundscape), 77–78, 82, 177, 179–81
diegetic space, 56, 79, 86–87, 97–98
diegetic storytelling, 67
Disque (Dulac), 18

La Dolce Vita (Fellini), 42, 43
Donaggio, Pino, 171, 173–75
Don't Look Now (Roeg), 175
Don't Torture a Duckling (Non si Sevizia un Paperino) (Fulci), 8–10, 47, 158–63
  abstract geometric form in the *giallo* in, 155*f*
  diegetic/nondiegetic sound in, 180–81
  the fragment and, 186
  intensified segmentation in, 158, 160*f*
  reflexive depth of field composition in, 161*f*
  simulated split diopter perspective in, 162*f*
  soundscape, 181*f*
Dressed to Kill (De Palma), 7, 8*f*, 8–10
  the fragment and, 186
  giallo film tropes in, 119
  imitation of *Psycho*, 171–73
  soundscape in, 171–75
  split frame in, 144–47, 145*f*, 147*f*, 151
Dulac, Germaine. *See also specific films*
  cinema pur films of, 18
  description of pure cinema, 23
  emphasis on image as rhythmic form, 118
  experimental works of, 32
  montages in films by, 17, 20
  montages of, 20
  Williams' analysis of, 217n16
Dumas, Chris, 214n13
Durgnat, Raymond, 44–45, 84

Eggeling, Viking, 89, 91–92, 209–10
Eisenstein, Sergei, 61–64
  Battleship Potemkin, noncontinuous cutting sequence, 79, 80*f*
  challenge of Kuleshov, 61–62
  comment on the montage, 164
  Deleuze's analysis of, 222n7
  De Palma's imitation of, 77–83
  dialectical dialogue of, 108
  influence on Hitchcock, 61, 62
  montage in films of, 108
  montages in films by, 61–64, 70–71, 79, 83
  on talking in movies, 164

total cinema myth and, 61–64
on "total film," 70–71, 137–38
use of counterpoint, 168–69
visual/sound counterpoint of, 169
Elder, R. Bruce, 89, 92
Elvis flicks, 49–50
Emak-Bakia (Man Ray), 16
Entr'acte (Clair), 16–17
"The Essence of Cinema-The Visual Idea" (Dulac), 18
evolution of cinema, 15–16
expanded contrapuntal sound, 168–71
exploitation cinema, 45, 49–50
expressionism, 15–17, 19
expressive frame, 85–89
expressive montage, 62–63, 135, 168

Fellini, Federico, 42, 43
Femme Fatale (De Palma), 6
  close-up without a frame, 202–6, 203*f*, 204*f*
  description/story line, 187–88
  the fractal image in, 77, 185–210
  frame breakdown, Notre Dame de la Croix sequence, 190, 191–200*f*
  shapes/patterns, Notre Dame de la Croix sequence, 188–90
  split gaze in, 207*f*
  use of the zoom in, 209–10
figural form
  in close-up, 204*f*
  Martin's analysis of, 226n2
  in *Vertigo*, 27–29, 47, 132–34
film direction, Hitchcock's comments on, 3–4
filone Italian film genre, 45, 158–59
Ford, John, 86–87, 224n7
Foreign Correspondent (Hitchcock), 75
  giallo tendency in, 73
  Hitchcock-Truffaut dialogue on, 68–69
formal segmentation, 63, 91–92, 225n32
Foster, Barry, 31
Four Flies on Grey Velvet (Argento), 129*f*, 129, 140
The 400 Blows (*Les Quatre cent coup*) (Truffaut and Godard), 42–43
fractal images
  in *Femme Fatale*, 77

fragments and, 185–88
split frame and, 138–39
the fragment
  in Argento's films, 71–72
  in Bava's films, 84–85, 111–12, 113–14, 186
  Deleuze's description of, 186
  in De Palma's films, 77–83, 173–74, 186
  description, 185
  fractals and, 185–88
  fragments within, 77–83
  frame/segmented frame and, 39–40, 55, 162–63
  in Fulci's films, 186
  gaze as, 206–9
  giallo and, 69
  in Hitchcock's films, 127–28
  montage and, 69–70, 114–15, 127, 146–47
  pure cinema and, 10–11
  split frame and, 127–28, 131–35, 139
  the zoom and, 163
frames (framing), 84–107, 114. *See also* frames within frames; schematic frame; segmentation
  abstraction, expression, and, 89–94
  adventurous frame compositions of, 117
  in Argento's films, 47, 72–73, 114
  in *Blood and Black Lace,* 46–47
  in *Breathless,* 43
  in *Carlito's Way,* 22, 50–52, 56
  in De Palma's films, 5, 7–8, 8*f*, 50–51, 51*f*, 55–56
  depth of field frame, 114–15
  expressive frame, 85–89
  as fragment, 84–85
  in *Frenzy,* 31–34
  geometric figuring within, 117, 190
  giallo and, 41–42, 49–50, 71
  Hitchcockian method and, 4, 18–19, 24–26, 63, 64, 69, 90
  in *The Lodger,* 26, 27–29
  in *Marnie,* 38–40
  mise en scène and, 16–17, 26–27, 85–87, 89–90, 97
  montage and, 23
  of the "other," 227n17
  in *Psycho,* 37–38

frames (framing) (cont.)
    in *Rear Window*, 1–2, 21, 86
    in *The Searchers*, 86
    split frame, 127–38
    theatre's influence on, 15
    topographic framing, 95–97, 225n28
    transgressive framing, 99f, 135, 140–44, 151, 227–28n9
    in *The Untouchables*, 53–54, 78, 82
    in *Vertigo*, 110–11
    frames within frames, 24–26, 98–102, 109, 112, 114–15, 118, 131–32, 146, 159–60, 198–201
Franco, Jesús, 156–57
Franklin, Richard, 5–6
The French Connection (Friedkin), 4
French New Wave cinema, 42
Frenzy (Hitchcock), 2, 3, 5, 30f
    close-up, fetishistic image in, 31f, 35f
    fast zoom in, 32
    geometric form experimentation in, 18
    graphic realism in, 30–32, 33f, 34–35
    libidinal cinematic gaze in, 36
    liminal close-up in, 109–10
    reflexivity in, 29–34, 36
Friedkin, William, 4
Fulci, Lucio. See also *Don't Torture a Duckling*
    Bava's influence on, 119f
    the fragment in films of, 186
    imitation of Hitchcock, 6, 186
    soundscapes in films of, 180–81
futurism, 15–16

Garcia, Andy, 77–78
gaze
    cinematic gaze, 26–27, 27f, 36
    diegetic gaze, 26–27
    as fragment, 206–9
    Hitchcockian gaze, 21f, 21–22
    scopophilic gaze, 137f
    split gaze, *Femme Fatale*, 207f
Genette, Gérard, 10–11
geometric figuring within frames, 117, 190
geometric form
    in Argento's films, 117–18
    expressionism and, 16–17
    geometric partitioning, 112f, 135

    in Hitchcock's films, 3, 18, 97, 100f, 102
    in line and movement, 100f
    in Richter's/Eggeling's films, 89
giallo, 8–10, 45–47
    in Argento's films, 45–47, 71–73, 72f
    in Bava's films, 45–47, 108–14, 120
    De Palma and, 10–11
    description, 8–10, 45, 113, 214n19
    diegetic/nondiegetic sound in, 179–81
    excessive stylistic excesses in, 68–73
    in Fulci's films, 45–47, 158–59
    giallo set piece, 68–73
    Hansen's comments on, 48–49
    Hitchcock's link to, 10–11, 16, 41–42, 73–75
    impact of aural excess in, 175–81
    Koven's comments on, 44–45, 48–49, 70–71
    medium specificity and, 48–49
    montages and, 71
    paracinema and, 49–50
    requirements in viewing, 70–71
    schematic frame in, 108–26
    Thomson's analysis of, 70–71
    as "vernacular cinema," 48–49
The Girl Who Knew Too Much (*a Ragazza che Sapeva Troppo*, Bava), 46–47, 73, 108, 113
Gleiberman, Owen, 6–7, 8–10
Goblin aesthetic, 178–79, 231n50
Godard, Jean Luc
    The 400 Blows, 42
    Breathless, 42, 43–44, 75
golden age of Hitchcock, 2
government hygiene films, 49–50
Greenwich Village, New York, 2
Griffith, D. W.
    models of affection-image of, 203–5
    montages in films by, 15

Halloween (Carpenter), 153
Hansen, Miriam Bratu, 48–49
Hanson, Curtis, 5–6
Hatchet for the Honeymoon (*Il Ross Segno Della Follia*, Bava), 47
Hays code, 30–31, 43–44
Hedren, Tippi, 170
Hemmings, David, 177

Herrmann, Bernard, 67–68, 171–75, 181–84
Herzog, UU, 121
Heyward, UU, 16–17
High Noon (Leone), 77
Hitchcock, Alfred. *See also* Hitchcockian method; *specific films*
　Allen's analysis of, 65–66
　antimodernist stance of, 43–44
　appearance in *The Lodger,* 24–26
　appropriation of European avant-garde, 18
　avant-garde's influence on, 165–66, 186
　Bellour's studies of, 64–65, 71–72
　beyond the shot/the part and the whole in, 3–10
　claim of "suspense film" monopoly, 90
　"classical style" in films of, 64–66, 68, 84–85, 90, 148–49, 186, 225–26n1
　comment on pure film, 19–20
　comments on Arbogast's death in *Psycho,* 91–92
　De Palma's imitation of, 7, 8–10, 41–42, 52–53, 119, 209
　description of pure cinema, 18
　on directorial method, 3–4
　discussions with Truffaut, 1–2, 68–69, 90
　Eisenstein's influence on, 61, 62
　European influence on, 217n21
　expressionism's influence on, 19
　fascination with geometric form, 3
　fascination with movement, rhythm, 19
　fetishization of film form by, 64
　"golden age" of, 2
　imitation of De Palma, 41–42
　opposition to visual image-sound synchronization, 18
　Rothman's comment on, 213n4
　self-reflection on career, 225n37
　shared vernacular visuality with De Palma, 48–49
　spectator immersion technique, 44–45
　Tarantino's criticism of, 5–6
　Thompson's analysis of, 4
　Wood's study of, 220n14
Hitchcockian method. *See also* frames (framing); gaze; split frame
　aural counterpoint, 93*f,* 218n37
　aural excesses, 175–81
　avant-garde influences, 165–66
　axial composition, 91*f,* 92
　Bellour's study of, 64, 66–67, 77, 227–28n9
　beyond the shot/the part and the whole in, 3–10
　compositional reflexivity, 86–87
　contrapuntal sound and, 171–75
　counterpoint, 168
　critics/filmmakers interests in, 4
　depth of field frame, 114–15
　description, 1–5, 16
　desire for abstraction in images, 89–90
　duality in, 84
　expanded contrapuntal sound, 168–70
　geometric form and, 18, 97, 100*f,* 102, 127–28
　geometric framing, 123
　Hitchcockian gaze, 21*f*
　imitators of, 5–11
　metteur en scène method, 29–30
　mise en scène and, 84–85
　montages in films, 4, 24–26, 61, 64, 67–70
　the reflected body in, 26
　schematic framing and, 64–65, 97–98
　schematic framing in, 64–65
　Scorsese on, 4
　split frame, 131–34, 137–40, 146–47, 148–49, 151–52
Hoffman, Dustin, 148–49, 149*f*

impressionism, 15–16
Inferno (Argento), 46–47, 113–14
Inglorious Bastards (Tarantino), 121
intensified segmentation, 158–63
investigative narratives, 46–47
Italy. *See also giallo*
　filone film genre, 45
　New Wave cinemas, 43
　poliziotteschi, crime film, 45
Ives, Charles, 181–83

Japanese monster movies, 49–50
Jaws (Spielberg), 150, 151*f,* 228n20
jazz films, 43
Jeux des reflets de la vitesse (Chomette), 17

Katz, Alex, 172–73
Keesey, Douglas, 123–24
Kermode, Mark, 120
kinesthetic elements (Sharff), 223n40
Koven, Mikel, 44–45, 48–49, 70–71
Kuleshov effect, 19–20, 61–62, 218n25

The Last Laugh (*Der Letzte Mann*, Murnau), 19
L'Avventura (Antonioni), 42–43, 46–47
Leone, Sergio, 48, 77. *See also specific films*
Levinson, Barry, 148–49, 149f, 150
line cross segmentation, 138–44, 142f
Lisa and the Devil (*Lisa e il Diavolo*) (Bava)
    abstract aesthetic form in, 113
    Nietzschean eternal return in, 113–14
    restrained visuality in, 113–14
The Lodger (Hitchcock), 3, 23–29
    avant-garde influence on, 165–66
    cinematic gaze in, 26–27, 27f, 146–47
    depth of field frame in, 114–15
    description, 23–24
    excessive point of view in, 28f
    experimental mise en scène in, 25f
    geometric form experimentation in, 18, 87
    Hitchcock's appearance in, 24–26
    mechanical visual form in, 23–29
    split-screen effect in, 146–47, 186
    Spoto's comment on, 23–24
    Truffaut/Hitchcock's discussion on, 23–24, 26
Lucas, George, 6–7

Man Ray (Emmanuel Radnitzky), 16
The Man Who Knew Too Much (Hitchcock), 2, 46–47, 97
Man with a Movie Camera (Vertov), 26
Marnie (Hitchcock), 2–3
    abstraction in, 39–40, 96–97, 135
    baroque color palette in, 46–47
    color as compositional element in, 112
    framing in, 38–40, 136f, 151–52
    geometric form experimentation in, 18
    Hitchcockian gaze in, 21–22
    intrinsic incompletion in, 186
    montages in, 135, 136–37
    scopophilic gaze in, 137f
    soundscape in, 175–76

Martin, Adrian, 7–8, 50–51, 85–86, 226n2
    analysis of *Carlito's Way,* 50–51
Massey, Anna, 31
Mean Streets (Coppola and Scorsese), 6–7
medium specificity, 15, 29–36, 48–49
metacinematic schematization, 120–26
metteur en scène method, 29–30
Michelson, Annette, 105–7
mise en scène
    alignment with montage, pure cinema, 19–23, 24–26, 84
    in De Palma's films, 7–10
    depth of field and, 24–26
    description, 8–10
    framing and, 26–27, 64, 85–87, 89–90, 97
    historical account of, 218n31
    in Hitchcock's films, 27–29, 84–85
    in *The Lodger,* 25f
    Martin and, 85–86
    Schroeder's study of, 218n37
    in *Un Chien Andalou,* 15–16
Mitchell, Tony, 231n42
modernism
    aesthetic modernism, 15–16
    avant-garde and pure cinema, 15–19
    in *The Birds,* 43–44
    evolution of, 16
    history of emergence of, 215n4
    modernist pictorial-cinematic space, 116f
    vernacular modernism, 48–49
montages
    abstraction in, 137–39
    abstract montages, 137–38
    alignment with mise en scène, pure cinema, 19–23
    in Argento's films, 71–72
    in Bava's films, 46–47
    Bazin's realist model and, 127
    in Chomette's films, 17
    cinematic form and, 23
    counterpoint and, 92
    in De Palma's films, 7, 8–10, 82, 83, 129
    description/uses of, 33–34
    dialectical montage, 108, 174–75
    in Dulac's films, 17, 20
    Dulac's theory on, 50–51
    Eisenstein's comment on, 164

in Eisenstein's films, 61–64,
70–71, 79, 83
expressive montage, 62–63, 135, 168
giallo and, 71
in Griffith's films, 15
in Hitchcock's films, 4, 19, 20–22, 24–
26, 61, 64, 67–70, 73, 75, 135, 136–37
intellectual montage, 137–38
Marxist dialectic context of, 62–63
parallel montage, 128–29, 144
pure cinema and, 19–22
in Soviet cinema, 16–17
Soviet montage, 16–17
in *Un Chien Andalou,* 15–16
Žižek's analysis of, 227n2
Murder a la Mod (De Palma), 52
Murnau, F. W., 19
influence on Hitchcock, 186
Nosferatu, 24–26
Sunrise, 27–29
Musante, Tony, 114–15
musical counterpoint, 165, 169, 174–75
myth of total cinema
of Bazin, 163, 227n1
of Eisenstein, 61–64

narrative parallelism, 128–29, 145–46
narrative patterning, 48
Ndalianis, Angela, 177–78
Necronomicon (Franco), 156–57
neo-baroque aesthetics (Italy), 8–10,
84, 222n18
neo-noir science fiction film genre, 118
New American Cinema, 94
Nicolodi, Baria, 177
Nietzschean eternal return, 113–14
nonsynchronic counterpoint, 170
North by Northwest (Hitchcock), 2, 5
abstraction in glass in, 106f
Bellour's analysis of, 64, 66–67
fragmented images in, 127–28
modernist line, pattern, color, in, 106f
schematic structure of, 103–5,
104f, 105f
soundscape in, 182–83
Truffaut's analysis of, 66
Norvello, Ivor, 26
Nosferatu (Murnau), 24–26
Notorious (Hitchcock), 85, 156, 228n22

Obsession (De Palma), 41–42, 151
Once Upon a Time in the West (*C'era una
Volte il West,* Leone), 77
Opera (Argento), 47
giallo in, 113
schematic framing in, 120
optical abstraction, in *Blackmail,* 103f
Orr, John, 43–44

paracinema, 49–50
parallel montage, 128–29, 144
patterning
formal patterning, 222n15
narrative patterning, 48
visual patterning, 68, 118f
Peckinpah, Sam, 94
Peretz, Eyal, 85
Peucker, Brigitte, 86–87, 114
pictorial-cinematic space, 116f
"plasticity" of images (Heyward), 16–17
Poe, Edgar Allan, 46
poliziotteschi, Italian crime film, 45
Pomerance, Murray, 95–97, 102,
105–7, 225n26
Psycho (Hitchcock), 2, 3, 5
as antimodernist aesthetic stance, 43–44
axial composition in, 91f
De Palma's admiration for, 52
Dressed to Kill comparison with, 8–10
Dressed to Kill's imitation of, 171–73
geometric form experimentation in, 18
Hitchcockian gaze in, 21–22
Hitchcock-Truffaut discussion
on, 90–92
medium-specific effects in, 37
mirror reflection symbolism in, 63
montage sequences, 67–69
relation of parts-whole in, 61, 68
Skerry's analysis of, 213–14n9
soundscape in, 169, 181–84
visual/aural counterpoint in, 93f
Pudovkin, V. I., 164–68
pure cinema *(cinéma pur)*
as "abstract filmmaking," 217n14
alignment with mise en scene,
montage, 19–23
classical form and, 42–45
De Palma's description of, 18
Dulac's description of, 19, 23

pure cinema (*cinéma pur*) (*cont.*)
   emergence of, 16–17
   Hitchcock's description of, 18, 19–20, 23
   Horak's analysis of, 216n8
   image plasticity in, 2
   modernist avant-garde and, 15–19
   qualities of, 185
   Rear Window as, 2
   self-reflexive approach in, 27–29
   Skerry's comment on, 22
   summation of argument in favor of, 185
   Vertigo as, 5
pure sound, 164–68

Raging Bull (Scorsese), 53
Rain Man (Levinson), 148–49, 149*f*, 150
Raising Cain (De Palma), 8–10
rear projection technique, 39–40, 120–22, 122*f*, 219n54, 219–20n56, 226n14
Rear Window (Hitchcock), 5
   aural excess in, 175–76
   Chion's analysis of, 170
   Hitchcockian gaze in, 21–22
   Hitchcock/Truffaut, discussion on, 1–2
   impact of aural excess, 176
   montages in, 21
   saccharine villainous acts in, 30
   sexual mores/generic subversion in, 65–66
Rebecca (Hitchcock), 68–69
reflexivity
   in *Frenzy*, 29–36
   self-reflexivity, 27–29
replicated figures, 63, 111*f*
representational art, 224n18
Reservoir Dogs (Tarantino), 180–81
Le Retour à la Raison (Man Ray), 16
rhythmic counterpoint, 175–76
Richter, Hans, 89–90, 91–92, 209–10
   Rhythm 21, 92
   Rhythm 23, 92
Roeg, Nicholas, 175
Rope (Hitchcock), 30
Rothman, William, 1, 213n4

Salt, Barry, 228n23
Scheider, Roy, 150
schematic frame, 225n32, 226n11
   in Argento's films, 108
   in Bava's films, 108–14, 120
   in De Palma's films, 51*f*, 55–56, 57*f*
   frames within frames, 109, 112, 114–15, 118
   in the *giallo,* 108–26
   Hitchcockian method and, 64–65, 97–98
   in Hitchcock's films, 97–103, 105–7
   metacinematic schematization, 120–26
   segmentation and, 225n32
   visual schematics, 51–52, 54, 55–56
Schroeder, David, 218n37
Sconce, Jeffrey, 49–50
scopophilic gaze, 137*f*
Scorsese, Martin. *See also specific films*
   art-house/New Wave sensibility of, 6–7
   Cape Fear, 175–76
   on the Hitchcockian method, 4
The Searchers (Ford), 86–87, 224n7
The Seashell and the Clergyman (La Coquille et le Clergyman) (Dulac), 16–17
Secret Agent (Hitchcock), 166–67
segmentation, 127–63. *See also* split frame
   Bellour on, 127, 129–31, 146–47
   compositional segmentation, 109*f*
   division and fragmentation, 127, 133*f*, 185
   formal segmentation, 63, 91–92
   in Fulci's films, 160*f*
   Hitchcockian method and, 84–85
   intensified segmentation, 158–63
   intensified split frame, 144–47
   line cross segmentation, 138–44, 142*f*
   schematic frame and, 225n32
   spatial segmentation, 77–78, 109, 141*f*, 148, 154, 160–61, 162–63
   split diopter image, 148–56
   subjective fragmentation and, 7–8
   the zoom, 156–58
The Seventh Seal (*Det sjunde inseglet*, Bergman), 42
Shadow of a Doubt (Hitchcock), 3, 5, 84–85, 97–98
   fragmented images in, 127–28
   geometric form experimentation in, 18, 100*f*

geometric form in line, movement in, 100*f*
Hitchcockian geometric framing in, 123
segmented depth of field in, 134*f*
split-screen effect in, 186
transgressive frame in, 99*f*
transgressive framing in, 99*f*
Shadows (Cassavetes), 43
Sharff, Stefan, 223n40
Shaviro, Steven, 70–71, 111–12, 118*f*, 176
Shaw Brothers, 156–57
Sisters (De Palma), 5–6, 52
De Palma's use of *giallo* film tropes in, 119
imitation of Hitchcock in, 186–87
split screen as narrative conceit in, 130*f*
Skerry, Philip J., 22, 137–38, 213–14n9
soundscape, 164–84
avant-garde influences, 166–68
Chion and, 167–68, 170, 175–76
contrapuntal sound, 168–75
De Palma's films and, 171–75
Donaggio and, 171, 173–75, 182
Fulci and, 180–81
Herrmann and, 67–68, 171–75, 181–84
Hitchcock/expanded contrapuntal sound, 168–71
Hitchcock's aural excesses, 175–81
impact of aural excess on *giallo*, 175–81
musical counterpoint and, 94, 169, 174–75
in *Psycho*, 169, 181–84
pure abstraction in, 181–84
"sensory encounters" (Ndalianis), 177–78
talkies and pure sound, 164–68
Weis and, 166–67, 168, 178–79
Soviet montage form, 16–17
space-as-whole, 109
spatial segmentation, 77–78, 109, 141*f*, 148, 154, 160–61, 162–63
spectator immersion method, 44–45
Spielberg, Steven, 6–7
Buckland's analysis of, 221n40
De Palma's admiration for, 53
use of split screen diopter, 150, 151*f*, 228n20
split diopter lens and images, 148–56

abstraction and, 148–56
Fulci's use of, 162*f*
the zoom comparison, 156–57
split frame, 127–38
in Argento's films, 129*f*
Deleuze and, 139
in De Palma's films, 144–47, 145*f*, 147*f*
in Hitchcock's films, 131–34, 134*f*, 136*f*, 137–40, 146–47, 148–49, 151–52
irrational split frame composition, 152*f*
as narrative conceit, 130*f*
narrative parallelism and, 128–29, 145–46
split diopter lens enhancement of, 148–56
the zoom comparison, 156–57
Spoto, Donald, 23–24
Stealers Wheel, 180–81
Sterrit, David, 213n8
Stewart, James, 1–2
Strangers on a Train (Hitchcock), 30
Allen's analysis of, 65–66
Truffaut's categorization of, 44–45
"Stuck in the Middle with You" (Stealers Wheel), 180–81
Summer, Elke, 47, 113–14
Sunrise (Murnau), 27–29
surrealism, 15–16, 113
Suspiria (Argento), 46–47, 71–73, 72*f*, 113–14, 120, 158

talkies (talking in movies)
Clair and, 164, 165–68
Hitchcock's comment on, 165–66
initial opposition to, 166
origins/development of, 164–68
Pudovkin and, 164–68
silent-film aesthetic philosophy and, 181–82
Tarantino, Quentin, 5–6, 121
Tatarkiewicz, Wladyslaw, 224n18
Taxi Driver (Scorsese), 6–7
Tenebrae (Argento), 8–10, 158
textual transcendence, 10–11
Théme et Variations (Dulac), 18, 27–29
The 36th Chamber of Shaolin (Shaw Brothers), 156–57
Thompson, Kristin, 4, 70–71, 166–67

To Catch a Thief (Hitchcock), 85, 86–87, 88*f*
topographic framing, 95–97, 225n28
Torn Curtain (Hitchcock), 30
transgressive frame, 99*f*
transgressive framing, 99*f*, 135, 140–44, 151, 227–28n9
transtextuality, 10–11
Tripp, June, 26
Truffaut, François. *See also specific films*
  analysis of *North by Northwest*, 66
  categorization of *Strangers on a Train*, 44–45
  comment *The Lodger*, 23–24
  discussions with Hitchcock, 1–2, 68–69, 90–92

The Untouchables (De Palma), 8–10, 53
  expressionist space in, 78*f*
  the fragment and, 186
  Odessa steps sequence, 77–83
  Sergio Leone zoom in, 79*f*
  split-diopter segmented framing in, 55*f*, 151
  split frame in, 148*f*, 151
  turning point in, 53–54
  two-shot dialogue in, 54*f*, 54–55

vernacular modernism, 48–49
vernacular visuality, 48–50
vertical axis, 90–91, 98–102, 117*f*, 117, 122, 132–34, 140, 153
Vertigo (Hitchcock), 2, 3, 5
  baroque color palette in, 46–47
  color as compositional element in, 112
  division and fragmentation in, 127, 133*f*
  exchange of gazes in, 26
  geometric form experimentation in, 18
  Hitchcockian gaze in, 21*f*, 21–22
  intrinsic incompletion in, 186
  montages in, 20–22
  reframed images in, 110–11
  soundscape in, 175–76, 182–83
Vertov, UU, 26
The Virgin Spring (*Jungfrukällan*, Bergman), 42
Visconti, Luchino, 46–47, 156–57
visual and aural counterpoint, 93*f*
visual counterpoint, 93*f*, 169, 218n37
visual patterning, 68, 118*f*
visual schematics, 51–52, 54, 55–56
Vivian Vaughan, B., 164–65

Wayne, John, 86
The Wedding Party (De Palma), 52
Weis, Elizabeth, 166–67, 168, 178–79
West Interior (Katz), 172–73
The Wild Bunch (Peckinpah), 94
Wild Strawberries (*Smultronstället*, Bergman), 42
Willeman, Paul, 156–57
Williams, Tami Michelle, 16–17, 217n16
wipe, 21, 56–57, 218n27
Wood, Mary P., 46–47, 114
Wood, Robin, 1, 29–30, 220n14
Wright, Basil, 164–65

Žižek, UU, 219n53, 227n2
the zoom, 156–58
  Argento's use of, 158
  Bava's use of, 111–12, 158
  Belton's comments on, 156–58, 163
  De Palma's use of, 82, 123–24
  description, 156–58
  in *Femme Fatale*, 209–10
  impact of using, 31
  Salt's study of, 228n23
  split screen/split diopter comparison, 156–57